Complete
Old English
(Anglo-Saxon)

Mark Atherton

For UK order enquiries: please contact Bookpoint Ltd,
130 Milton Park, Abingdon, Oxon OX14 4SB.
Telephone: +44 (0) 1235 827720. *Fax:* +44 (0) 1235 400454.
Lines are open 09.00–17.00, Monday to Saturday, with a 24-hour
message answering service. Details about our titles and how to
order are available at www.teachyourself.com

For USA order enquiries: please contact McGraw-Hill Customer
Services, PO Box 545, Blacklick, OH 43004-0545, USA.
Telephone: 1-800-722-4726. *Fax:* 1-614-755-5645.

For Canada order enquiries: please contact McGraw-Hill Ryerson
Ltd, 300 Water St, Whitby, Ontario L1N 9B6, Canada.
Telephone: 905 430 5000. *Fax:* 905 430 5020.

Long renowned as the authoritative source for self-guided
learning – with more than 50 million copies sold worldwide – the
Teach Yourself series includes more than 500 titles in the fields of
languages, crafts, hobbies, business, computing and education.

British Library Cataloguing in Publication Data: a catalogue record
for this title is available from the British Library.

Library of Congress Catalog Card Number: on file.

First published in UK 2006 as **Teach Yourself Old English** by
Hodder Education, part of Hachette UK, 338 Euston Road,
London NW1 3BH.

First published in US 2006 by The McGraw-Hill Companies, Inc.

This edition published 2010.

The *Teach Yourself* name is a registered trade mark of
Hodder Headline.

Typeset by MPS Limited, A Macmillan Company.

Printed in Great Britain for Hodder Education, an Hachette UK
Company, 338 Euston Road, London NW1 3BH by CPI Group
(UK) Ltd, Croydon, CR0 4YY.

The publisher has used its best endeavours to ensure that the URLs
for external websites referred to in this book are correct and active
at the time of going to press. However, the publisher and the
author have no responsibility for the websites and can make no
guarantee that a site will remain live or that the content will remain
relevant, decent or appropriate.

Hachette UK's policy is to use papers that are natural, renewable
and recyclable products and made from wood grown in sustainable
forests. The logging and manufacturing processes are expected to
conform to the environmental regulations of the country of origin.

Impression number   10 9 8
Year   2014

Contents

Acknowledgements

I would like to thank the following people for their helpful comments on sections of this book: Dr Stephen Baxter, Ginny Catmur, Dr Catherine Clarke, Julie Dyson, Tony Harris, Peter Jackson, Professor Barbara Raw, colleagues and students at Regent's Park College, and the students who participated in the Old English language classes and lectures at the English Faculty, University of Oxford.

Meet the author

A teacher at my school once wrote the Old English word **cyning** (*king*) on the board at the start of a lesson – and **cyning** is the first word in Unit 2 of this book. In its short form **cing**, very like modern English *king*, it appears in the first Old English sentence in Unit 1. Though I cannot remember the rest of that school lesson, clearly the word must have stuck, for I work now as a lecturer in English and the history of English. Just one word kindled a spark of interest in languages and their literature: French, Latin and German at school, then German, some Russian and Old English at university. I taught English and translation studies, mainly in Germany and Austria, and did teacher training in Wales and Spain. With that came the realization that real learning is not only about grammar and translation but also about developing skills of contextual reading and comprehension, about doing things with words and thinking in the language. These skills can be acquired and practised: I see them as equally relevant whether you are learning modern languages or a language of the past.

Mark Atherton

Only got a minute?

Old English (Anglo-Saxon) is the language of a thousand years ago, with a rich literature; it is also the language of many historical records. By learning Old English, you equip yourself to:

▶ explore the literature, like *Beowulf* or *The Battle of Maldon*

▶ do the history, like the life of King Alfred or Edward the Confessor, or

▶ do etymology, like the names of fields, hedges, streets, towns and the people who named them.

You learn how people a thousand years ago thought, felt, organized society and lived their lives.

They called it **englisc** (pronounced 'enn-glish'), and you can see from the spelling and pronunciation how English has changed since then. Its fascinating story starts with Old English – the language spoken in the period from post-Roman times to the 11th century.

The main difference between their English and ours is structural. Old English is an **inflected** language: words change their shape or ending according to meaning. Modern English uses an ending *-ed* to distinguish *we love* from the past meaning *we loved*. Old English has many more endings and inflections.

English spelling has changed radically over the centuries: there was, for instance, no letter *v*, so *f* had two values. But you need learn only two new letters before you start this book: þ, an old runic letter called 'thorn', and ð called 'eth' (an adapted letter **d**); both letters are pronounced like our 'th'.

Now you are in a position to read two short sentences in Old English: **se cyning lufað** *the king loves* and **se cyning lufode** *the king loved*. To say *he loves* you use the old *-th* ending, written with the letter 'eth'. For the past you change the ending to **-ode**, which corresponds to our *-ed* in *loved*.

5 Only got five minutes?

What is Old English?

Old English is the language written and spoken from the fifth or sixth century onwards in the part of southern Britain that eventually became the united kingdom of England under such kings as Athelstan and Edgar, descendants of Alfred the Great (king of Wessex, 871–899). Old English stopped being used for writing in the 12th century, giving way to Latin and French, but regional varieties of everyday spoken **englisc** (it was called 'enn-glish') continued to be widely used, and these changed and developed into the varieties of spoken English of the present day. We can distinguish broadly two kinds of Old English: literary and everyday.

Archaic, poetic Old English

You can see this sentence from king Alfred's time on display in the Ashmolean Museum in Oxford:

> AELFRED MEC HEHT GEWYRCAN
> literally: 'Alfred me ordered to make'
> i.e. King Alfred ordered me to be made

This inscription is on the edge of the Alfred Jewel, a ceremonial object that held a pointer for guiding a reader's eye along the line of writing in a book (see front cover of this book for an illustration). Its language is formal and archaic: the word **mec** by then also existed as **me** *me*, and the word **heht** also had a newer form **het**; it meant *ordered*, and is related to our word *behest*. The name **Aelfred** meant the *rede* or *advice* of *the supernatural being*. Shakespeare spelt his name in different ways, and so did **Ælfræd**: spelling, though much more phonetic than modern English, was not fixed. The verb **ge-wyrcan** *to make, work* (e.g. metalwork) with past participle **ge-wroht** (cf. the term *wrought* iron) – from a root-word **wyrc**, related to **weorc** *work* – illustrates a further characteristic of Old English: much more so than present-day English, the shape of the word would change according to its meaning or use in the sentence. The **ge-** prefix (pronounced 'yuh') added a meaning of completedness to the action, while the ending **-an** on the root **wyrc** shows that that this is the infinitive *to make*.

Everyday Old English

This is found in chronicles, lawsuits, legal agreements and land transactions, in religious writings such as sermons and stories of saints, and other documents. For example, in a manuscript of rules for a monastery, we find an account of the sign language used by the monks – for instance, when they had to keep silence at certain meals in the rectory. In the extract below, we slightly modernize the spelling, but – with the possible exception of **bralinga,** which means *flat* (from **bradlinga,** which contains the root **brad** *broad*), and **swilche** *as if* (related to modern English *such*) – all the words are recognizably connected with present-day ones. For instance **cyse**, also spelt **cese**, was pronounced with a 'ch' and in the later medieval period came to be written **chese** or **cheese.**

Lightly modernized text: Thonne thu chese habban wylle, sete thonne thine twa handa togædere bradlinga swilche thu wringan wylle.

Word-for-word translation: Then thou cheese have will, set then thy two hands together flat as if you will wring.

Idiomatic translation: When you want to have cheese, then put your two hands flat together as if you were pressing it out (i.e. in the process of separating the cheese from the whey).

Original Old English: Þonne þu cyse habban wylle, sete þonne þine twa handa togædere bralinga swilce þu wringan wylle.

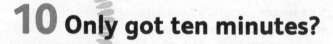

10 Only got ten minutes?

Characteristics

Compared to the present-day language, the word order is varied and free. Old English is more compact in its vocabulary, and the shape of words was altered by endings, so that many common words such as *love*, *like*, *fall* usually have two syllables rather than one: **lufu**, **lician**, **feallan**. It is harder to be monosyllabic in Old English.

Sounds

The letters **þ** and **ð** both represent the modern English 'th' sound; **g** before **e** was pronounced 'yuh'; and **c** before **e** was 'tch'; sc was 'sh' – examples are: **þing** *thing*, **gear** *year*, **ceas** *chose*, **scir** *shire*. Between vowels, **f** sounds as 'v': **lufu** i.e. 'lu-vu' means *love*. If you get the sounds of the language right, it recreates the authentic words of the texts, making them more memorable and easier to learn.

Vocabulary

Much of our present-day core vocabulary is Old English: *hands* and *feet; hearts* and *minds; love* and *goodness; fall, fell, fallen; one, two, three; Monday, Tuesday, Wednesday;* the personal pronouns *he, his, him, her, it, thou, ye, you;* and basic words like *is, are, was; have, had; to, for, with.*

Compounds

Old English personal names are often two-word compounds: **Ead-weard** *blessed guardian*, **Ead-gar** *blessed spear*. Place names also have two elements: **Oxena-ford** *crossing-place of the oxen* is Oxford, **Æppeltun** *apple farm* is Appleton. More complex or abstract ideas are formed in a similar way: **scir-gerefa** *shire-reeve* i.e. *sheriff*, **scir-ge-mot** *shire-moot* i.e. *shire assembly*, **þrinnes** *three-ness* i.e. *trinity*, **word-hord** *wordhoard* i.e. *vocabulary*.

Actions in time

The present tense is recognised by **-þ** or **-ð**, the ending -th that we still see in Shakespeare's *the rain it raineth every day*. The past is marked in two ways: by **-od-**, that is to say, the **-d** ending that we see in *it rained yesterday*; or by the change of vowel, as in *she chese a husband, he fell from his horse*.

Three words for the

We find the basic forms **se, seo, þæt** like the three broad groups of masculine, feminine and neuter in German or the two words *le/la* in French. The noun **brocc** *badger* was masculine; so if you wanted to say *the badger* you said **se brocc,** but for *the adder* you said **seo næddre,** and *the horse* was **þæt hors**. These gender markers make words more distinctive within a phrase or sentence.

Cases

Old English had endings to mark the role or function of words in the sentence. This survives in our pronouns to some extent – so we cannot say, for example, of a reputedly amorous king *Edgar loves she*; instead the feminine word has to change its form to *her*, as *Edgar loves **her***. In Old English the definite article – the determining word *the* – also changes its form. The basic expression *the queen* is **seo cwen,** but if we write *Edgar loves the queen*, this becomes **Eadgar lufað þa cwene**. And **se cyning** *the king* changes in its accusative case in the same way to **þone cyning**. Note what a liberating effect this has on the word order: **se cyning þa cwene lufað** and **þa cwene se cyning lufað** both mean *Edgar loves the queen*. Similarly: **seo cwen lufode þone cyning** and **seo cwen þone cyning lufode** and **þone cyning seo cwen lufode** could all mean *the queen loved the king*.

Introduction

Old English, or Anglo-Saxon as it is sometimes called, was the
language spoken and written in England until the 12th century.
Its rich literature ranges from the epic *Beowulf* to the visionary poem
The Dream of the Rood to the varied writings of the Anglo-Saxon
Chronicle. As the language of historical record, Old English opens
an invaluable window on the early history of England: on the
political events that shaped the land, on the culture and spirituality
of the writers of the time, on landscape history and the layout of
towns and villages, on the history of institutions. Through the
study of their language these documents can be made to speak their
own voices and express their concerns. All languages have their
own phrases and modes of expression, and by learning Old English
you can appreciate how the men and women of the time actually
thought and felt.

Beginning as a set of dialects spoken in the provinces and petty
kingdoms of southern Britain, Old English eventually became the
standard written language used by the rulers of England from
Alfred the Great to king Harold. In many respects, this language
is with us today, in the very names of the towns and villages in
which we live. These place names reflect the shape of the land and
relate how it was used: *Longridge* and *Revidge* (i.e. Rough Edge)
near the dark or shining stream of *Blackburn*, *Swindon* the hill
where the pigs were grazed, *Oxford* the river crossing suitable for
oxen, *Bury St Edmunds* the *borough* or town with a monastery
church dedicated to St Edmund, patron and defender of its rights.
It is significant that Old English had a core vocabulary that we
still use in our everyday speech and writing. *Head* and *heart*,
hands and *feet*, *sticks* and *stones* all go back to Old English in a
different spelling; *sun*, *moon* and *stars* or *thunder* and *lightning*
are originally Old English words, as are *love* and *hate*, *strength*
and *weakness*. The basic grammar of present-day English has older
roots: the way we talk about the past by ringing the changes in

the vowels of *sing, sang, sung* or *choose, chose, chosen*, the way we express moods of volition and obligation with auxiliary verbs such as *will–would, may–might, shall–should*, the way we refer intimately to ourselves and others with personal pronouns such as *me* and *you, his* and *hers*, or even *I* and *thou*.

In the poem 'Bone Dreams' from his book *North*, the Irish poet Seamus Heaney pictures the history of the English language as a kind of archaeological dig: the excavator explores the many layers or accretions that the language has gathered over the centuries. Digging down from the present time, the archaeologist uncovers layer after layer of influences that have affected the English lexicon:

Colonialism	Asian, American, African words come into English
Enlightenment	Latin and Greek scientific terms
Renaissance	Latinate learned words
Middle Ages	French literary and cultural influences
	Norman French administration
	Old Norse everyday words especially in the north and east
	Old English – the foundation

At the base of his trench, the poet–archaeologist finds **ban-hus** (pronounced 'bahn-hoos'); this is the poetic compound *bone-house*, an image or metaphor from *Beowulf* that signifies the body, where the spirit lives. For Heaney, as translator of *Beowulf*, this is one of the attractions of the Old English poetic line, the compression of its imagery. Other modern poets and writers have felt similarly drawn: W.H. Auden and Ted Hughes to its strength and craftedness, Gerard Manley Hopkins to the lilt of its alliterative rhythms, J.R.R. Tolkien to its strong contrasts of light and dark and its myth-making power.

The aim of this book is to help you to gain an efficient reading knowledge of Old English. It offers a graded progressive course in Old English based on authentic texts selected from the rich archive of poems, prose and historical documents that have survived from the libraries of early medieval England. Passages from famous poems such as *Beowulf* will be presented, but there are also extracts from the writings of great prose writers such as archbishop Wulfstan of York, and whole texts from the administrative records of the period, chosen for their cultural and historical interest. The passages are presented with minimal adaptation, so that you may, if you wish, go back to the original editions and read them with confidence.

In reading these texts, you will at the same time also explore the political, cultural and literary contexts in which they were written.

How to use this book

The course units

In each unit there are four sections: a specific text for reading and study, a set of grammar explanations, further texts and vocabulary and practice exercises. These are interspersed with various other short sections of information and explanatory material.

Pronunciation

Pronouncing the pieces out loud is important for appreciating the literature, whether poems or prose documents, and for recreating their dramatic and rhetorical effects. It also makes the language easier to learn and it helps to make clear the correspondences between Old and modern English. A reference guide to spelling and pronunciation is provided at the beginning of the book and it will help to refer to this frequently, especially at first. Further guidance is given in the units. The accompanying recording provides recordings of major pieces of prose and poetry used in the course.

Texts

Each unit takes one authentic document as a study text, with help and guidance on vocabulary and cultural background, and grammar. Usually it will be accompanied by supplementary texts and materials. For instance, the study texts in one unit include a personal letter and a poem, both dealing with the same events in the reign of a king. All texts appearing on the recording are marked with an arrow in the left margin of the page.

Grammar

Three or four points of grammar are explained in each of the earlier units, in non-technical language and with the main focus on increasing the ability to read the study texts in the original. Later units give more grammatical information, using more traditional tables and paradigms to sum up what has already been learned and to fill in any gaps.

Vocabulary

The vocabulary of the texts is presented in a number of ways. In the sections **old–modern correspondences,** you will be shown how words in Old English are related in form or meaning to their modern English equivalents. In **cultural contexts,** you study the meaning and connotations of words against the social and intellectual background of the period. The sections marked **wordhoard,** based on the Old English term for a thesaurus or treasury of words, present a theme-based way of recording and learning the words and phrases of the language.

Reading

The **reading** sections in each unit are intended to supplement the study texts with passages of verse and prose selected for similarity of theme or vocabulary. These are accompanied by a parallel translation but no vocabulary list. The aim is to encourage a lighter, more extensive kind of reading where you read for gist and improve your passive knowledge of the language.

Language and style

This section serves especially in later units to provide insights into the different techniques used by writers in this period, whether they are writing prose or poetry. Information will be given on choice of word or phrase, the use of rhythm and metre, the frequent use of alliteration (e.g. *light and life*) by Old English writers. By studying such devices, along with sentence structure, word order and rhetoric, you will begin to recognize the style of a particular author, for example the distinctive 'voice' heard in the writings of archbishop Wulfstan, and to make connections with other texts you have read.

Practice

Within each unit, you are given the opportunity to practise the forms and patterns acquired in a series of translation, fill-in-the-gap and comprehension exercises, with a key at the end of the book.

Select word index

The **word index** at the back of the book lists all the words and phrases that appear in the study texts and practice exercises, with cross-reference to the unit(s) where the word is explained or discussed. At first, in order to give as much primary assistance as possible, words are given exactly as spelled in the texts themselves, as well as in the base form with which they would appear in a dictionary. To encourage the discursive use of the supplementary reading texts, their vocabulary is not given specific listings in the index at the back, since the parallel translations should provide all the help that is needed.

The focus, then, is on the study text; in the units you can read or listen to the texts, learn the meanings of their vocabulary and grammar and explore their literary, historical and cultural contexts.

Insight

This book aims to provide material for as many different interests, and as many different kinds of learner, as possible. Some learners like systematic grammar, others like to take in the patterns of the language gradually as they appear in the texts; some like to start reading and thinking in the language immediately, others like to translate; some like to acquire the natural rhythms of the language and learn 'chunks' and naturally occurring phrases. In this book, you are encouraged to try out different approaches – for instance, to the learning of vocabulary in Unit 12 – and extend your own repertoire of language-learning techniques into territory with which you are not yet familiar.

The study of Old English

The study of Old English opens a window on the past and illuminates the history and the literature. Through the texts we gain glimpses of the people of the time and hear snatches of their talk.

In one historical document, for instance, a lawsuit takes place between a man and a woman over a piece of land. The woman calls on the aid of the queen herself and a whole group of women attend the assembly of the shire court to support her (see Unit 19). The assembly meets at Cwichelm's Low, an ancient mound at the junction of the old Ridgeway and the road to West Hendred in Berkshire. Now known as Scutchamer Knob, partly obscured by trees and damaged by a pre-20th-century archaeological dig, the mound is still accessible; it is possible to stand on the site where those people met to argue their case, as recorded on a slip of parchment a thousand years ago. In another, heard by the shire court in Herefordshire, a woman was sued by her own son. In this instance no women attended the hearing, and perhaps they were prevented, but the indignant mother sent a message to the assembly, which was ratified by the men present (see Unit 20). And the presiding official Thorkell the White, husband of the woman's kinswoman, rode to Hereford and had her exact words recorded in a blank space of a Latin gospel book at the cathedral, where it remains to this day. Here is a tangible material connection between the present and the past.

Byrhtferth, one of the Old English writers presented in this book, regarded his branch of study as a journey across the waves to the salt sea strand (Unit 5). And texts associated with the court of king Alfred express a view of learning in terms of striking images: of thoughtful study as drawing from a well without letting the water run to waste; or tracing the tracks of those who went before; or exploring the forest for good building materials. For the rulers and writers of the period, the ancient language to be explored was Latin, but this imagery applies equally well to teaching yourself Old English. Such exploration can bring many rewards: a renewed sense of past connections, new historical insights, even new ways of seeing the English language and its literature.

Some linguistic terms used in the book

Adjective: a word that describes or qualifies a noun (*fearful, green, happy*)

Adverb: a word that qualifies a verb (*swam quickly*) or modifies an adjective (*extremely easy*); it expresses the time, manner or place of an action (*then, quickly, here* etc.)

Cognate: related to a word in another language (English *two* is cognate with German *zwei* – they both come from a common ancestor in primitive Germanic)

Noun: a word referring to a person, thing or idea (*man, tree, friendship*)

Preposition: a short connecting word, such as *to, for, by, with, from*

Verb: a word denoting an action in time (*swim, arrived, sang*)

Prefix: a meaningful syllable or short word affixed to the beginning of a word; the prefix changes the meaning of the root word, e.g. *mis-take, be-come, under-stand.*

Suffix: a similar affix added to the end of a word, e.g. *good-ness, holi-ness, lord-ship, lady-ship*

Pronunciation

A short introduction

The pronunciation of Old English has been carefully worked out by a process of historical and comparative research. In the overview here, many linguistic facts have been omitted, but further distinctions and fine tunings will be made in the course of the book. For those interested in phonetics, some further reading on the sounds of the language will be given at the end of the book.

The following is a **quick guide** to sounding broadly correct. It is important to learn the basic sounds of the language, so that the texts and poems can be read fluently and with their original rhythmical effects. In addition, once the basic sounds are learnt the connections with modern English become much clearer and the language is much easier to learn.

In the vocabularies, the Old English is given in **bold**, the meaning in *italics*. Where appropriate a rough pronunciation based on modern English is indicated by inverted commas: e.g. **rice** *kingdom* 'ree-cheh'.

> The basic rule is to pronounce every letter as written, including **-e** on the end of words. The letters **þ** and **ð** were pronounced as modern 'th'; **g** adjacent to **e** or **i** becomes a 'yuh' sound and **ic** is 'itch'. Vowels sound very like those in modern English: pat, pet, pit, pot, put, or like continental European vowels when lengthened; **ea** is a one-syllable 'e-a'.

A reference guide for later study

Further details on pronunciation are given below and these are pages to which you should return frequently for reference purposes. However, it is suggested that you do at least the first three units of the book before you study the details below any further.

Many consonants sounded as in modern English: **b, p, t, d, l, r, w, m, n, x.**

The consonants **f, s** and **þ** have two pronunciations:

▶ *Initially and finally they sound like 'f', 's' and 'th' in 'thin'.*
▶ *In the middle of a word, between vowels, they take on the voiced pronunciation: 'v', 'z' and 'th' in 'that'.*

Thus **heofon** and **freosan** sound more like their modern equivalents *heaven* and *freeze* than they might appear at first sight and the medial -þ- will sound like 'th' in 'bathing', not like the voiceless 'th' in 'mathematics'.

The letter **c** represents 'k' in **cyning** *king* and **candel** *candle*, but when adjacent to the vowels e and i in **ceap** *goods*, **cild** *child* and **cirice** *church* or names in -ic like **Ælfric** and **Godric**, it had the modern 'ch' sound. Similarly **g** is 'g' in **god** *good* but becomes a 'y' sound in **gif** *if* 'yif' and **geong** *young* 'yeong' and **dæg** *day* 'dæy'. In the middle of words, such as **boga** *bow*, g later came to be pronounced 'w', but in the Old English period it was pronounced like a Dutch 'g' or a German voiced 'ach' sound heard in north German 'sagen Sie'. The letter combination **cg** is equivalent to the modern spelling *dge*; thus **ecg** and **brycg** sound very like modern *edge* and *bridge*. Similarly, **sc** is the digraph for 'sh' as in **scip** *ship*, pronounced 'ship'.

In the middle of words **h** sounded like the medial -ch- in German **Sicht** while in final position it sounded like the '-ch' in Scottish 'Loch Ness'.

The letter **a** represents a back vowel like 'a' in 'psalm'. It contrasts with the front vowel spelt **æ**, pronounced as in southern English or standard American 'man'.

There are two diphthongs, written **ea** and **eo**. Again, each letter should be pronounced, but the tongue should glide quickly from one vowel to the next so that the diphthong remains one syllable.

Each vowel and diphthong has a short and long sound. The long vowel has the same quality of sound as the short vowel; the difference is basically one of extension: the short vowel is drawled out to make it long. Listen carefully for long vowels in the recordings. In Old English, the word is with a short vowel (pronounced roughly as 'iss') means *is*, whereas is with a long vowel (pronounced 'ees') means *ice*. Similarly, note the difference between the short vowels in **mann** *person*, **full** *full* and **god** *god* compared with the long vowels in **man** *evil*, **ful** *foul* and **god** *good*, pronounced 'mahn', 'fool' and 'goad' respectively.

Sometimes the scribes marked length with an accent, e.g. ís and gód, but this was done only occasionally and often inconsistently. Especially for poetic texts, many modern textbooks of Old English employ a macron over the long vowel, e.g. īs and gōd. In keeping with the aim of this book to present texts unencumbered and with minimal adaptation, macrons will not be used in the study texts of the units. In explanations, however, occasional use of the macron will mark the long vowels of words like īs and gōd. Attention to long vowels helps to make connections with modern English, and is particularly important when reading the **poetry**, where precise distinctions of length are necessary for the correct study of the metre of the poems.

Insight

Most traditional textbooks of Old English are arranged as a systematic grammar, covering separately pronouns, adjectives, nouns, verbs and sentence structure, all in a set order: in verbs, for instance, the full rules of the present tense are taught before those of the past tense, regular verbs are given before irregular, and so on. There is a rationale to this, but as one 19th-century educationist put it, 'Would you teach dancing by giving rules for dancing and keeping the learner fixed in his seat?' (Joseph Payne, *Monthly Journal of Education* 1874, p. 306).

Language learning is a skill or an integrated set of skills. Even though each element can (and should, to a certain extent)

(Contd)

be taught separately, when you actually experience the language, by reading a text, say, all its elements, from its sounds and spellings to its pronouns, verbs and case-endings to its vocabulary and phraseology, are present simultaneously. Keeping this in mind, you will see that each unit in this book takes as a basis a certain type of text or genre, such as a chronicle entry, a riddle or a king's declaration, and teaches some essentials for reading that particular text in context. The aim is to provide an integrated approach to the learning of the language.

1

Here Edward was consecrated as king

This unit will cover:

texts
- *the coronation of Edward the Confessor as reported in the Anglo-Saxon Chronicle*

first steps in reading Old English
- *word recognition*
- *pronunciation*
- *spelling*

vocabulary
- *introduction to personal names*

◄ **TR 1**

Her wæs Eadward gehalgod to cinge
Here Edward was consecrated as king

The use of English

In 1040 Edward the atheling – prince and heir to the throne – returned to England after twenty-four years of exile on the Continent. Two years later he succeeded to the throne of England

and in the following year the Anglo-Saxon Chronicle reports that Edward was consecrated king at *Winchester on the first Easter Day with great honour.*

Edward the Confessor, as he came to be called by his successors, ruled a stable and prosperous England for twenty-four years. Yet during his lifetime, the country became subject to a bewildering variety of cultural influences: from Norse and Anglo-Danish to Norman and French. One constant in all this period of change was the large and central role played by the Old English language in the political, literary and spiritual life of the country. Unlike most of Europe at this time, where Latin was the only written language in use, England had developed a considerable literature in the vernacular, and much of its everyday administration was also conducted through the medium of written English.

The C version of the Chronicle

It so happened that a new version of the Anglo-Saxon Chronicle was started around the time of Edward's accession. The Chronicle was a year-by-year record of the nation's affairs probably begun in the time of king Alfred in the ninth century. The new recension of the 1040s, known as version C, was made perhaps at Abingdon

Abbey or at an ecclesiastical centre in Mercia, the Midland region of Anglo-Saxon England. The compiler copied the earlier Chronicle up to his own day and then began entering new records in the annual list of events. By adding his own stories, he was essentially acting as a contemporary observer of political events. The following short Old English text is his own, typically brief, account of the coronation of 1043.

◀» TR 1, 00:20
The year 1043

1043

Her wæs Eadward gehalgod to cinge on Wincestre on forman Easterdæig mid myccelum wyrðscype, and ða wæron Eastron .iii. *Nonas Aprelis*. Eadsige arcebisceop hine halgade, and toforan eallum þam folce hine wel lærde, and to his agenre neode and ealles folces wel manude. And Stigant preost wæs gebletsad to bisceope to Eastenglum.

AD 1043

Here Edward was consecrated as king at Winchester on the first Easter Day with great honour, and that year Easter fell on the third of the nones of April. Archbishop Eadsige consecrated him, and before all the people instructed him well, and for his own need and that of all the people admonished him well. And the priest, Stigand, was blessed as bishop to the East Angles.

Insight
The phrase **mid myccelum wyrðscype** meaning *with great honour* is much closer to modern English than it might first appear. Remember that the letter ð (called 'eth') represents a modern 'th' and that **sc** is modern 'sh'. The last word is therefore the compound *worth-ship*, the origin of the modern word *worship*.

Strategies for reading Old English

(a) The first strategy to employ when tackling a text written in an **inflected** language like Old English is to mark up (with hyphens or by underlining) the **inflections**, i.e. all the endings which the language uses to mark grammatical meanings in the text; it is useful also to highlight the root or stem of each word by marking any prefixes. An example of an ending is -e on **cing** *king*, a prefix **ge-** occurs before **halgod** *hallowed, consecrated*; in the same word the -**od** ending corresponds to the modern ending -*ed*.

(b) Try doing a literal word-for-word translation of the text. This helps to understand the structure of the language.

(c) Next, hear the text read out loud on the recording (or by someone familiar with the language); this will help with comprehension. Many words (e.g. **Easterdæig**) become instantly recognizable once they are heard and the connections between Old and modern English start to emerge. Using the guide to pronunciation (in the introduction) you can also try reading out loud on your own; it is possible to learn to pronounce the basics of Old English surprisingly quickly. At first, remember that ð, þ represent the modern 'th' sound in 'thorn'. Next, careful attention should be paid to the letter–sound correspondences of **æ, g, c, cg** and **sc**.

(d) Start observing the patterns of the language: its frequent meaningful endings, its word order, its typical modes of expression and idioms. When reading texts from the Chronicle for instance, you will soon find that a typical word-order is *Here was Edward... Here commanded the king..., Here came Cnut...* etc. As you gradually acquire more knowledge of the rules of grammar, this may seem less necessary, but in fact a good habit of observation is always essential: it will strengthen your grasp of the language and enrich your knowledge of the resources of the language.

(e) One further option is to experiment with transcribing the text in a slightly modernized spelling, in order to become familiar with the form and shape of the words. An example would be transcribing **Wincestre** as **Winchestre**.

◀) **TR 3** [*listen again, phrase by phrase, with a translation*]

Reading strategies in practice

Taking a sentence at a time, we can apply the above strategies to our text from the Anglo-Saxon Chronicle.

Highlight inflections and prefixes
Her wæs Eadward ge-halg-od to cing-e on Wincestr-e on forma-n Easterdæig mid myccel-um wyrð-scype.

Do a literal translation
Here was Edward hallowed to king on Winchester on former Easterday with mickle (i.e. great) worthship.

The literal translation can then be turned into natural modern English:

Here Edward was consecrated as king at Winchester on the first Easter Day with great honour.

Pronounce out loud
Pronounce every letter and syllable. For finer points, use the pronunciation guide in the introduction; the following are some hints:

Her: pronounce 'hayr' with a long, close vowel like French *été*. The long vowel points to its later modern form *here*.

wæs: the letter æ represents a medium-low front vowel like '-a-' in standard English 'cat'.

Eadward: 'Aird-ward'.

ge-halgod: pronounce 'yuhHALgod' (note that the capital letters represent the stressed syllable); make the **a** a long back vowel. The **g** was a guttural or fricative like in Dutch, but a later pronunciation was 'w', which perhaps makes the connection with modern English *hallowed* more obvious.

to: rhymes with 'tow' not with 'too'.

-dæig: 'dæi' (glide from the 'æ' to the 'ih' sound). To British ears this may sound rather like an Australian 'G'day!'.

myccelum: 'MÜTCH-eh-lum' (pronounce y as French 'u' or German 'ü').

wyrðscype: 'WÜRTH-shih-peh' (**sc** sounds like modern English 'sh').

◀» **TR 4** [*listen again*]

Observe linguistic patterns

Note the word order: *here was Edward hallowed...* In present-day English the natural sequence is to place *Edward* before the verb *was hallowed*, but Old English often placed the verb in second position with the subject following.

Observe also the use of the prepositions *to, on, mid*. In Old English it was natural to say that someone was *hallowed to king* rather than *as king*; the preposition still makes perfect sense in modern English, but the idiom is no longer used. From the evidence of this sentence, note also the use of *on* + location in the phrase *on Winchester*, as well as *on* + time in *on Easter Day*.

Experiment with modernized spellings

Try modernizing the spelling, replacing þ and ð with **th**, soft c with **ch**, soft g with **y** or **i**, and medial guttural g with **w**:

Her wæs Edward i-halwod to kinge on Winchestre on forman Easterdæi mid michelum worthshipe.

If you transcribe the text on these principles, it begins to 'look like' English, or at the very least like a kind of Middle English, and the exercise helps you to become familiar with the orthography or spelling system of Old English.

Insight

The words **biscop** *bishop* and **preost** *priest* are originally Greek **epi-skopos** (literally *over-seer*) and **presbuteros** (*elder*) borrowed into the Church Latin of Rome as *episcopus* and *presbyter,* and then into the older Germanic languages when these came into contact with the late Roman empire. The earlier a word is borrowed or taken into the language, the more thoroughly it is assimilated, and takes on a new phonetic identity.

Cultural contexts

In contrast to the relative peace and stability of his period of rule, Edward the Confessor's earlier life had been far from secure. Born in about 1005 at Islip near Oxford on an estate later owned by his mother, Emma of Normandy, he grew up in a country devastated by Viking wars and divided by the alleged misrule of his father Æthelred 'the Unready'. In 1009, for instance, Oxford, an important trading port on the old border of Wessex and Mercia, was burned to the ground. In 1013–14 the Danes seized power and the royal family fled abroad. The following year the situation was reversed and, though still a young boy, Edward was sent back to England on a mission to negotiate with the Council for his father's return to power. But in 1016 Æthelred died and the Danish Cnut became king. As the new Anglo-Danish dynasty consolidated its power Edward again fled the country for refuge with his Norman relatives.

As a modern biographer and historian has pointed out, Edward was probably resigned to the life of an exile and may never have expected to succeed to the throne when he did. There are some hints about this in our source text. The Chronicle text for the year 1043 suggests that archbishop Eadsige made a special point of instructing the king in his royal duties. Perhaps he thought that Edward was unprepared for the greatness that had been thrust upon him, and possibly the archbishop was concerned about Edward's reputation as a son of Æthelred the Unready.

> ### Insight
>
> Edward's father is known to history as Ethelred the Unready – a modernization of the personal name **Æþelræd** and the negative byname **Unræd** given him by others (though presumably not in the presence of the king himself). The word **ræd** means *advice* or *counsel* and **æþel** means *noble*, whereas **un-** is the negative prefix. So **Æþelræd Unræd** is a pun; it is a later, negative assessment of the reign of the 'ill-advised king'.

It would be intriguing to know the content of archbishop Eadsige's speech before the king and people at the coronation. One text that we can be fairly certain was used at the ceremony was the Old English coronation oath, the same oath that Edward's father Æthelred had sworn many years before, in AD 978 (for the text, see Unit 22). It is possible that the king repeated the words of the oath after the archbishop. But Eadsige probably had more to say than simply this. The chronicler's choice of the past tense verbs **lærde** and **manude** (*instructed* and *admonished*) is reminiscent of opening formulas from sermons and it is likely that the archbishop preached a set-piece sermon on that solemn occasion. The most influential writer of political sermons in this period was archbishop Wulfstan, a prominent churchman and administrator of the previous generation. His writings were in widespread circulation through the eleventh century and it is perhaps one of these that Eadsige used for his sermon. An ideal text for his purposes would have been archbishop Wulfstan's so-called *Institutes of Polity*, a treatise on the duties of all the ranks of society, with a recommendation that the king should be a shepherd of the people and *carefully keep God's commands and frequently seek out wisdom with the Council* (a pointed critique of Æthelred, one is tempted to think). (For a full translation of this passage from the *Institutes of Polity*, see Michael Swanton, *Anglo-Saxon Prose*, in the **bibliography**.)

Reading

In the reading section of each unit you are invited to read and browse through some passages supplementary to the main study texts of the unit. The reading texts are chosen for similarity of theme, outlook or vocabulary, but it is not necessary to understand every word or study them intensively.

The opening words of an 11th-century sermon

Leofan men, ure Drihten, ælmihtig God, us þus singallice manað and læreð þurh his ða halgan bec þæt we riht and soð don her on worulde in urum life.

Dearly beloved, our Lord, almighty God, thus continually admonishes and instructs us through his holy books that we should do right and truth here in this world in our life.

Old English personal names

In the early Middle Ages, most men and women simply had one name. This meant that many people tended to have the same name, with obvious potential for confusion, although **bynames** or even nicknames were used to distinguish them. Sometimes a set of related names tended to run in an important family. This is certainly true of the West Saxon royal dynasty, in which a recurrent name element is **Ead-** (modern English *Ed-*), found in the tenth-century kings **Eadmund, Eadred, Eadwig, Eadgar, Eadward**.

The common type of Old English personal name is referred to as **dithematic** because, like a compound, it is made up of two meaningful words put together. Thus the name **Eadward** consists of two elements, **ead** *blessed* + **weard** *guardian*, an apt name for a man intended to be a *shepherd of the people*.

A typical woman's name **Godgifu** pronounced 'GOD-yi-vuh' (later spelling **Godiva**) consists of **god** *god* + **gifu** *gift*. In the following table (**Test Yourself (2)**), most of the elements can be combined productively to give common Old English names.

TEST YOURSELF (1)

Using the instructions as a guide, apply some of the reading strategies outlined above to the remaining two sentences from the text. Some suggested answers for the exercise will be found in the **Test Yourself answers** at the back of the book.

1 Eadsige arcebisceop hine halgade, and toforan eallum þam folce hine wel lærde, and to his agenre neode and ealles folces wel manude.

2 And Stigant preost wæs gebletsad to bisceope to Eastenglum.

Tasks:
- **a** do a very literal translation first
- **b** then retranslate into idiomatic, natural-sounding English
- **c** identify potential pronunciation difficulties involving þ, ð, æ, c, g, cg and sc
- **d** make a note of any patterns you can observe in the language of the text, such as use of prepositions (e.g. *to*, *for*), or frequent endings on words or word order
- **e** transcribe the first sentence with a modernized spelling; omit any endings you can.

TEST YOURSELF (2)

Making names

Identify five famous men and five women among the names in the tables below. Check your results in the **Test Yourself** answers at the back of the book. For help, consult the *Blackwell Encyclopedia of Anglo-Saxon England* or Stenton (1998).

Men's names

first element	second element
ælf *supernatural, elf*	**gar** *spear*
æþel *noble*	**heah** *high*
ead *blessed*	**ræd** *advice*
eald *old*	**ric** *powerful*
god *god*	**sige** *victory*
leof *dear*	**stan** *stone*
	weard *guardian*
	wine *friend*

As either first or second element: **beorht** *bright*, **os** *god*, **wig** *battle*, **wulf** *wolf*.

Women's names

first element	second element
ælf *supernatural, elf*	**flæd** *beauty (used only in names)*
æþel *noble*	**gifu** *gift*
ead *blessed*	**þryþ** *power*
god *god*	**gyð** *battle*
wyn *joy*	

2

A king must hold a kingdom

This unit will cover:

texts
- *extracts from the poem* Maxims II

grammar
- *infinitives*
- *the auxiliary* shall, must
- *introduction to cases*

vocabulary
- *introduction to place names*

◀) TR 5

Cyning sceal rice healdan
A king must hold a kingdom

The poem *Maxims II*

The genre

Maxims II is a collection of proverbial sayings arranged into a poem to form a series of reflections on the order of things in the natural world and human society. Generically, maxims and proverbs are a traditional form of oral literature; their purpose is to preserve for posterity the cherished beliefs and wisdom of a society. In the poem *Maxims II* you can find key aspects of Anglo-Saxon material culture, the social hierar chies, traditions and customs, views of the natural world and religious and historical attitudes.

The manuscript

The poem *Maxims II* is known to us only from one manuscript – in the mid-11th century a scribe copied the text and placed it at the beginning of version C of the Anglo-Saxon Chronicle, along with another poem (called *Menologium*) on the festivals of the Church calendar. As we saw in Unit 1, version C was written around the time of Edward the Confessor's accession to the throne in 1042 and coronation in 1043. Since the Chronicle was the main annual record of political events in the kingdom, it looks as if the two poems serve as a preface: a thematic commentary on the history of England that follows in the rest of the book.

The manuscript itself is now preserved in London, in the Cotton Collection of the British Library (shelfmark Tiberius B. i). For some more texts from the same chronicle, see Unit 4.

◀) **TR 5** Cyning sceal rice healdan

cyning *king* pronounce 'KÜ-ning'
sceal *must* a one-syllable 'SHÉal'
rice *kingdom* 'REE cheh'
healdan *rule, hold* 'HÉal-dan'

Cultural contexts

The king's place in society

The king was the mainstay of Old English society. Later shortened to **cyng** or **cing**, the word **cyning** in its original meaning is connected with the idea of *kin*, Old English **cynn** (*kindred*).

In very early Old English times therefore, the *king* was the leader of a small group of people who were familiar to him, like the chief of a clan. The traditional role of the king, therefore, was to form a strong bond of loyalty between himself and his followers. The verb **sceal** expresses necessity, and can usually be translated *must*, but in some contexts also *will* or *shall* or even *belong*, since proverbs express the idea of where something naturally must belong in the right order of things.

The king's role in the world

To understand the maxim *a king must rule a country* we need to see the larger context of the poem in which it occurs. Here is a translation of the opening section:

> *The king must rule over a realm. Cities are conspicuous from afar, those which there are on this earth, the ingenious constructions of giants, ornate fortresses of dressed stones.*

*The wind in the sky is the swiftest thing and thunder in
its seasons is the loudest. The powers of Christ are great:
Providence is the most compelling thing.*

(translation by S.A.J. Bradley)

The chain of associations continues through the opening lines
of the poem. We hear talk of the seasons and the fruits of the year,
the fickleness of truth, the value of gold, wisdom and the clouds
flitting by. The poet then explores the necessary qualities of a young
nobleman before exploring people and things in their requisite
locations. This is a poem about the rightful place of smaller things
in the wider whole, the spear held in the hand, the jewel on the
ring, the mast on the ship, the sword on the lap, the dragon in its
cave, the fish in the water.

Insight

In **cyning sceal rice healdan**, the word **healdan** *to hold* is
classed as an infinitive and is identified by the ending **-an**.
In many languages, infinitives are marked by an ending:
compare French **ten-ir** or German **halt-en** with Old English
heald-an. This is one advantage of an inflected language i.e.
one that marks most of its words with inflectional endings:
the function and meaning of a word is shown by its form.

Notes on spelling and pronunciation

▶ Practise the pronunciation of the first maxim **cyning sceal
rice healdan**. Remember the general principle of Old English
spelling that every letter represents a sound.
▶ Exceptionally, the combination of two letters **sc** in **sceal** is
pronounced as one sound, like *sh* in English *shall*.
▶ The letter **c** is pronounced **k** in **cyning** (sometimes spelled
kyning). But in **rice** the letter **c** sounds like the *ch* of modern
English *rich*. Avoid pronouncing c like the 's' sound that it
often takes in modern English.
▶ **Rice** itself is a two-syllable word **ri-ce** sounding rather like
'REE cheh' (i.e. with stress on the first syllable). **Healdan** is
also two syllables, **heal-** and **-dan**.

▶ The combination **ea** is a falling diphthong, in which the tongue glides quickly from the prominent vowel **e** to the weaker vowel **a**; accordingly **heald-** sounds rather like 'HAYald' or HÉald' run together as one syllable. Other examples of one-syllable diphthongs occur in **beag, eald** and **eorl**.

Old–modern correspondences

The noun **rice** *kingdom* or *kingship* is connected with the ending *ric* in present-day English 'bishopric'. It is also cognate with the adjective **rice** *powerful*, which gradually took on the meaning *rich and powerful* and then simply *rich*. Under later Norman influence, the change in meaning was reinforced by French *riche*.

Cyning sceal on healle beagas dælan
A king in hall must deal out rings

After the lines about the dragon in the cave and the fish in the water, the poem *Maxims II* continues as follows:

◀) **TR 5, 00:13**

> Cyning sceal on healle
> beagas dælan. Bera sceal on hæðe,
> eald and egesfull. Ea of dune sceal
> flodgræg feran.

QUICK VOCAB

heall *hall* one-syllable 'HÉal'
on healle *in a hall* 'HÉal-leh'
beag *ring* one-syllable 'BÉag'
beagas *rings* 'BÉa-gas' (plural form)
dælan *to share out, apportion* 'DÆH-lan' (pronounce the long **æ** here like the open sound in modern British English 'air'; when short, **æ** is like the 'a' in 'cat')
bera *bear* 'berra'

on hæðe *on the heath* (**hæð** is also written **hæþ** –
pronounce **þ** and **ð** like Modern English 'th', voiced between vowels in
hæðe and voiceless at the end of a word as in **hæð**)
eald *old* a one-syllable 'Éald'
egesfull *terrible* 'EH-yes-full'
ea *river* 'éa'
dun *mountain, hill* 'doon'
of dune *from the hill* 'off DOO-neh'
flod-græg *flood-grey* 'fload-græy'
feran *to go, travel* 'FÉ-ran'

Cultural contexts

The hall or **heall** was the central meeting place of the town or
settlement, the seat of government, the place of feasting and
festival; in literature it becomes a symbol of right living in the
world. In poetry such as *Beowulf*, **beag** (also spelled **beah**) means
a ring in the sense of *treasure, wealth* given by a **beah-gifa**, the
ring-giver or king; it probably refers to large rings of precious
metal that could be looped onto the pommel of a sword. In later
Old English, the word is used for an armlet or arm-ring, normally
made of silver and often of considerable weight. It was used by the
king to reward loyalty and must have been equivalent to a large
sum of money. For a picture of an arm-ring in an eleventh-century
manuscript, see Unit 8.

◄) TR 6

Fyrd sceal ætsomne *A host must ride together*
Fyrd sceal ætsomne,
tirfæstra getrum. Wudu sceal on foldan
blædum blowan. Beorh sceal on eorþan
grene standan. God sceal on heofenum,
dæda demend.

18

fyrd *army, militia* 'fürd' (pronounce **y** like German 'ü')
ætsomne *together*
getrum *troop* 'yuh-TRUM'
tirfæstra *of the glorious* (**tir** *glory* + **fæst**)
wudu *wood*
folde *earth* (poetic word for **eorþe** *earth*)
blædum *with fruits* (dative plural of **blæd, bled** *fruit*)
blowan *flourish*
beorh, beorg *hill, mountain* (cf. *iceberg*)
grene *green* 'GRÉ neh'
on heofenum *in the heavens* (dat. pl. of **heofenas** *heavens* from
  heofon *heaven*)
dæda *of deeds*
demend *judge* 'DÉ-mend'

Grammar

The infinitive

Old English is an inflected language. This means it uses inflections,
i.e. endings on words, to indicate the meaning and role of words in
the sentence. The base form of the verb (as listed in dictionaries)
is the infinitive, in modern English *hold* or more often *to hold*.
In Old English the infinitive is indicated by the ending -an.

verb		stem	ending	pronunciation
healdan	*(to) hold*	**heald-**	**-an**	'HÉal-dan'
dælan	*(to) share*	**dæl-**	**-an**	'DÆ-lan'
feran	*(to) travel*	**fer-**	**-an**	'FÉ-ran'

Other infinitives include: **biddan** *to pray*, **bringan** *to bring*, **cyðan**
to proclaim, **gretan** *to greet*, **niman** *to take*, **scinan** *to shine*,
standan *to stand*, **wyrcean** or **wyrcan** 'wür-chan' *to work, create*;
an exceptional form is **beon** *to be*.

The auxiliary

Because it normally takes an infinitive, **sceal** is known as an
auxiliary (i.e. a 'helping' verb). Examples of auxiliaries in modern
English are *can, may, must, shall, will* – these are followed
immediately by the infinitive: a king must *rule*, a bear shall *dwell*
on a heath, a wood will *blossom*. Old English auxiliaries include:

sceal *must*   **mæg** *can*   **mot** *is allowed*   **wile** *will, wants*

Word order with auxiliary and infinitive

Unlike in modern English the infinitive can come much later in
the Old English sentence, as seen in the typical sentence structure
(syntax) of the proverbs in this unit:

subject	auxiliary	adverbial	object	infinitive
Cyning	sceal	on healle	beagas	dælan

subject	auxiliary	adverbial	complement	infinitive
Beorh	sceal	on eorþan	grene	standan

In the above scheme, the subject is the doer of the action expressed
by the verb; the object is the person or thing directly affected by
the action of that verb. An **adverbial** qualifies the verb in some
way giving information about time, manner, or place of the action.
The **complement** in this sentence refers back to the subject.

In brief, as the two examples show, the auxiliary often sends the
infinitive to a position at or near the end of the sentence. Having

the infinitive at the end of the sentence may seem strange at first, but you may have come across this word order in German and it is quite common that the reader or listener anticipates what the infinitive is going to be before they hear it. This phenomenon of anticipation means that in some cases the infinitive can be omitted by ellipsis, because it is 'understood'. Ellipsis usually happens when the expected verb after **sceal** is a form of *to be* (**beon** or **wesan**), or a related idea such as *to remain* or *to dwell* (**gewunian**):

Treow sceal on eorle, wisdom on were.

treow *loyalty*
on *on, in*
on eorle *in an earl* (from **eorl** *nobleman, earl*)
on were *in a man* (from **wer** *man*)

In these cases, **sceal** can be translated in various ways:

> Loyalty must be in a warrior, wisdom in a man.
> Loyalty belongs in an earl, wisdom in a man.
> Loyalty will remain in a warrior, wisdom in a man.

Introduction to cases

Note again the endings in the following phrases:

of dun-e	*from the hill*
on glof-e	*on a glove* (e.g. a falcon)
on hæð-e	*on the heath*
on wer-e	*in a man*
dæd-a demend	*judge of deeds*
on heofen-um	*in the heavens*

Nouns and adjectives decline, i.e. take endings, to show their meaning and function in the sentence. For now, some basic distinctions will be made and more will be given on the uses of cases in later units. The nominative is the base form of the word and the subject of a sentence, while the accusative is usually the recipient of the action (see Units 5 and 6 for more detail).

The genitive case expresses a general idea of possession and can usually be translated as *of* (see Unit 7). The ending -a in **dæd-a** marks the genitive plural *of deeds*. In the phrase **on eorl-e** the ending -e marks the dative case, which is used here after the preposition **on**. Prepositions (short relational words such as *on, of, for*) force the following noun to take a case ending, usually the dative:

on + singular **hæð** *heath* = **on hæð-e** *on the heath*
on + plural **heofenas** *heavens* = **on heofen-um** *in the heavens*

A further meaning of the dative is *to* or *with,* as in **blæd-um blowan** *to flourish with fruits* (other uses of the dative are discussed in Unit 8).

Wordhoard

Old English place names

The former Roman city of Bath had two names, **Baþanceaster** and **Akemannesceaster**, and from there the **Akemannesstraet** led to **Lunden** (Latin *Londinium*), otherwise known as **Lundenburh** or (dative) **Lundenbyrig**. While **ceaster** endings derive from Latin **castra**, the alternative **-burh** indicates a *fortified settlement* or *walled town* and derives from the verb **beorgan** *to protect*. The *-ton* endings originate in Old English **tun**, which must have originally meant *enclosure* (cf. Dutch **tuin** *garden*, German **Zaun** *fence*), and in Old English place names came to mean *farm* or *estate*.

Old English **burh**

Old English	Modern English	Etymology
Bebbanburh	Bamburgh	*Bebba's fortress*
Burh	Peterborough	*fortified town*
Ealdelmesbyrig	Malmesbury	*Aldhelm's town*

Old English **ceaster**

Old English	Modern English	Etymology
Legeceaster, Ceaster	Chester	*city of legions*
Wintanceaster	Winchester	*unknown* (Latin *venta*)
Wigoraceaster	Worcester	*city of the Wigora tribe*

Old English **tun**

Old English	Modern English	Etymology
Hamtun	(South) Hampton	*home farm*
Middeltun	Milton	*middle estate*
Æppeltun	Appleton	*orchard or estate where apple trees grow*

TEST YOURSELF

1 Alliteration. Listen to a reading of the extract from the poem *Maxims II* and note the words in each line that alliterate e.g. **b**eagas and **b**era, or **ea**ld and **ea**.

> Cyning sceal on healle
> beagas dælan. Bera sceal on hæðe,
> eald and egesfull. Ea of dune sceal
> flodgræg feran. Fyrd sceal ætsomne,
> tirfæstra getrum. Treow sceal on eorle,
> wisdom on were. Wudu sceal on foldan
> blædum blowan. Beorh sceal on eorþan
> grene standan. God sceal on heofenum,
> dæda demend.

2 Translate the proverbs:
   a A bear belongs on a heath, old and terrible.
   b A river must flow, flood-grey down the mountain.
   c A wood belongs on the earth, flourishing with leaves.
   d A hill must stand green upon the earth.

3 Etymology. Use the **word index** at the back of the book to work out the derivation of the following place names. What original Old English words lie behind them?
   a Kingston   b Somerton   c Norton
   d Sutton   e Acton   f Merton
   g Shipton   h Oxford   i Hereford
   j Hertford   k Newbridge

24

3

Say what I am called

This unit will cover:

texts
- *riddle 66 from the Exeter Book*

grammar
- *personal pronouns*
- *the verb* **to be**
- *introduction to the present tense*

vocabulary
- *a comparison with* **King Lear**
- *names of countries and people*

◀)) **TR 8**

Saga hwæt ic hatte
Say what I am called

Cultural contexts

Leofric bishop of Exeter

Edward the Confessor's succession to the throne in 1042 was, naturally enough, accompanied by a number of changes. After his long years of exile in Normandy he brought with him a number of Continental friends and supporters and he appointed some of these to work as chaplains and clerks in the royal household. When posts became available, these men were promoted, and in 1044 Leofric, a man of English descent from Lotharingia (Lorraine), was appointed bishop of Devon and Cornwall. In 1050, he moved the see of the bishopric to Exeter. Anxious to use English in his pastoral work, he collected a large set of books, listed in the record of his donations to the cathedral in 1069–72. One of them is described as **mycel englisc boc be gehwilcum þingum on leoðwisan geworht** *a large English book on various matters made in verse*, clearly a description of the late tenth-century Exeter Book, which, through his gifts to the cathedral, was preserved for posterity.

Riddles from the Exeter Book

The Exeter Book anthology owned by bishop Leofric contains a number of famous Old English poems: *The Advent Lyrics*, a set of religious lyrics exploring the advent and life of Christ, hagiographic poems on the hermit *Guthlac*, an elegiac search for wisdom in *The Wanderer*, the poem of exile and pilgrimage known as *The Seafarer*, and two thematically connected lyrics of loss and reconciliation called *The Wife's Lament* and *The Husband's Message*. As well as these, there are ninety-five riddling poems that describe many aspects of the human and natural world, in a spirit sometimes of playful humour but usually also of wonder and exploration.

> ## Insight
> Modernizing the spelling assists the learning process. Compare the following transcription of the beginning of the study text: **Ich eom mare thonne thes middan-yeard, læsse thonne hondwyrm, leoghtre thonne mona, swiftre thonne sunne.**

Ic eom mare þonne þes middangeard
I am more than this middle earth

The following text is riddle 66 from the Exeter Book. Take a
moment to read it through, remembering the basic pronunciation
rule that every letter counts, that the letters þ ('thorn') and ð ('eth')
represent a 'th' sound, that ge- is pronounced 'yuh-', that c is a 'ch'
sound in words like **ræce** *reach* 'RÆ-cheh'.

．．

◀) **TR 8, 00:08**

Ic eom mare þonne þes middangeard,
læsse þonne hondwyrm, leohtre þonne mona,
swiftre þonne sunne.

I am more than this middle world,
less than a mite, lighter than the moon,
swifter than the sun.

◀) **TR 8, 00:30**

Sæs me sind ealle
flodas on fæðmum ond þes foldan bearm,
5a grene wongas.
The seas to me are all
floods in my embrace, and this earth's lap,
the green plains.
5b Grundum ic hrine,
helle underhnige, heofonas oferstige,
wuldres eþel,
To the depths I touch
hell I sink below, heavens I soar above,
the glory land,
wide ræce
ofer engla eard, eorþan gefylle,
ealne middangeard ond merestreamas

(Contd)

10 side mid me sylfum. Saga hwæt ic hatte.
widely I reach
over the angels' land; the earth I fill –
all the world and the ocean streams –
widely with myself. Say what I am called.

Old–modern correspondences

Although written in an ancient form of verse, the poem uses a good number of words that still belong to the core vocabulary of the English language:

> **grammar words:** am, and, less, me, more, on, than, this, what
> **content words:** all, angel, earth, fathom, fill, flood, green, ground, hand, heaven, hell, mere, mid, moon, over, reach, under, say, self, stream, sun, wide.

Some words are recognizable when the variable endings are removed: **sæ-s** *sea-s*, **flod-as** *flood-s*, **swift-re** *swift-er*.

From what was said in the previous unit, you may recognize the dative endings after prepositions **on** and **mid**: line 4 **on fæðm-um** *in my embrace, in my encircling arms* and line 10 **mid me sylf-um** *with myself,* while **grundum ic hrine** means literally *I touch to the depths.*

Other words have endings that do not survive in modern English: **midd-an** mid, *middle,* **gren-e** *green* or even a prefix ge- (pronounced 'yuh-') which should be removed to get at the root of the word: **ge-fyll-e** *fill*.

Other words may sound broadly similar, but have a different modern spelling: **geard** *yard, enclosure* (pronounced 'YÉard'), **ofer** *over* (pronounced 'over'), **hwæt** *what* (pronounce each letter; rhymes with 'cat').

Occasionally a word may still exist in English, but its meaning will have changed over centuries of use. This is true of *yard* just quoted, and **fæðm** *embrace* – here there are connections with modern English *fathom* which originally meant 'to stretch out the arms wide and so make a measurement'. Such changes in meaning can be explored by consulting the word in the multi-volume or online version of the Oxford English Dictionary.

The verb **stige** (pronounced 'STEE-yuh') in **ofer-stige** *climb over* connects with the noun **stigel** (pronounced 'STEE-yul'); this is modern English *stile* – the wooden steps for climbing over farm walls and fences.

Old English vocabulary

This leaves a set of words that have no modern equivalents. First some compounds:

line 1: **middangeard** = **middan** *middle* + **geard** *enclosure* = *world*
2: **hondwyrm** = **hand** *hand* + **wyrm** *worm, reptile* = *mite, insect*
6: **underhnige** = **under** *under* + **hnige** *sink* = *sink under*
6: **oferstige** = **ofer** *over* + **stige** *climb* = *climb over*

then some purely Old English nouns and phrases:

line 4: **foldan** from **folde** *earth*
4: **bearm** *lap, bosom*

5: **wong-as** plural of **wong** *field, plain*

7: **þes wuldres eþel** *this land of glory* (**wuldor** *glory* +
eþel *homeland*)

8: **engla eard** *region of angels*

and finally some verbs:

sind *are*, **ic hrine** *I touch*, **ic hatte** *I am called*.

Often German, Dutch or Scandinavian languages provide parallels.
For instance in line 6, the verb **hnige** comes from **hnigan** cognate
with German **neigen** *to incline*, while Old English **stigan** parallels
German **steigen** *to climb* and **ic hatte** is like German **ich heisse**.

Riddle formulas

Old English has a verb **hatan**, which means *to call* or *to be called*.
The sentence formula **saga hwæt ic hatte** *say what I am called*,
usually at the end of the poem, is a challenge to the listener to guess
the name of the speaker and so arrive at the solution of the riddle.
In this case the consensus solution is *creation*, Old English **gesceaft**.
Another common formula, often at the beginning of the riddle, is **ic
wiht geseah** *I saw a creature* (**wiht** *creature, wight*; **geseah** *saw*).

Rhythm and sounds

Listen next to a reading of the whole of riddle 66, paying attention
to the letters highlighted in **bold** in each line. There are four accents
or beats to the line, and their varying patterns set the rhythm and
metre of the poem. By modern editorial convention, each line is
divided by a space, the caesura, into its two half-lines, known as
the a-verse and the b-verse and connected by alliteration:

◄) TR 9

Ic eom mare   þonne þes middangeard,
læsse þonne hondwyrm,   leohtre þonne mona,

swiftre þonne sunne.   Sæs me sind ealle
flodas on fæðmum   ond þes foldan bearm,
5   grene wongas.   Grundum ic hrine,
helle underhnige,   heofonas oferstige,
wuldres eþel,   wide ræce
ofer engla eard,   eorþan gefylle,
ealne middangeard   ond merestreamas
10   side mid me sylfum.   Saga hwæt ic hatte.

Alliteration is an important stylistic device in Old English writing, far more important than rhyme. Because it is associated with traditional poetry and song, it was used for rhetorical effect by prose writers in charters, chronicles, laws, saints' lives etc.

Insight

Alliteration in Old English texts, especially in the poems, is governed by rules of style and metre. The only significant alliteration falls on the heavy syllable of content words – semantically important nouns *sun, sea, flood, fathom,* and adjectives *more, less, light, swift* – and occasionally on verbs, rather than on lighter grammatical words such as *and, this, than, me, on, over.*

Grammar

Introduction to personal pronouns
(I, you, he, she, we, they)

Different languages find different ways of doing personal pronouns and it is worth remembering that the modern English system of interpersonal address is not the only one possible. There were more personal pronouns in Old English than in modern English, chiefly because there were three words for *you*. In fact, these are different ways of conceiving of the concept 'you': þu and ge, pronounced 'thoo' and 'yay', correspond to *thou* (the singular *you*)

and *ye* (the plural *you*). There was also a dual pronoun **git**,
pronounced 'yit', *you-two* and **wit** to refer to *we-two*:

	singular		dual		plural	
1st person:	**ic**	*I*	**wit**	*we-two*	**we**	*we*
2nd person:	**þu**	*thou*	**git**	*you-two*	**ge**	*you*
3rd person:	**he,**	*he,*	[ ]		**hi,**	*they*
	heo,	*she,*			**hig**	
	hit	*it*				

In the story of Joseph in Genesis, for example, two Egyptian officials
are thrown into prison with Joseph; eventually they tell him, '**Wit
gesawon swefn** (*we-both saw a dream*)', to which Joseph replies,
'**Secgaþ me hwæt git gesawon** (*Tell me what you-both saw*)'. For
another example of the use of this dual pronoun, to address the king
and queen together, see archbishop Wulfstan's letter in Unit 18.

On pronunciation, note that the combination of letters in -**ig** was
always pronounced 'ee' and corresponds to the modern -*y* ending
in *bloody*, *greedy* etc. (Old English **blodig**, **grædig**). Thus the word
for *they* was pronounced 'hee' whether it was spelt **hi** or **hig**. The
pronoun **ic** was pronounced 'itch' and later written **ich** (note that it
did not have or need an initial capital letter). The pronoun **heo** *she*
was occasionally spelt **hio**.

Insight

The pronoun **þu** *thou* is simply the standard word for
singular *you* in Old English. Only later in the Middle Ages
did it become a marker of informal address, on the model of
French **tu** cf. German **du**, or Italian and Spanish **tu** (in these
languages the word is singular and informal).

Old–modern correspondences

In Shakespeare's time, **thou** and **ye** were clearly still current; but less
obviously **ich** was also in limited use: the pronoun survived in dialect
as the contracted form **'chill** (= ich will) and **'chould** (= ich would).
In the following extract from *King Lear* (Act IV, scene 6) Edgar,

disguised as a peasant and leading the blind, outlawed Gloucester by the arm, affects a rustic dialect as he is challenged by Oswald:

Oswald Wherefore bold peasant
Dar'st thou support a publish'd traitor? Hence;
lest that th' infection of his fortune take
like hold on thee. Let go his arm.

Edgar Chill not let go, zir, without vurther 'casion.

Oswald Let go, slave, or thou di'st.

Edgar Good gentleman, go your gait, and let poor volk pass.

The equivalent of *thou dar'st* in Old English was **þu dearst,** with the same **-st** ending on the verb. For the forms *me, thee, you, his* and *him*, which change according to case, i.e. their function in the sentence, see especially Units 8 and 18.

Introduction to the present tense

The present tense varies its endings according to the person and number of the subject doing the action:

ic ræce	*I reach*	'ich RAEcheh'
þu ræcst	*you* (sing.) *reach*	'thoo RAEch(e)st'
he, heo ræcþ	*he, she reaches*	'hay, héo RAEch(e)th'
we, ge, hig ræcaþ	*we, you, they reach*	'way, yay, hee RAEchath'

Present tense of the verb to be (I am, you are, she is ...)
There were two forms of the verb *to be*: **wesan** and **beon.** They form their present tense as follows:

sg.	1	**ic**	**eom**	OR	**beo**	*am*
	2	**þu**	**eart**		**bist**	*are*
	3	**he, heo, hit**	**is**		**bið**	*is*
pl.	1–3	**we, ge, git, hi**	**sind**		**beoð**	*are*

To remember the form **beoð** it may be helpful to visualize it as the verb *be* with the present tense ending *-eth* as found in Shakespearean English, e.g. *maketh*.

There is room for variation in the above. Just as the two ways of representing the 'th' sound can alternate, so do the vowels i and y, so that we also find **ys**, **byð**. Similarly, instead of **sind** other writers use **synt**, **sindon**, or even **sindan**.

Wordhoard

Countries and people

Regions or countries tended to be named after the people who lived there: **West-Seaxe** meant *West Saxons* rather than simply the region Wessex. Other names are similar: **Suð-Seaxe** *South Saxons* for Sussex, **East-Seaxe** *East Saxons* for Essex, **Eastengle** *East Angles* for East Anglia. In the north of the country was **Norðhymbre**, another plural noun meaning primarily *Northumbrians* and hence *Northumbria*. In writings from the time of king Alfred the various regions came to be called collectively **Angelcynn** *the Angle kindred*, as opposed to the **Wealhcynn** or **Wealas** *the Welsh*. The neighbours of the Welsh, in what is now central England, were the **Mierce** (pronounced 'Meer-cheh') meaning *Borderers* hence *Mercia*, the March or Border Land (for map see Appendix II).

By a process of phonetic change the term **Angle** *the Angles* became **Engle** *the English*, who spoke the language **englisc**. The older term **Angelcynn** still had an ethnic meaning when Cnut raised a tax for **eal Angelcynn** in the D version of the Chronicle for the year 1017, but it was not generally the name for the whole country. Instead, the process of political change that brought about the nation state in the tenth century gave rise to a new name: **Engla-land** *Land of the English*.

Further afield are the following names: **Scottas** *the Scots*, **Scotland** *Scotland*, **Francland** *Frank-Land* i.e. France, **Ealdseaxe**

Old Saxons i.e. Saxony, **Dene** *the Danes*, **Denemearc** *the Dane March* i.e. *Denmark*, **Norðweg** *North Way* i.e. *Norway* – sometimes occurring as a plural noun e.g. **into Norðwegon**, *into the Northways*, the name partly retaining its literal, topographical sense.

Insight

On maps of this period, the island of Britain (**Brytene igland**) was located at the edge of the world, in the encircling ocean (**garsecg**). At the centre of the world was Jerusalem (**Hierusalem**), and the Mediterranean was known as the **Wendelsæ**.

TEST YOURSELF

More riddles

As you read and listen to these riddles selected from the Exeter Book, practise pronunciation, particularly of consonants c, g, h, ð and þ and vowels æ, e, ea and eo. What are the solutions? (For suggested answers see the end of the book.)

◀) TR 10

(a) riddle 69
Wundor wearð on wege; wæter wearð to bane.
A wonder happened on the wave; water turned to bone.

◀) TR 10, 00:13

(b) riddle 75
Ic swiftne geseah on swaþe feran.
I saw a swift one travel on the track.

◀) TR 10, 00:24

(c) riddle 76
Ic ane geseah idese sittan.
I saw a lady sit alone.

4

Here in this year

This unit will cover:

texts
- *the Anglo-Saxon Chronicle*

grammar
- *introduction to past tenses*
- *weak and strong verbs*
- *the prefix ge- (pronounce 'yuh-')*

vocabulary
- *descriptive titles*

◀) TR 11

Her on þissum geare
Here in this year

Annals 1019–1031 from the Anglo-Saxon Chronicle

The Anglo-Saxon Chronicle is a unique contemporary record of early English history. Written by monks at important ecclesiastical centres like the New Minster Winchester or Christ Church Canterbury, its immediate purpose was commemorative – to record major events such as the succession of a new king or bishop, the marriage of a king and queen, the arrival of a comet, journeys, battles, harvests, famines. It was unique at this time because most chronicles in western Europe were written in Latin. In appearance a typical page of the Chronicle has a list of Roman numerals down the left margin signifying the years; the scribe selects any significant or eventful year and writes a short text or annal beside it on the page.

◀ TR 11, 00:07
The year 1019

1019   Her gewende Cnut cyng to Denemearcon, and ðær
        wunode ealne þone winter.

Insight
Each verb consists of two parts: stressed ROOT + inflexion. The root is the base form and when spoken it is stressed, i.e. pronounced with greater prominence (in this book capital letters indicate a stressed syllable). The inflexion is a (weakly stressed) variable ending; it shows the use and meaning of the verb in the context of the sentence: **WUN-ian** *to remain*, **WUN-ode** *(he) remained*.

Cnut's early reign

As a young Danish Viking, Cnut came to the throne after the long Anglo-Danish wars, which intensified in the 990s during the reign of Æthelred the Unready and culminated in the Danish victory at **Assandun** (*Ashingdon*) in 1016. A peace ceremony followed æt

Olanige wið Deorhyrste, at the island of Olney near the town of Deerhurst, where an Anglo-Saxon church still stands to this day. At first Cnut was king in the north only, while Æthelred's son, king Edmund Ironside (**Eadmund Irensid**), ruled in the traditional heartlands of Wessex. But Edmund was short-lived, and in 1017 Cnut **feng ... to eall Englalandes rice** *succeeded to all the kingdom of England.* Rivals to the throne like Edmund's half-brother the young Edward (the Confessor) fled into exile and Cnut married Æthelred's royal widow Emma of Normandy. In 1018 he imposed a large tax on **eall Angelcynn** *all the English nation,* paid off the Danish fleet, and brought about an Anglo-Danish agreement **æt Oxnaforda** *at Oxford.* His power and influence were growing and, from 1019, when he inherited the Scandinavian empire from his brother, Cnut had to divide his time and attention between the two kingdoms of England and Denmark. In the texts it will be seen that the compiler of Chronicle C writes annals for the years up to 1023, but not for 1024–27; he thus emphasizes the period when Cnut was proving his credentials as an English king. Highlighted in this account are Cnut's co-operation with the famous Wulfstan, archbishop of York, his consecration of a church at Ashingdon in Essex at the site of his victory in 1016 and his honouring of the English martyr saint Ælfheah, or St Alphege as he came to be called, the heroic archbishop of Canterbury during the years 1006 to 1012.

◄》 TR 11, 00:18
The year 1020

1020   Her on þissum geare forðferde Lyfing arcebisceop.

And Cnut cyning com eft to Englalande, and þa on Eastron wæs mycel gemot æt Cyringceastre, þa geutlagode man Æþelweard ealdorman and Eadwig 'ceorla cyngc'.

And on ðisum geare se cyng for to Assandune, and Wulfstan arcebisceop and Þurkil eorl and manega bisceopas mid heom, and gehalgodan þæt mynster æt Assandune.

on þissum geare *in this year* 'on THI-sum yéar-reh' (dative case)
forðferde *departed, passed away*
Lyfing pronounced 'Lüving' (also known as archbishop Ælfstan)
com *came* 'cohm'
eft *again, afterwards*
þa ... þa *when ... then*
ge-mot *meeting, assembly* 'yuh-MOAT'
ge-utlagode man *(they) outlawed* 'yuh-OOT-lagoduh'
ealdor-man *nobleman*
ceorl *free peasant* 'CHÉorl'
ceorla cyncg *king of peasants* (a nickname, note variant spelling)
for *went*
manega *many*
mid heom *with them*
ge-halgodan*(they) consecrated* (from the adjective **halig** *holy*)
þæt *the* (neuter)
mynster *church, minster*

Cultural contexts

Descriptive titles

It was normal Old English practice when stating a person's title to give the name first, followed by the rank:

Cnut cyning	king Cnut
Lyfing arcebisceop	archbishop Lyfing (of Canterbury)
Wulfstan arcebisceop	archbishop Wulfstan (of York)
Æþelweard ealdorman	ealdorman Æthelweard
Þurkil eorl	earl Thorkell

This was also true of the nicknames that apportioned praise or blame and the many bynames, which were useful for distinguishing between people of the same name:

Æþelræd Unræd	Æthelred the Ill-advised
Eadmund Irensid	Edmund Ironside
Æþelstan Healfcyning	Æthelstan Half-king
Eadwig ceorla cyng	Eadwy king of the peasants
Þurkil Hwita	Thorkell the White
Ælfgyfu seo hlæfdige	Ælfgyfu the Lady (Emma's adopted English name)
Ælfgyfu seo Hamtunisca	Ælfgyfu of Northampton (lit. the Northamptonian)

Another Thorkell appears later in the reign of Cnut; his name is always given distinctively as **Þurkil Hwita** Thorkell the White (see Unit 20). Cnut's first wife happened to have the same English name as his royal wife Emma of Normandy. This was the noble name Ælfgyfu ('ÆLF-yi-vuh'). To distinguish them the chroniclers called the first wife *Ælfgyfu of Northampton* or simply **seo oðre Ælfgyfu** *the other Ælfgyfu,* while the honorific title **seo hlæfdige** ('HLÆF-di-yuh') was reserved for **Ælfgyfu Imme** i.e. Ælfgyfu Emma.

There was some difference between the old rank of **ealdorman** held by the exiled Æthelweard and the new rank of **eorl** as held by earl Thorkell, a former commander of the Danish army. While there had been around a dozen ealdormanries in the tenth century, the earldoms were fewer in number at the beginning of Cnut's reign, just the four great provinces of Wessex, East Anglia, Mercia and Northumbria. The rank of earl, then, was higher than the normal ealdorman, because he governed a larger territory. This situation had arisen once before in the early tenth century, when

the powerful super-ealdorman was known as Æþelstan healfcyning
Æthelstan Half-king.

Insight

The term **eorl**, which originally meant *brave man, warrior*
in the poetry, gained popularity because it sounded like **jarl**,
the equivalent word in Cnut's mother tongue Old Norse. In
fact, the two languages were similar enough for some mutual
comprehension (for more discussion, see Unit 20).

In 1016 Cnut had appointed Thorkell as earl of East Anglia,
although, as it turned out, there were personal difficulties
between the two of them.

◀) TR 12
The years 1021 to 1023

1021	Her on ðissum geare to Martines mæssan Cnut kyning geutlagode Þurkil eorl.
1022	Her Cnut kyningc for ut mid his scipon to Wiht, and Æþelnoð arcebisceop for to Rome.
1023	Her Cnut cyning com eft to Englalande, and Þurcil and he wæran anræde. And he betæhte Þurcille Denemearcan and his sunu to healdenne, and se cyning nam Þurciles sunu mid him to Englalande. And he let ferian syððan Sancte Ælfeges reliquias of Lundene to Cantwarabyrig.
1024	– [the scribe left a space but wrote nothing]
1025	–
1026	–
1027	–

ut *out* 'oot' (sometimes written **út**; pronounce long)
for ut *travelled out of the country, sailed out to sea*
mid his scipon *with his ships* (dative plural after **mid**)
Wiht *Isle of Wight*

wæran *were*

an-ræd *reconciled, of single counsel* (pronounce both vowels long)

betæhte *entrusted* 'be-TÆHte'(pronounce with a fricative 'h')

to healdenne *to hold, rule*

se *the* (masc.)

nam *took*

sunu *son*

let *ordered* 'late' (pronounce with a long close 'é' sound)

ferian *carry, convey*

syððan *afterwards*

reliquias *relics*

Insight

Old English 'borrowed' or assimilated religious vocabulary from Church Latin e.g. **sanct** from Latin **sanctus** *holy*. The word **reliquias** is originally Latin **reliquiae**, where the **-qu-** spelling is retained from the Latin but the Old English plural **-as** ending is added to the word. The noun **mæsse** is assimilated into the language from Latin **missa** and thoroughly anglicized.

Grammar

Talking about the past

Some of the basics of the present tense of verbs have already been touched on in Units 2 and 3, and more will be explained in Unit 5, but by definition, of course, a chronicle deals with past events. There are two basic ways of forming a past tense in English. One is to add a consonant -*d* as an ending -*ed* to the stem of the verb:

I play → *I played*

the other is to change the vowel in the stem of the verb:

I drink → *I drank*

Both these means of forming the past tense go back to the early stages of the language. Their Old English equivalents are as follows:

ic plegie → **ic plegode**, adding **-ode** to the stem **pleg**
ic drince → **ic dranc** changing the vowel in the stem **drinc**

Verbs of the first type are known as consonantal, or 'weak' verbs, while the others are vocalic (i.e. vowel-changing), or 'strong', verbs. Further examples of weak verbs you will meet are **feran** *depart* **ferde** *departed* and **ahnian** *own* **ahnode** *owned*; two strong verbs are **healdan** *hold* **heold** *held* and **adrifan** *drive out* **adraf** *drove out*. Although numerically there are far more of the first type, so many, in fact, that they are termed the 'regular' verbs in modern English, nevertheless many common verbs, which you will come across frequently, belong to the vocalic type. Some other past tenses already seen are:

weak verbs:	**heo hæfð** *she has*	→	**heo hæfde** *she had*
strong verbs:	**ic seo** *I see*	→	**ic seah** *I saw*
	hit wyrð *it becomes*	→	**hit wearð** *it became*
	hig sittað *they sit*	→	**hig sæton** *they sat*

Note on long and short vowels

Old English scribes rarely indicated vowel length, so that a phrase **god sceal wið yfele** in the poem *Maxims II* can be taken to mean either *God must fight with evil* or *good must fight with evil*. But occasionally for clarity's sake a scribe could write **gód** with an accent or even **good** with a double vowel to indicate a long pronunciation (like 'goad') and to emphasize that the word here means *good*. Another case is **sittan** *to sit,* said with a short 'i', whereas **ridan** *to ride* is pronounced long as 'ree-dan'. Many strong past tenses have a long vowel; so **com** *came* and **for** *travelled* are pronounced with a single long vowel sound, as though written **cóm** and **fór** (or in text books often **cōm** and **fōr**).

In a section on rhetoric in his *Handbook* (for which, see Unit 5), the author Byrhtferth writes of barbarism. The example he gives is a person who wishes to insult someone by calling him a fool but instead of using the correct form þu sott *you fool,* with a short 'o' vowel, he mistakenly pronounces a long vowel and says þu sot *you soot*! The reason for the mistake is that sott with a short vowel was a new expression in the language, a fashionable insult perhaps, influenced by the equivalent word in French. The example is humorous, but it illustrates very well the distinction between long and short vowels.

The prefix ge- ('yuh-')

For the past tense many Old English writers liked to attach an optional ge- prefix to the verb. This is pronounced 'yuh-' and is weakly stressed: the emphasis falls on the stem of the word, e.g. ge-wende is pronounced 'yuh-WENde'.

As far as meaning is concerned the ge- is a perfective prefix which conveys the idea of result or completeness; often it is prefixed to the past tense merely to emphasize the idea of a completed action in the past:

ic seah	and	**ic geseah**	both mean *I saw*
ic nam	and	**ic genam**	both mean *I took*

With some verbs, however, the perfective prefix adds to the meaning:

ahnian *to own*	**geahnian** *to take possession, prove ownership*
áscian *to ask*	**geáscian** *to discover*
ridan *to ride*	**geridan** *to occupy, i.e. ride round and occupy*
sittan *to sit*	**gesittan** *to settle, inhabit*

In modern dictionaries of Old English, it is usual to ignore the prefix for reference purposes and to look up a word such as **sittan** or **gesittan** under the letter 's'.

The prefix **ge-** before nouns

The prefix **ge-** is also used with nouns derived from verbs, again to indicate a completed action, such as **ge-sceaft**, derived from **scieppan** *to create*, which means *that which has been created*, i.e. *creation*, or in the plural as **þa feower gesceaftas** *the four elements* (for which see Unit 5).

Before other nouns **ge-** conveys an idea of grouping together or association:

ge-mot	*assembly* (cf. modern English *folk-moot*)
ge-trum	*troop*
ge-fera	*comrade, travelling companion*
	(from **feran** *to travel*)

On the same pattern, the singular **broðor** *brother* has the simple plural **broðru** *brothers*, but the plural with prefix **gebroðru** indicates a *group of brothers* hence also *co-religionists* or *monks*.

> **Insight**
>
> Old English **genog** or **genoh** *sufficient* was written with an **i-** prefix from the 12th century, to give forms in Middle English such as **inug, ynug, ynough**. The adjective *enough* is one of the few modern English words to preserve the old **ge-** prefix.

Irregular past tenses

As well as the two basic types of verb, the weak and strong conjugations, there are also a good number of verbs that do not fit the standard pattern. Some are common verbs such as *be, do, go* or *know*. As in many languages, these occur so frequently in people's speech that they take on irregular forms in present and past tenses:

is	*is*	'iss'	→	**wæs**	*was*	
deð	*does*	'day-th'	→	**dyde**	*did*	'dü-deh'
gæð	*goes*	'ga-th'	→	**eode**	*went*	'éo-deh'
wat	*knows*	'wah-t'	→	**wiste**	*knew*	

Comparing present and past tenses of *to be*

			Present			*Past*	
sg.	1	**ic**	**eom**	**beo**	*am*	**wæs**	*was*
	2	**þu**	**eart**	**bist**	*are*	**wære**	*were*
	3	**he, heo, hit**	**is**	**bið**	*is*	**wæs**	*was*
pl.	1–3	**we, ge, git, hi**	**sind**	**beoð**	*are*	**wæron**	*were*

The plural past tense ending in **-on** or **-an**

In modern English we distinguish singular *was* and plural *were* but
not a singular *did* from a plural *did*, since with most verbs the form
does not change. But in Old English the distinction **wæs/wæron** is
invariably made with other verbs too: **dyde/dydon, eode/eodon,
wiste/wiston.**

A simple rule is that the past tense plural takes the ending -on:

wiste = *he/she knew*   **wiston** = *they knew*

As can be seen from the study texts, however, the scribes
sometimes write **-an**, because in late Old English the **-on** ending
was pronounced as in modern English 'button' and so the earlier
distinction between **-an** and **-on** could no longer be heard.

Cultural contexts

The adverb *here*

The first word of a typical annal is pronounced 'hay-r' with a
long close vowel like French 'é' and means literally *here* i.e. *now at
this point* in the series of annals marked by the list of numbers in
the left margin of the manuscript page. The same demonstrative
adverb *here* is used in the Old English titles written over narrative
illustrations in Anglo-Saxon religious manuscripts; these captions
explain to the viewer what happened *here* in the picture.

The equivalent Latin word **hic** appears in the Latin titles of the Bayeux Tapestry, which was most probably made by Anglo-Saxon artists and embroiderers.

The calendar

The dates in the Chronicle and other Old English writings follow the Roman calendar in using the system of ides, nones, and kalends, except that feast days are usually named individually, e.g. **midwintres dæg** *Christmas Day*. The ides (Latin **idus**) fall on the 15th day of March, May, July and October and on the 13th day of the other months. The kalends are the first day of the month. The twelfth of the kalends – the day of the solstice and the equinox – is found by counting backwards. The system can be illustrated by looking at the second half of December schematically:

December

13	the ides of December (Latin **idus Decembris**)
14	nineteenth of the kalends of January
15	eighteenth of the kalends of January
16	seventeenth of the kalends of January
17	etc.
18	
19	
20	
21	twelfth of the kalends of January (the solstice, Old English **sunstede**)
22	
23	tenth of the kalends of January
24	

25	Christmas (Old English **midwintres dæg**)
26	St Stephen's Day
27	
28	fifth of the kalends of January
29	fourth of the kalends of January
30	third of the kalends of January
31	second of the kalends of January

January
1   the kalends of January (Latin **kalendas Ianuarii**)

Similarly, the nones (Latin **nonas**) can be defined as the ninth day by (inclusive) counting backwards from the ides. In March, May, July and October the nones fall on the 7th of the month, and on the 5th of the other months.

Reading

In a further extract from *Maxims II*, the introductory poem in the C version of the Chronicle, the poet presents his reflections on the struggles of life in the world (lines 48b–55a). The compiler of the Chronicle perhaps considered it suitable wisdom to ponder as his readers read about the deeds of the kings in their own generation:

> Tungol sceal on heofenum
> beorhte scinan, swa him bebead Meotud.
> God sceal wið yfele; geogoð sceal wið yldo;
> lif sceal wið deaþe; leoht sceal wið þystrum;
> fyrd wið fyrde, feond wið oðrum,
> lað wið laðe ymb land sacan,
> synne stælan. A sceal snotor hycgean
> ymb þysse worulde gewinn.

A star belongs in the heavens, shining brightly as the Lord commanded. Good must fight with evil, youth with age, life

(Contd)

with death, light with dark, army with army, enemy with
another, foe against foe, dispute the land, accuse of wrong.
Ever a wise man must meditate on the struggles of this world.

Insight

Modernization of the spelling can point up the 'Englishness' of Old English, which the different orthographic conventions can hide. The above text in modernized spelling could read: **Tungol shal on hevenum beorghte shinan, … Good shal with yvele, lif shal with deathe; leoght shal with thystrum.** Most of the words then seem familiar apart from the first and last: **tungol** an expressive synonym for **steorra** *star*, and the archaic-poetic **thyster** or **thester** *darkness*.

TEST YOURSELF (1)

Comprehension and interpretation

The aim of the following questions is to check comprehension and explore interpretations. The **Test Yourself answers** may be found at the back of the book.

1 What happened to Thorkel on the Feast of St Martin in 1021?

2 What reasons could you suggest for the travels of king Cnut and archbishop Athelnoth in the year 1022?

3 Why did the king take Thorkel's son back with him to England?

4 What happened to the relics of St Alphege?

TEST YOURSELF (2)

1 **Past tenses** Reread the study texts paying particular attention to the tenses of the verbs. For each infinitive in the list below supply the corresponding past tense:

Infinitive	Past tense
e.g. **wendan** *to return*	**gewende** *returned*

    a   gewunian *to remain*
    b   niman *to take*
    c   forðferan *to depart*
    d   lætan *to order*
    e   gehalgian *to consecrate*
    f   betæcan *to entrust*

2 Choose the correct missing verb:
    a   Her Cnut kyningc_____ út mid his scipon to Wiht [com/for].
    b   Ic wiht _____ on wege feran [geseah/wiste].

c Her on ðissum geare Cnut kyning _____ Þurkil
eorl [geutlagode/geutlagodon].

d Wulfstan arcebiscop and oðre biscopas ... _____
þæt mynster æt Assandune [gehalgode/gehalgodon].

3 The following annals from the D chronicle (which do not
appear in C) reveal an interest in contacts with Rome and
journeys to the papal court. Translate, using for assistance the
grammar notes in this unit and the word index at the back.

D 1026   Her for Ælfric biscop to Rome, and onfeng
         pallium æt Iohanne papan on .ii. Idus Nouembris.

D 1031   Her for Cnut cyng to Rome. And sona swa he
         ham com, þa for he to Scotlande, and Scotta cyng
         eode him on hand, and wearð his man, ac he þæt
         lytle hwile heold.

4 **Two versions of the story of king Olaf** Compare and contrast the
annals for 1028–30 in manuscripts C and D of the Chronicle.
What differences can be seen in the two versions of the narrative?

Version C

C 1028   Her Cnut cing for to Norwegon mid fiftig scipum.

C 1030   Her wæs Olaf cing ofslagen on Norwegon of his
         agenum folce, and wæs syððan halig. And þæs
         geres ær ðam forferde Hacun se dohtiga eorl on sæ.

Version D

D 1028   Her for Cnut cyng of Englalande mid fiftig
         scypum to Norwegum, and adraf Olaf cyng of
         þam lande, and geahnade him eall þæt land.

D 1029   Her com Cnut cyng eft ham to Englalande.

D 1030   Her com Olaf cyng eft into Norðwegon, and þæt
         folc gegaderade him togeanes and wið him fuhton,
         and he wearð þær ofslægen.

5

About the four seasons

This unit will cover:

texts
- *the four seasons*
- *Byrhtferth's* Handbook

grammar
- *more on the present tense*
- *the nominative case*
- *grammatical gender*

vocabulary
- *numerals*
- *the seasons*
- *dates*

🔊 **TR 13**

Ymbe þa feower timan
About the four seasons

Byrhtferth's *Handbook*

An extract from the writing of Byrhtferth (c.970–c.1020), a monk and teacher at Ramsey Abbey, and an author of historical and scientific writings. In his position as **magister** (*teacher*), Byrhtferth compiled a bilingual Latin and English **handboc** or *manual* known otherwise by a Greek title *Enchiridion*. This was a textbook on the science of **gerim-cræft** *computus*, i.e. the mathematics of the calendar, which involved arithmetic, geography, astronomy and rhetoric. Byrhtferth's readership was made up partly of the young monks and pupils of his own monastery, who knew Latin, but more widely also of the ordinary priests and clerics of the unreformed minsters and parishes, who used mainly English. Byrhtferth's secondary aim therefore was to teach some basic Latin to those who did not know the language. But his main purpose was to teach computus and convey his enthusiasm for it: in his colourful prose Byrhtferth described the beauty of computus as **þære lilian blosman** *the blossom of the lily* and its profundity as **þære rosena swæc** *the fragrance of roses*. And he was full of respect for the institution that had fostered him: **þas þing we gemetton on Ramesige, þurh Godes miltsiendan gife** *these things we found at Ramsey, through God's merciful grace*.

> ### Insight
> *He* and *they*. The pronunciation of the pronoun **he** meaning *he* is close to 'hay' or 'hé' (in phonetics /he:/). The plural equivalent **hi** meaning *they* was pronounced like 'hee', to rhyme with modern English 'tea' (phonetics /ti:/). Because the digraph **-ig** was pronounced 'ee', the word for *they* could also be written **hig**.

> ◀) **TR 13, 00:09**
>
> **Ymbe þa feower timan** *About the four seasons*
>
> Ymbe þa feower timan we wyllað cyðan iungum preostum ma þinga, þæt hig magon þe ranclicor þas þing heora clericum geswutelian.

54

About the four seasons we wish to proclaim to young priests more things, so that they can explain the more boldly these things to their clerics.

ymbe *about* 'üm-beh'
þa *the* 'thah' (with long vowel) (plural)
tíma *time, season* 'tee-ma'
we wyllað *we want* 'wé wüllath'
cyðan *proclaim, make known* 'kü-' (with a long vowel) + '-than'
iung-um preost-um *to young priests* 'yun-gum préas-tum' (dative plural)
ma *more* 'mah' (with long vowel) (comparative adverb)
þæt *that, so that*
hig magon *they can* 'hee maggon' (plural of **mæg** can)
þe ranclicor *the more boldly*
ge-swutelian *clarify* 'yuh-SWOO-tuh-leean'
þas þing *these things* 'thahss' (long vowel)
heora cleric-um *to their clerks* (dative plural in **-um**)

◀》 TR 14

(1) Lengtentima *Spring*

Ver ys lengtentima, and he gæð to tune on .vii. idus Februarii, and he byð wæt and wearm, and þry monðas he byð betwux mannum, and he hæfð an and hundnigontig daga, and he hæfð emniht.

ys = is *is*
lengten-tima *springtime, Lent time* (masculine noun)
gæð *goes from* **gan** *to go* (pronounce vowels long)
tun *estate, town* (see **reading** below)
.vii. = seofon *seven* 'séo-von'
on .vii. idus Februarii *7th February*
monð-as *months* 'mohn-thass' (plural)

be-twux *among, betwixt*
mannum *men, people* (dative plural)
an *one* 'ahn' (long vowel)
hundnigontig *ninety* 'hund-NEE-ghonti'
daga *of days* (genitive plural)
emniht *equinox*

🔊 **TR 15**

(2) Sumor *Summer*

Se oðer tima hatte *æstas*, þæt byð sumor. On lengtentima
springað oððe greniað wæstmas, and on sumera hig weaxað
and on hærfest hig ripiað. Sumor byð wearm and drigge, and
þes tima byð þry monðas, and he hæfð hundnigontig daga, and
he gæð to mannum on .vii. idus Mai, and he hæfð sunstede.

se *the* (masculine singular definite article)
oðer *second*
springað from **springan** *to spring up*
oððe *or* (conjunction)
greniað *flourish* 'gré-niath' (from **grenian**, cf. **grene** *green*)
wæstm-as *fruits* 'wæst-mas' (plural noun)
weaxað from **weaxan** *wax, grow*
ripiað from **ripian** *ripen*
drigge *dry* 'drih-yeh'
þes *this* (masculine nominative singular)
.vii. idus Mai *9th May*
sunstede *solstice*

QUICK VOCAB

Insight
The **-ð** or '-th' ending on verbs is a sure sign of present tense
meaning. In early modern English the verbs in the above text
'Summer' would be **springeth**, **greeneth**, **waxeth** and **ripeneth**.

(3) Hærfest *Autumn*

Se þridda tima ys *autumnus* on Lyden gecweden and on
Englisc hærfest. Boceras getrahtniað þæne naman for þære
ripunge oððe for þære gaderunge. Hig cweðað '*autumnus*,
propter autumnationem uel propter maturitatem'. Se gæð
on .vii. idus Augusti to tune, and he byð þry monðas, and he
hæfð emniht, and he hæfð twa and hundnigontig daga, and
he byð drigge and ceald.

se þridda tima *the third season*
Lyden *Latin*
gecweden *called* (past participle of **cweðan**)
bocer-as (plural of **bocere** *scholar*, cf. **boc** *book* 'bohk')
getrahtniað *explain* (present tense)
þæne *the* (masculine accusative case; see Units 5 and 10)
nama *name*
for *because of*
þære *the* (feminine dative; see Units 8 and 10)
ripung *ripening*
gaderung *gathering*
cweðað *say* (present tense of **cweðan** *say*)
.vii. idus Augusti *7th August*
ceald *cold*

QUICK VOCAB

[The Latin etymology 'autumnus propter autumationem uel
propter maturitatem' can be translated as '*autumn*, because of
autumatio or *maturity*'.]

(4) Winter *Winter*

Se feorða tima ys genemned hiemps on Lyden and winter on
Englisc. He hæfð sunstede and twa and hundnigontig daga,
and he byð þry monðas, and he byð ceald and wæt.

Old–modern correspondences

The verb cyðan

The verb cyðan *make known, proclaim* derives from cuð *known*; this still exists in modern English as the negative adjective *uncouth*, which initially meant *unknown, strange*, whence it later came to mean *unattractive in manners and language* and in some situations *uncultured*.

Emniht *Equinox*

Although early medieval Europeans knew nothing of a heliocentric universe, they inherited a sophisticated knowledge of the sun and the planets from Roman astronomy. The equinox (from Latin aequus *equal* and nox *night*) is the time when the sun crosses the equator making the night and the day equal in length. The Old English emniht captures very well the sense of equi-nox, being a compound of emn a phonetic assimilation from efn i.e. efen *even, equal* + niht *night*.

The latter word, like byrht, briht, beorht *bright* (the first element of Byrhtferth's name) and leoht *light,* has the fricative '-h-' sound still found in German *Licht*. In modern English, this older pronunciation is reflected in the now silent -gh- spelling, but even up to Shakespeare's time there were speakers who still pronounced it. Eventually, the -gh- ceased to sound, but in some words it resolved to another fricative: the 'f' sound of *rough* and *enough*, from Old English ruh and ge-noh. In parts of Scotland, of course, the '-h-' sound still survives in words like *light* and *night*.

Sunstede *Solstice*

The solstices are the two turning points, one in summer and one in winter, when the sun, in the gradual shifting of its course through the sky, reaches its maximum distance from the equator. In summer the sun follows a more northerly course and 'stands' at the solstice on 21st June, thereafter following a daily more southerly course until it reaches its position at the winter solstice on 21st December. The Old English word sun-stede is again an elegant rendering of the Latin, a compound meaning literally *sun-place* or *sun-stead*, the second element occurring in modern English *homestead*, *farmstead* and *bedstead*, as well as in adjectives like *steady* and *steadfast*.

Grammar

The basics of the present tense

It is hardly necessary to emphasize the importance of knowing whether a writer is talking about the present or the past and, like many European languages, English makes a basic formal distinction between present and past in its system of tenses. In Old English the present tense can often be recognized in the third person, i.e. when the subject is *he, she, it, they,* by the ending in **-ð** or **-þ**. This is the same '-th' ending that we find in the King James Bible or Shakespeare's 'the rain it raineth every day' or in old proverbs such as 'manners maketh the man'. Examples in Old English are:

singular

byð *is,* **hæfð** *has,* **gæð** *goes,*
cymð *comes,* **drincð** *drinks,* **selð** *gives*

plural

wæstmas **springað, greniað, weaxað, ripiað**
the fruits spring up, flourish, grow, ripen
we wyllað cyðan iungum preostum ma þinga
we want *to tell young priests more things*

The nominative

The nominative is the normal form of the noun and the pronoun, the headword that is listed in the dictionaries. In the following typical examples, a noun in the nominative case is the subject of the sentence, i.e. the person or agent that carries out the action:

<u>cyning</u> sceal rice healdan
a king must rule a country (seen in Unit 2)

Her gewende <u>Cnut cyng</u> to Denemearcon
here <u>king Cnut</u> returned to Denmark (seen in Unit 4)

In the singular, a noun in the nominative case is unmarked by any ending, but when it refers to more than one the noun **declines,** i.e. takes an ending, to show that it is nominative plural. Again the nominative shows the <u>subject</u> of the verb, i.e. the doers of the action:

<u>boceras</u> getrahtniað þæne naman for þære ripunge
<u>scholars</u> explain the name as ripening

Grammatical gender

Languages like Old English and German distinguish three fundamental categories of noun and with each category use a different word for the definite article. In Old English the three base forms for the definite article are **se, seo, þæt**:

> the article **se** is used with masculine nouns such as **tima** *season*
> **seo** is used with feminine nouns such as **gaderung** *gathering*
> **þæt** goes with neuter nouns such as **mynster** *minster*

In the same way, there are three words for *it*; these are the personal pronouns **he, heo,** and **hit**: the pronoun **he** means *he* as a personal pronoun or *it* when referring to a masculine noun; similarly, **heo** is either *she* or *it*; while **hit** means *it* in the neuter.

To give some quick examples of masculine nouns: **se nama** means *the name*, **se here** *the army*, **se mona** *the moon*, **se monað** *the month*, **se hafuc** *the hawk*, **se bera** *the bear* (note that the word **se** in these instances can also mean *that*. For feminine nouns, **seo tid** means *the hour* or *that hour*, **seo heall** means *the hall*, **seo glof** *the glove*, **seo eorþe** *the earth*, **seo sunne** *the sun*. Similarly, with neuter nouns: **þæt hus** means *the house*, **þæt scip** means *the ship*, **þæt ger** 'yér' *the year*. All these examples show the base form or the nominative.

It has been calculated that roughly forty-five percent of the nouns you will meet are masculine, thirty-five percent are feminine and twenty-five percent neuter (Quirk and Wrenn, p. 20). It is not usually possible to predict the gender of a noun from its form, although knowledge of the equivalent words in German will help.

In the late Old English period a new article **þe** developed and this became the modern *the*. But until that process of gradual change had completed itself, speakers always made a distinction between the three grammatical genders of nouns. And the gender of a noun affected not only the article *the* but other relevant words in the sentence.

So when Byrhtferth discusses the second season of the year he writes **se** because **tima** is masculine:

> **se oðer tima hatte æstas, þæt byð sumor**
> *the second season is called aestas, that is summer*

And when he refers to this season a little later, Byrhtferth uses the corresponding word for *it*, which has to be masculine **he**:

Sumor byð wearm and drigge, and **þes tima** byð þry monðas, and **he** hæfð hundnigontig daga, and **he** gæð to mannum on .vii. idus Mai, and **he** hæfð sunstede.

*Summer is warm and dry, and this season is three months, and it (Old English **he**) has 90 days, and it (Old English **he**) goes to men on 9th May, and it (Old English **he**) has a solstice.*

If he were writing about the sun, **seo sunne,** a feminine noun, the corresponding pronoun would be **heo**, and if he were writing about a neuter noun **þæt ger** *the year*, the pronoun would be **hit**. So although it sounds like Byrhtferth is personifying the season, this is not necessarily the case, since he is using **he** according to the rules of grammatical gender.

Here is Byrhtferth writing about *the day*, in Old English **se dæg**, and its divisions and hours (in Old English **todælednys** and **tid** 'teed' are feminine nouns); note the variation in the definite article according to gender:

Se dæg hæfð þreo todælednyssa: **seo** forme hatte mane, þæt ys ærnemerigen, and **seo** oðer ys gecweden meridies, and **seo** þridde ys geciged suppremum, þæt ys on æfen oððe **seo** ytemeste tid (*Handboc*, II.3, ll. 127–30).

The day has three divisions: the first is called 'mane', that is early morning, and the second is called 'meridies', and the third is termed 'suppremum', that is in the evening or the last hour.

From now on, to help with the learning of gender along the lines of many modern language textbooks, the vocabulary lists in each unit will list nouns together with their requisite definite article **se, þæt, seo** (meaning *the* or *that*). This is followed as before by the meaning in italics, where necessary the pronunciation in inverted commas and any further information in brackets.

Examples are:

> **se tima** season, *time* 'tee-ma' (modern English *time*)
> **seo tid** hour, *time* 'teed' (cf. the proverb *time and tide wait for no man*)

Insight

In **cyning sceal beagas dælan** in Unit 2, the verb **dælan** means *to distribute* or *deal out*. With a prefix **to-** added to give a sense of completion, **todælan** means *to deal apart, to scatter, to divide*, the adjective *divided* being **todæled**. To turn this into a noun, the suffix **-nes** or **-nys** is added. By this process of word-formation, known as derivation, the abstract idea of *division* or 'dealt-apart-ness' is expressed in Old English by the noun '**to-dæl-ed-nys**'.

Reading

As in other units the reading section allows you to browse, to read some well-known texts discursively without worrying about the meaning of every word.

1 From *Maxims II*

In some lines from the beginning of the poem, the poet ponders **wyrd**, a term derived from the verb **weorðan** *to become*. A common word for *fate* in Old English poetry, **wyrd** means here *the becoming of events* and the poet links it with the passing of the seasons. The passage can be seen as a set of associations and interconnections, in a modern punctuation best presented as a set of clauses joined by commas:

> Wind byð on lyfte swiftust,
> þunar byð þragum hludast, þrymmas syndan Cristes myccle,
> wyrd byð swiðost, winter byð cealdost,
> lencten hrimigost, he byð lengest ceald,
> sumor sunwlitegost, swegel byð hatost,
> hærfest hreðeadegost, hæleðum bringeþ
> geres wæstmas þa þe him God sendeð,
> soð bið swutolost, since byð deorost,
> gold gumena gehwam, and gomol snoterost
> fyrngearum frod, se þe ær feala gebideð.

> *Wind in the air is swiftest,*
> *thunder sometimes is loudest, the glories of Christ are great,*
> *fate is strongest, winter is coldest,*
> *spring the frostiest – it is cold the longest –*
> *summer brightest with sun, sky is hottest,*
> *autumn most glorious – brings to men*
> *the fruits of the year which God sends them –*
> *truth is clearest – treasure is dearest,*
> *gold to everyman – and an old man most prudent,*
> *wise with distant years, who has experienced much.*

2 From the Exeter Book

The Seafarer

The Seafarer, a poem about pilgrimage and exile, presents vivid images of winter and summer. Note the hyperbole of the following passage (lines 14–17):

> hu ic earmcearig iscealdne sæ
> winter wunade wræccan lastum
> winemægum bidroren,
> bihongen hrimgicelum. Hægl scurum fleag.

how I, wretched on the ice-cold sea,
remained the winter on the exile paths,
deprived of kinsmen,
hung round with icicles. Hail flew in showers.

A well-known passage is the image of the cuckoo or **geac**
described as **sumeres weard** *summer's ward*, i.e. *the guardian*
of summer (lines 53–55a):

Swylce geac monað geomran reorde
singeð sumeres weard sorge beodeð
bittre in breosthord.

The cuckoo too serves warning by its mournful cry; summer's
herald sings and foretells cruel distress at heart.
                                  (trans. Bradley 1982, p. 333)

The Wife's Lament
Another Exeter Book poem, *The Wife's Lament*, also an elegy on
the theme of exile, speaks ambivalently of the summer-long day
(lines 37–8):

þær ic sittan mot sumorlangne dæg,
þær ic wepan mæg mine wræcsiþas...

There I must sit the summer-long day.
There I may weep for the ways of my exile... (trans. Bradley)

Insight
As we saw in Unit 3, annal C 1019 of the Chronicle tells us
that king Cnut spent the winter of 1019–20 in Denmark.
There were practical as well as political reasons for his stay.
Because of adverse weather conditions, winter normally put a
stop to travel until the sailing season could begin again at the
end of the spring.

3 From the Anglo-Saxon Chronicle

Naturally enough, winter was a very conspicuous season. Perhaps because of this, people tended to count the winters rather than the number of years that a king lived or reigned. Thus the Chronicle, version F, writes about the founding of Normandy by the Viking Rollo:

> **F 876 Her Rodla ðurhferde Normandi mid his here, and he rixade fifti wintra.**
>
> *Here Rollo took over Normandy with his army, and he ruled fifty winters.*

4 From the Middle English Harley Lyrics

Byrhtferth writes that the spring **gæð to tune**, literally *goes to town* – in other words that it comes among the dwelling places or arrives in the world. A similar turn of phrase occurs in a famous Middle English poem, written long after the Old English period, in an anthology known as the Harley Lyrics. Made about 1340, forty years or so before the time of the great Chaucer, the collection preserves a whole set of diverse early English poems. This stage of Middle English sits roughly halfway in the development of the language between Old and early modern English. Although Middle English has lost the many case endings and gender distinctions of Old English, most of the words in this passage are Old English in origin. Pronunciation is very similar to Old English, but there are a different set of spelling conventions, for example, -ou- in **toune** regularly represents the same 'oo' sound as -u- in Old English **tun**):

> Lenten ys come wiþ love to toune,
> Wiþ blosmen ant wiþ briddes roune,   [**blosmen** *blossoms*]
> þat al þis blisse bringeþ.
> Dayeseges in þis dales,   [**briddes roune** *birdsong*]
> notes swete of nyhtegales,   [**dayeseges** *daisies*]
> uch foul song singeþ.   [**uch foul** *each bird*]

There are Old English equivalents for most of the words in this text: **lengten** *spring*, **ys (ge)cumen** *is come*, **wiþ** *with*, **lufe** (dat.) *love*, **to** *to*, **tun** *farmstead*, **blostm** *blossom*, **and** *and*, **bridd** *young bird*, **run** *mystery, counsel, runic letter*; **þæt** *that*, **eal** *all*, **blisse** (acc.) *bliss*, **bringeþ** *bringeth*, **dæges-eage** *'the day's eye'* i.e. *daisy*, **swet** *sweet*, **nihtegale** *nightingale*, **ælc** *'æltch'* *each*, **fugol** (later pronunciation 'foo-wol') *bird*, **sang** *song*, **singeþ** *singeth*. Only two or three words in the passage do not fit: the meaning of Middle English **roune** has changed to 'song'; **dale** meaning *valley* comes from Old Norse rather than Old English **dæl** *part*; and **note** is from Old French.

Cultural contexts

In 1016 came the Battle of Ashingdon. Byrhtferth's noble patrons – Eadnoth bishop of Dorchester (formerly abbot of Ramsey from 992 to 1006) and Wulfsige (who succeeded as abbot) – both fell in the fighting. Ramsey came under the jurisdiction of the new king and it was probably he who appointed a new abbot. Wythmann was a foreigner from Germany, unused to the ways at Ramsey, and the monks reacted against his severe regime. In 1020 he was driven out. After going on pilgrimage to Jerusalem, he returned to Ramsey, resigned his position and became a hermit at Northeya. In the meantime, Cnut had decided to disperse the unruly monastery community, but was persuaded to change his mind by the abbot of Peterborough.

In these times of unrest there is a possibility that Byrhtferth also chose to leave his alma mater for voluntary exile elsewhere. In one of his later works, a Latin **Life of Saint Ecgwine,** Byrhtferth tells the legendary story of the founder of Evesham Abbey in Worcestershire and the book is respectfully dedicated to the monks of that abbey, almost as though he knew them. As Baker and Lapidge (1995) suggest, it is possible that during the troubles the abbot of Evesham, a former monk of Ramsey, invited Byrhtferth to join him there.

TEST YOURSELF

1 Fill in the correct form of the present tense.
   a We _____ cyðan iungum preostum ma þinga [wyllan].
   b Lengtentima ____ to tune on .vii. idus Februarii [gan].
   c He _____ an and hundnigontig daga [habban].
   d On lengtentima _____ wæstmas [springan].
   e On sumera _____ wæstmas [weaxan].
   f On hærfest hig _____ [ripian].
   g Winter _____ ceald and wæt [beon].

2 Translate:

> Be ðære sunnan
>
> Be ðære sunnan cweðe we þus. Ðonne heo uparist, þonne
> wyrcð heo dæg. Þonne heo nyðer byð astigen, þonne bringð
> heo þa niht (Byrhtferth, *Handboc*, II.3, lines 124–6).

3 The following passage comes from an anonymous eleventh-
   century schooltext on gemstones and minerals. Read the
   extract and fill in the missing words in the translation below.
   a Asbestus hatte sum stancynn on Claudea rice. Gif he wyrð
      onbyrnende, ne mæg hine wæter ne wind adwæscan.
   b Sum stan is on Persa rice; gif þu hine mid handa ahrinest,
      he birneð sona. Se stan is haten piriten.
   c Seleten hatte sum stan þæs gecyndu sind þæt he mid
      wexsendan monan wexseð and mid waniendan wanað.
      Se stan bið gemet on Persa rice.
   d Sum stan hatte alexandrius. Se bið hwit and cristallum
      gelic.

   a *A certain type of stone* _____ *asbestos in the*
      kingdom of Claudea. If _____ *starts (lit. becomes)*
      burning, neither water nor wind _____ *extinguish* ____.
   b *A certain stone is in the kingdom of the Persians; if you*
      _____ *it with the hand it immediately* _____ .
      The stone is called pyrites.

c *Seletes is the name of a stone whose characteristics are that _____ waxes with the waxing moon and _____ with the waning one. The stone is found in Persia.*

d *A certain stone is called alexandrius; it _____ white and like to crystal.*

6

I saw in a dream

This unit will cover:

texts

- **extracts from the Old English version of the story of Joseph and his brothers in Genesis**

grammar

- **the past tense of hatan** to command
- **the use of the construction þa... þa** when... then
- **the accusative case**
- **me þuhte** it seemed to me

🔊 **TR 18**

> **Ic geseah on swefne**
> *I saw in a dream*

Joseph and his brothers

The story of Joseph and his brothers from the Book of Genesis is a compelling account of betrayal and reconciliation. It has had many retellings over the centuries, and it appears to have been popular in the Old English period. A translation of Genesis was made by a team of translators and a group of artists made an illustrated version of the

Hexateuch (the first six books of the Bible). The story of Joseph also circulated as a separate text: in one manuscript now in Cambridge it occurs at the end of a collection of archbishop Wulfstan's legal and political writings. Evidently there were political resonances to the story, for as we will see in later units a biblical story of fraternal rivalry had much to say to an age when brothers and half-brothers vied for the throne, suffered exile or worse and, at times, seemed to struggle towards a hard-won reconciliation.

TR 18, 00:08

Ða Iosep wæs syxtynewintre *When Joseph was 16*

Ða Iosep wæs syxtynewintre, he heold hys fæder heorde mid hys broðrum. And he wæs mid Balan sunum and Zelphan hys fæder wifa. He gewregde his broðru to hira fæder ðære mæstan wrohte.

QUICK VOCAB

ða *when* 'thah'
seo heord *herd*
mid hys broðrum *with his brothers* (dative plural after **mid**)
þæt wif *woman, wife* 'weef' (note the neuter gender)
wifa *wives* 'wee-va' (plural)
gewregde *accused* (past tense of **ge-wregan**)
heora *their*
ðære mæstan wrohte *of the greatest wrongdoing* (nominative **seo wroht**)

Check your comprehension against this translation:

When Joseph was 16, he kept his father's herd with his brothers. And he was with Bala's sons – and Zelpha's – his father's wives. He accused his brothers to their father of the greatest wrong.

TR 19

Soþlice Israel lufode Iosep ofer ealle hys suna for þam ðe he hine gestrynde on hys ylde, and het him wyrcean hringfage tunecan.

soþlice *truly* 'sothe-li-cheh'
lufode *loved* 'LU-vo-deh' (from **lufian** *to love*)
for þam ðe *because*
strynan *to gain, beget* (also spelt **strienan, streonan**)
yld *old age* (also spelt **ield** *age*)
het *ordered* 'hét' (with long vowel) (from **hatan**)
wyrcean *to make* 'wür-chan'
hringfag *variegated, of many colours, decorated with coloured rings*
hring *ring*
fag *variegated, stained* (also spelt **fah**)

Truly Israel [i.e. Jacob] loved Joseph over all his sons because he had him in his old age, and he ordered a ring-coloured tunic to be made for him.

Insight

The idea of *truly* is expressed by **soþlice** ('soth-liche'), which survives in early modern English as **forsooth** and in the noun **soothsayer,** which occurs for example in Shakespeare's *Julius Caesar*.

Wordhoard

The verb *hatan* **and its two past tenses**
het **and** *hatte*

Meanings

The past tense **het** *(he) ordered* comes from the unusual verb **hatan** 'hah-tan' *to call, order, promise,* which had several forms. One of these, **ic hatte,** meaning either *I am called* in the present or, alternatively, *I was called* in the past tense, occurred in Unit 3 in the riddle formula **saga hwæt ic hatte.** Another form will be seen in

Unit 22 in the king's coronation oath **ic þreo þing behate** *I promise three things*. With the prefix **be-** the verb means *to promise*, and there is a related word **seo behæs** *vow*, which became Middle English **behest** *promise, vow*. In the modern expression **at my behest**, meaning *on my instructions* the sense of **hatan** as *call, order* is still present.

The past tense *het*
Linked to the meaning of modern English *behest* is the other past tense form **het**, pronounced with a long vowel 'hét' which means *he/she ordered something to be done*. Like **sceal** (see Unit 2), **het** is followed by the infinitive. A classic example of **het** and how it is used comes at the beginning of the poem *The Battle of Maldon*, where Byrhtnoth, the East Anglian ealdorman, orders the deployment of his men:

> **Het þa hyssa hwæne hors forlætan, feor afysan**
> *Then he ordered each of the warriors to abandon (his) horse, drive (it) away*

A scene from the Bayeux Tapestry seems to illustrate the same situation: it has been used as evidence that the Anglo-Saxons did not use cavalry, that they rode to battle on horseback but always *fought* on foot.

The construction **het** can also occur without a direct object, so conceivably the above sentence could have been:

> **het þa hors forlætan**
> *he then ordered the horses to be abandoned*

In older texts, or poems in an archaic style, **het** appears as **heht**; a celebrated instance is the inscription AELFRED MEC HEHT GEWYRCAN *Alfred ordered me to be made* on the famous Alfred Jewel, now in the Ashmolean Museum in Oxford (see cover of this book).

The wording of the Alfred Jewel language mirrors a similar pattern in the Joseph text:

and het him wyrcean hringfage tunecan
and he ordered a tunic of many colours to be made for him

In this sentence, the father's full authority is implied in the choice of the verb **het**.

Insight

The Alfred Jewel depicts an iconic figure; the large eyes and emblems of authority in his hand symbolizing divine insight and royal wisdom (see front cover of this book). The boar's head was common on Anglo-Saxon metalwork; here its open jaws were designed to grasp a wooden pointer that could be used by a reader to point to the line of text being read. Such a reading would take place on a formal occasion, from a book placed on a lectern.

Reading

🔊 **TR 20**

þa hys broðru þæt gesawon *When his brothers saw this*
Ða hys broðru þæt gesawon, þæt hys fæder hyne swyðor lufode þonne hys oðre suna, ða onscunodon hi hyne and ne mihton nane freondrædene wið hyne habban.

When his brothers saw this, that his father loved him more than his other sons, then they shunned him and could not have any friendship with him.

Witodlice hyt gelamp þæt hym mætte, and he rehte þæt hys gebroðrum; þurh þæt hi hyne hatodon þe swyðor.

So it happened that he had a dream, and he told that to his brothers; because of that [literally through that] they hated him the more.

ða... ða *when... then*
gesawon *saw* 'yuh-SA-won' (plural of **geseah** *saw*)
hyne *him* (accusative pronoun)
swiðor *more* (comparative of **swyðe** *strongly,
very much*; also spelt **swiðe**)
onscunian *shun* 'on-SHUN-yan'
mihton *they could* (past tense of **magon** *they can*)
seo freondrǣden *friendship*
habban *have*
witodlice *indeed, so* 'WI-tod-lee-cheh' (sentence adverb)
rehte *told*, narrated (past tense of **reccan**)
hatian *to hate*

Insight

The two basic words for *friend* are

▶ **wine** in archaic-poetic contexts, including personal names, and
▶ the everyday **freond**, with compounds **freondrǣden**, **freondscype** 'FREOND-ship-uh', and **freondlice** *in a friendly manner* 'FREOND-li-chuh'.

The opposite of **freond** is **fynd** *enemy* (which has become modern English *fiend*).

Grammar

Uses of þa

The definite article þa (pronounced with long 'ah') and the adverb
þa are technically homonyms, since they both have the same sound
and spelling, but a different meaning and origin. Directly before
a noun phrase, as seen in Unit 5, the word þa can be identified as
the definite article, either the plural *the*, as in: (1) ymbe þa feower
timan *about the four seasons*, or the feminine accusative: (2) þonne
[seo sunne] nyðer byð astigen, þonne bringð heo þa niht *when the
sun is gone down then it brings the night*.

But at the beginning of a sentence, þa is usually either a time
indicator *then*, or a connecting word *when*. The context usually
helps us to decide. In examples (3) and (4) below the word þa
simply marks the adverb *then*: (3) Þa cwædon hys gebroðu, 'Byst
ðu ure cyning?' *Then his brothers said, 'Are you our king?'* (4) þa
geutlagode man Æþelweard ealdorman (Unit 4) *then they outlawed
ealdorman Æþelweard.*

Note 'second-place' position of the verb. This is typical of clauses
beginning with her and þa: the verb follows immediately after þa
when it means *then*.

In example (5), however, the first þa means *when* while the
second is *then*: (5) Þa hys broðru þæt gesawon, þæt hys fæder
hyne swyðor lufode þonne hys oðre suna, ða onscunodon
hi hyne.

Again, note the word order in the *then* clause: ða is followed
immediately by the verb **onscunodon**. But in the first part,
where þa means *when*, the verb is sent to the end of the
clause:

> Þa hys broðru þæt gesawon, þæt hys fæder...
> [literally] *When his brothers that saw, that his father...*

This pairing up of the same word to connect two parts of a sentence is known in Old English grammar as correlation. Another instance is the correlation of þonne... þonne in sentence (2) above: (2) þonne [seo sunne] nyðer byð astigen, þonne bringð heo þa niht.

The accusative

In the typical structure of a sentence, the key elements are a subject (the doer), the verb (the action) and the object (the thing or person acted upon by the verb), for example:

subject	verb	object	
(1) Israel	lufode	Iosep	*Israel loved Joseph.*
(2) He	gewregde	hys broðru	*He accused his brothers.*

In these two sentences the word order subject + verb + object (SVO) helps us to identify the doer of the action and distinguish him from the object of the sentence. The pattern here is the same in both Old and modern English.

Insight

It is important to remember that the object of a sentence is a grammatical rather than a literal notion. We are not talking about objects in the real world, but simply about ways of expressing relationships between words in a sentence. In modern English the object nearly always follows the verb. In Old English the object is a word given a specific shape by the endings of the accusative case.

As an inflected language, Old English has a way of indicating the object other than by the order of the words. This is the main function of the accusative case (although it has other uses after a preposition or in time phrases). The accusative is marked by various endings which vary according to the gender and type of word. Of all the accusative endings, the ending -ne is the easiest to distinguish and marks various words that refer to a masculine noun in the singular. It is found on the pronoun **hyne,** also spelt **hine,** the accusative form of the word **he,** as in the sentence:

> **witodlice ðurh his swefen hi hyne hatedon**
> *so because of his dream they hated him*

Note that the case ending allows the writer to be freer with the word order of the sentence – the accusative pronoun tends to be placed before the verb:

adverbial	subject	object	verb
Witodlice ðurh his swefen	hig	hyne	hatedon

Note the word order also in the clause **for þam ðe he hyne gestrynde on his ylde,** after the conjunction **for þam ðe** *because*:

conjunction	subject	object	verb	adverbial
for þam ðe	**he**	**hyne**	**gestrynde**	**on his ylde**
because	*he*	*him*	*begat*	*in his old age*

Other occurrences of the *-ne* ending

The accusative ending **-ne** is also found on 'strong' adjectives qualifying a masculine noun; it marks the noun phrase as the grammatical object of the sentence:

ic ... gefylle eal**ne** middangeard *I ... fill <u>all the world</u>* (Unit 3)

The **-ne** ending is also found on the definite article:

> boceras getrahtniað þæ**ne** naman for þære ripunge
> *scholars explain <u>the name</u> [autumn] as 'ripening'* (Unit 5)

Insight

Impersonal verbs are verbs without a grammatical subject. These do not exist in present-day English because we supply a meaningless subject *it*, as in the phrase *it seemed to me that…*, which in Old English is expressed by **me þuhte þæt…**.

Me þuhte *it seemed to me*

Comparison with Chaucer

In Chaucer's dream vision *The Book of the Duchess*, a Middle English poem written about 1370, the poet narrator begins his dream as follows (as you read the passage, look for words or expressions that it shares with the account of Joseph's dream):

Loo, thus hyt was; thys was my sweven.	[**hyt** *it*]
Me thoghte thus: that hyt was May,	
And in the dawenynge I lay	[**dawenynge**
(Me mette thus) in my bed al naked	*dawning*]
And loked forth, for I was waked	
With smale foules a gret hep	[**foules** *birds*;
That had affrayed me out of my slep,	**hep** *multitude*]
Thorgh noyse and swetnesse of her song.	[**her song**
	their singing]

Chaucer's Middle English contains many words of Old English origin. It will be seen that his word for *dream* is **sweven**, spelled differently but pronounced the same as Old English **swefn**. Chaucer also uses two **impersonal verbs** that both occur in the Joseph passage; in both instances the Old English construction consists of the dative **me** *to me* (pronounced 'may') followed by the verb:

me þuhte *it seemed to me*	Chaucer **me thoghte**
me mætte *it dreamed to me*, i.e.	Chaucer **me mette**
I dreamed	

It follows therefore that the common Shakespearean expression **methought** (equivalent to Old English **meþuhte** as written by some scribes) does not, strictly speaking, mean *I thought* but *it seemed to me*.

In classic Old English, by contrast, the two meanings *seem* and *think* were kept apart, for the language distinguished the two verbs by their form:

	infinitive	present	past
	þyncan *seem* 'thün-chan'	**þyncð**	**þuhte**
and	**þencan** *think* 'then-chan'	**þencð**	**þohte**

In later English, both these verbs then coalesced as **thinketh** (*thinks*) in the present and **thought** in the past tense.

Reading

The Dream of the Rood

The Dream of the Rood is a poem contained in the religious anthology the Vercelli Book, so called because its owner seems to have left the manuscript in Vercelli (where it is still kept in the cathedral library). Vercelli is in northern Italy, on the pilgrimage route to Rome; no other reason is known for the presence of the book in Italy. The poem belongs to the medieval genre of the dream vision, and begins as follows; again note the use of words and phrases that echo the vocabulary of *Joseph*:

> Hwæt, ic **swefna** cyst secgan wylle
> hwæt **me gemætte** to middre nihte,
> syðþan reordberend reste wunedon.
> **Þuhte me** þæt ic gesawe syllicre treow
> on lyft lædan leohte bewunden
> beama beorhtost.
>
> *Listen, the best of dreams I will say, what I dreamed in the middle of the night, after human-beings remained in sleep. It seemed to me that I saw a wonderful tree taken into the air, surrounded with light, the brightest of beams.*

TEST YOURSELF (1)

In the following exercise the story of Joseph continues. The task is to supply the missing past tenses from the following list: **abugon, bundon, cwædon, cwæð, hæfdon, hatedon, stodon, ðuhte.** Answers as usual, are at the back of the book and some of the sentences will be discussed in the grammar below.

Joseph's first dream And he (a) _____ to him: 'Gehyrað min swefn, ðe me mætte. Me (b) _____ þæt we (c) _____ sceafas on æcere and þæt min scef arise and stode upprihte on middan eowrum sceafum, and eowre gylmas (d) _____ ymbutan and (e) _____to minum sceafe.' Ða (f) _____ hys gebroðu, 'Cwyst ðu la, byst ðu ure cyning oððe beoð we ðine hyrmen?' Witodlice ðurh his swefen and þurh þas spræca hi hyne (g) _____ , and (h) _____ andan to him.

And he said to them: 'Hear my dream which I dreamed. It seemed to me that we were binding sheaves in the field and my sheaf seemed to arise and stand upright among your sheaves, and your sheaves stood about and bowed down to my sheaf.' Then his brothers said, 'Are you saying you are our king or we are your retainers?' So because of his dream and because of these conversations they hated him and had enmity towards him.

þæt swefn *dream* 'sweven' (also spelt **swefen,** cf. Middle English **sweven**)
þe *which*
me mette *I dreamed*
se sceaf *sheaf* 'SHÉaf' (also spelt **scef**, cf. the mythical name **Scyld Scefing Shield Sheafson** in the poem *Beowulf*)
se æcer *field* 'acker' (cf. modern English **acre**)
on middan *in the midst*
ymbutan *round about*
hyrmen *retainers* 'hür-men' (**se hiereman** *retainer, subject*)
oððe *or*
hyne *him*

TEST YOURSELF (2)

1 Uses of þa. Translate the following sentences:

    a Ða Iosep wæs syxtynewintre, he heold hys fæder heorde mid hys broðrum.

    b Þa hys gebroðru þæt gesawon, ða onscunodon hi hyne.

    c Þa cwædon hys gebroðru, 'Byst ðu ure cyning oððe beoð we ðine hyrmen?'

2 Joseph's second dream

Oðer swefen hyne mætte, and he rehte þæt hys broðrum, and cwæð, 'Ic geseah on swefne swylce sunne and mona and endleofan steorran, and ealle onbugon me.' Þa he þæt hys fæder and hys broðrum rehte, ða aðreatode se fæder hyne, and cwæð: 'Hwæt sceal ðis swefen beon þe ðu gesawe? Sceolon we abugan þe, ic and ðin modor and ðine gebroðru?'

Comprehension question: why would Joseph's family take exception to his telling of the dream?

Vocabulary: many of the words in the above text have appeared in this or preceding units, but make note of the following:

> **se steorra** *star* (plural **steorran** *stars*)
> **aðreatode** *rebuked* (past tense of **aðreatian**)
> **þe ðu gesawe** *which you saw*
> **seo modor** *mother*

3 Etymologies

In Shakespeare's play *Richard III*, the Duke of Clarence, brother of Richard (Duke of Gloucester) – and his potential rival – is imprisoned in the Tower of London, where he has a dream (Act I, scene iv), an extract of which is given below. Read through the passage and then, using glossary and dictionary, identify words deriving from Old English. List any of these originally Old English words whose meaning has changed over the course of time. For example: *dream*, Old English **dream** *joy* (the Old English **swefn** is now archaic).

Keeper What was your dream, my lord? I pray you tell me.
Clarence Methoughts that I had broken from the Tower,
And was embark'd to cross to Burgundy;
And in my company my brother Gloucester,
Who from my cabin tempted me to walk...
Methought that Gloucester stumbled, and in falling,
Struck me (that thought to stay him) overboard
Into the tumbling billows of the main...
Methoughts I saw a thousand fearful wrecks;
Ten thousand men that fishes gnaw'd upon;
Wedges of gold, great anchors, heaps of pearl,
Inestimable stones, unvalu'd jewels,
All scatter'd in the bottom of the sea.

7

King Cnut greets his archbishops

This unit will cover:

texts
- *royal writs by king Cnut*

grammar and usage
- *the strong noun declension*
- *plurals*
- *the relative pronoun þe*
- *more on the genitive case*

vocabulary and usage
- *frith illustrated in a passage from* The Battle of Maldon
- *the meaning of* lord, thegn *and other ranks of society*
- *greetings in letters*

◀) **TR 22**

> **Cnut cyning gret his arcebiscopas**
> *King Cnut greets his archbishops*

Additions to the York Gospels

While in Denmark in the winter of 1019–20, Cnut sent a remarkable proclamation to the English people in which he promised to be a **hold hlaford** *gracious lord* and to uphold the

peace that had now been established in the kingdom. A copy of
this document is written, along with some of archbishop
Wulfstan's impassioned Old English sermons, at the back of the
famous York Gospels – the *de-luxe* late tenth-century and early
eleventh-century gospel book kept at York Minster Library. Latin
gospel books were often kept for display on the altars (**weofod**)
of important churches, and for permanent safekeeping other
important documents such as charters and title deeds were copied
into them.

Insight

Some present tenses in Old English have lost the standard **-th**
ending in the 3rd person. The reasons are phonetic. If the stem
or root of the verb ends in **t** or **d** it tends to assimilate the regular
-th that would follow it. Examples are **stent** *stands* for the
expected **standeð** and **gret** *greets* instead of **greteð** (the latter
form, however, occurs in poetry, e.g. **greteð gliwstafum** *he greets
joyfully* in *The Wanderer* line 52).

◀) TR 22, 00:08

From Cnut's proclamation of 1020

Cnut cyning gret his arcebiscopas and his leodbiscopas and
Þurcyl eorl and ealle his eorlas and ealne his þeodscipe,
twelfhynde and twyhynde, gehadode and læwede, on
Englalande freondlice.

And ic cyðe eow þæt ic wylle beon hold hlaford and
unswicende to Godes gerihtum and to rihtre woroldlage.

Ic nam me to gemynde þa gewritu and þa word þe se
arcebiscop Lyfing me fram Papan brohte of Rome, þæt ic
scolde Godes lof upp aræran and unriht alecgan and full frið
wyrcean be ðære mihte þe me God syllan wolde.

gret *greets* 'grét' (present tense)

leodbiscop *bishop* (**leode** *people*)

se þeodscipe *nation*

twelfhynde and twyhynde *high- and low-ranking* (pronounce with short vowels)

gehadode *ordained* 'yuh-HAH-do-de' (from **gehadod** past participle)

læwed-e *lay* 'LÆ-weh-de'

freondlice *in a friendly manner* (adverb)

ic cyðe eow *I inform you, I proclaim to you*

unswicende *faithful, undeceitful*

ðæt geriht *right, justice, obligation*

riht *just*

seo worold *world*

seo lagu *law*

seo ge-mynd *mind, memory*

a-ræran *raise* 'ah-RÆ-ran'

þæt unriht *injustice* 'UN-riht' ('riht' rhymes with German 'nicht')

a-lecgan *put down, lay down* 'ah-LEDGE-an' (became *allay* in modern English)

se frið *peace*

seo miht *power* (modern English *might*; pronounce to rhyme with **riht**)

Check your comprehension of the passage against the following translation:

> *King Cnut greets his archbishops and bishops and earl Thorkell and all his earls and all his nation, high-ranking and low-ranking, clergy and laity, in England with friendly greetings. And I proclaim to you that I will be a loyal lord and faithful to God's laws and to just secular law. I took to mind the writings and the words which archbishop Lyfing brought to me from Rome, that I would raise up God's praise and bring down injustice and work full peace by the power which God wished to give me.*

Grammar

The relative pronoun þe *(which he brought me from Rome)*

The relative pronoun þe is a connector; it opens a clause beginning with *which* or *who*:

> þa gewritu þe se arcebishop me fram papan brohte of Rome
> *the letters which the archbishop brought me from the Pope*
> *from Rome*
> on manegra goddra manna gewitnysse þe me mid wæron
> *with the witness of many good men who were with me*

After the relative pronoun, the verb tends to come later in the sentence than it does in modern English:

> be ðære mihte þe me God syllan wolde
> *by the power which God wished to give me*

Old–modern correspondences

Hlaford

The etymology of modern English *lord* is a set piece in cultural history, stretching from pagan 'dark-age' England to late feudal Scotland. The original Old English word has been reconstructed as a combination of **hlaf** *loaf* and **weard** *guardian*, so that the lord's original honorific title as head of household was *warder of the loaf*. By the time texts came to be written, **hlafweard** had coalesced to **hlaford**, which is the usual form up to the 11th century – although not without a competitor. Old English had another word for *lord* in **dryhten**, the leader of a **dryht**, an old poetic word for a company of men. In the tenth century, however, **dryhten** tended to be used mainly for *the Lord* in a religious sense, while **hlaford** remained secular. But as English competed for status with Latin and French in the Anglo-Norman period, the process of change accelerated. **Drihten** became reserved for poems in an archaic style and, with feudalism on the increase, **hlaford** extended its range to both the religious and the secular. By the 12th century the initial **h-** had disappeared and the **-f-** (which probably sounded as 'v' anyway) came to be spelt with a **-u-** as **lauerd**. From this we get *lord* in southern English and *laird* in Scottish English.

Frith

One of several words for peace is **frið**, cognate with German *Frieden*, and in the compound **friðsocn** it implies the seeking out of a place of peace as sanctuary. **Frith** meaning *sanctuary* is connected then with the strong medieval reverence for sacred spaces protected by the authority of Church and state. Describing the altar and reliquary of the saints at Hexham, a 12th-century historian wrote in Latin of the 'stone chair which in English is called the *frith-stool*'. As Richard Fletcher points out in his book *Bloodfeud* (2003, p. 37): 'This sanctuary chair, simple, solid and dignified, can still be seen at Hexham, as can a similar one at Beverley. They are tangible reminders of one of the ways in which a violent society sought to limit and control aggression.'

Reading

From *The Battle of Maldon* (lines 36–9)

The Battle of Maldon is a poem about lordship and loyalty, about making a choice between appeasement and war. In the following passage, during the negotiations before the battle, the Viking messenger lays down his ultimatum:

> Gyf þu þat gerædest þe her ricost eart
> þæt þu þine leoda lysan wille,
> syllan sæmannum on hyra sylfra dom
> feoh wið freode, and niman **frið** æt us,
> we willaþ mid þam sceattum us to scype gangan,
> on flot feran and eow **friþes** healdan.

If you who are most powerful here advise
that you will ransom your people
and pay to the seamen at their own judgement
money for peace, and take protection from us,
we with the money will go to ship,
travel on the sea, and keep peace with you.

Grammar

The strong noun: a brief introduction

The main type of noun in Old English is the so-called 'strong' noun; here the word strong indicates the declension, i.e. the way the noun changes its endings to show case. The strong masculine noun, for example, has the following set of case endings:

	singular		*plural*	
nominative	**se eorl**	*the earl*	**þa eorlas**	*the earls*
accusative	**þone eorl**		**þa eorlas**	
genitive	**þæs eorles**	*of the earl*	**þara eorla**	*of the earls*
dative	**þam eorle**	*to the earl*	**þam eorlum**	*to the earls*

There are other patterns of noun declension: e.g. the strong feminine (which has a different set of endings) and the weak noun (weak nouns tend to end in **-n** in most cases except the nominative singular). The full details of noun declension can be learned in time; the important thing is to grasp some essentials first.

Insight

Many languages have different ways of forming the plural of nouns. The most common plural in Old English is **-as,** and this has survived in present-day English, with influence from the very common **-s** plural found in French.

Plurals

The basic nominative plural ending for the main type of ('strong')
masculine nouns is formed by adding -as:

se biscop *the bishop*	þa biscopas *the bishops*
se eorl *the earl*	þa eorlas *the earls*
se freols *the privilege*	þa freolsas *the privileges*
se heofon *heaven*	þa heofonas *the heavens*
se flod *flood* 'flód'	þa flodas *floods*
se wer *man*	þa weras *the men*

Strong neuter plurals end either in -u or like modern English *sheep*
the plural remains unchanged as the 'zero' ending:

þæt gewrit *the letter*	þa gewritu *the letters*
þæt scip *the ship*	þa scipu *the ships*
þæt heafod *head*	þa heafdu *heads*
þæt scep *the sheep*	þa scep *the sheep* (plural)
þæt word *the word*	þa word *the words*
þæt þing *the thing*	þreo þing *three things*

Strong feminine nouns have a plural in -a:

seo glof *the glove*	þa glofa *the gloves*
seo benn *the wound*	þa benna *the wounds*
seo wynn *joy*	þa wynna *the joys*

A small group of common nouns have a plural in -e:

seo dæd *the deed*	þa dæde *the deeds*
seo wyrd *fate*	þa wyrde *the fates*

The plurals of 'weak' nouns have the common weak ending -an:

þæt eage *the eye*	þa eagan *the eyes*
þæt eare *the ear*	þa earan *the ears*

An irregular noun is found as in modern English in **fot** *foot* (pronounced 'foat') with plural **fet** (pronounce long as 'fate').

Two additions to the Royal gospel book

On the adjoining pages of another gospel book (now in the British Library at shelfmark Royal I D.ix), in the characteristically 'handsome hand' of the Canterbury scribe Eadui Basan, there occur two texts relating to Cnut's dealings with Christ Church cathedral and monastery. The first of these is an agreement with the monks of Christ Church, the second a royal writ or message to Lyfing, who was archbishop of Canterbury when Cnut came to the throne. Both seem to date from 1018, when Cnut was in Kent granting the land at Hazelhurst to Christ Church (see Unit 10) and before he departed for Denmark.

A confraternity notice

A confraternity agreement for mutual support between, on the one side, Cnut and his brother Harald, who may have been with Cnut in England between 1016 and 1018 and, on the other side, the monks of Christ Church Canterbury. The first sentence *In the name of our Lord Jesus Christ* is a rubric in Latin, the rest is Old English. Two of the other three names feature elsewhere in the charters.

+ In nomine domini nostri Iesu Cristi. Her is awriten CNUTES kynges nama, þe is ura leofa hlaford for worulde and ure gastlica broðor for Gode, and Harold þæs kinges broðor.

Ðorð ure broðor. Kartoca ure broðor. Thuri ure broðor.

From King Cnut's writ to archbishop Lyfing

The following extract from Cnut's writ or letter to archbishop Lyfing and others begins, like his proclamation to the English

nation, with a formula of greeting to the recipients **Cnut cing gret ...**
freondlice, *King Cnut greets ... in a friendly manner,* followed
by a solemn statement of purpose and **ic cyðe eow þæt ...** *and*
I make known to you that ... But beyond the formalities an
actual dialogue is reported in this extract and the voices of king
and archbishop can be heard in debate. The main topic under
discussion is the freedom of Christ Church (**Cristes cyrice**),
the cathedral in Canterbury. For some questions on the text,
see **Test Yourself** (1) below.

> Cnut cing gret Lyfing arcebiscop, and Godwine biscop, and
> Ælmær arcebiscop, and Æþelwine scirman, and Æþelric,
> and ealle mine þegnas, twelfhynde and twihynde, freondlice.
> And ic cyðe eow þæt se arcebiscop spæc to me ymbe Cristes
> cyrcean freols þæt heo hæfð nu læsse munde þonne hio
> hwilan ær hæfde. Þa lyfde ic him þæt he moste niwne freols
> settan on minan naman. Þa cwæð he to me þæt he freolsas
> genoge hæfde gyf hi aht forstodan. Þa nam ic me sylf þa
> freolsas and gelede hi uppan Cristes agen weofod on þæs
> arcebiscopes gewitnysse and on Þurkilles eorles and on
> manegra goddra manna þe me mid wæron...

scirman *shire governor* 'sheer-man' (**seo scir** *shire, province*)
þegn *thegn, official,* minister 'thane' (cf. **þegnian, þenian** *to*
 minister)
seo mund *security, protection* (**mund-e** accusative)
hwilan, hwilum *sometimes, once* 'hwee-lum' (dative plural of **seo**
 hwil *time*)
ær *before, previously*
lyfde *granted, conceded* (past tense of **lyfan,** also spelt **liefan**)
moste *be allowed, might* (from **motan** *to be allowed*)
niw-ne *new* (masculine accusative strong ending)
gyf *if* (sends verb to end of clause)
aht *anything*
forstodan *were worth, stood for* (past of **forstandan**)
sylf *self*
ge-lede *laid* (also **gelegde,** past of **lecgan**)

QUICK VOCAB

92

hi *them* 'hee' (the nom. and acc. of **hi** *they* is the same)
se weofod *altar*
seo (ge)witnys, witnes *knowledge, witness*

Insight

After the preliminary formula, the main message of Cnut's writ begins with the words **se arcebiscop spæc to me** *the archbishop spoke to me*. Note the phrase **ymbe Cristes Cyrcean freols** *about Christ Church's privilege*. Grammatically, the word **cyrcean** is genitive, corresponding to the base form **seo cyrice** *the church* and also spelt **cirice** (pronounced 'chiriche'). Because **seo cyrice** is a feminine noun, the two following pronouns **heo** and **hio** *she, it* (variant spellings of the same pronoun) refer back to **Cristes Cyrice**.

Cultural contexts

The king's writ

The legal document known as a writ (from Old English **ge-writ** *letter*) was a type of short administrative notice that probably came into use in the ninth century; there are many examples from the tenth and eleventh centuries. Very like a letter, the writ was composed on one side of a piece of vellum (parchment), which could then be folded and a wax seal attached. The issuing party, very often the king, sent the writ accompanied by his authenticating seal to the shire court, where its instructions could be put into force.

Insight

All writs and charters of the Anglo-Saxon period have been catalogued by P.H. Sawyer (see **bibliography**). For convenience, in histories of the period, documents are identified by the Sawyer catalogue number. In the case of Cnut's writ to archbishop Lyfing, the catalogue number is S 985.

Thegns

The assembly or court of this writ is presided over by the **scirman** (often called the sheriff, Old English **scir-ge-refa** *shire reeve*), and attended by bishops as well as by thegns, who were officials and landed nobility akin to later medieval knights. Thegns could inherit their status or be appointed to serve this position (the noun derives from **þegnian, þenian** *to minister* or *serve*). According to a treatise by Wulfstan, as copied in a set of laws at Rochester, a man needed the following attributes in order to be granted thegnly status: **fif hida agnes landes** *five hides of their own land*, **cirican and kycenan** *a (private) church and kitchen*, **bellhus and burhgeat** *a bell-house and a castle-gate* and **setl and sundernote on cynges healle** *a seat and special office in the king's hall*. A hide was a unit of land measurement roughly equivalent to the land that could support one household, but was used as a means of tax assessment. Without the five hides of land, as another text states, the **ceorl** ('cheorl') could not advance his status, even if he possessed other attributes, such as the armour and gold-decorated sword that marked out a thegn by his personal appearance, much as a knight would have horse, armour and spear in later centuries. The thegns mentioned in Cnut's writ are distinguished according to their wergild (lit. *man payment*), the amount of money their status was worth in the legal system based on compensation.

So, for example, if a man were the victim of a feud, a settlement could be reached by paying his family the value of the wergild. In the long legal tradition going back to the laws of the West-Saxon king Ine, the wergild of a nobleman (**cyninges geneat** *king's companion*) was 1,200 shillings, whereas that of an ordinary freeman was 200 shillings.

Grammar

Friendly greetings in writs and declarations

In the opening protocol of a letter or writ, the adverb goes to the end of the sentence:

> Wulfstan arcebiscop gret Cnut cyning his hlaford
> and Ælfgyfe þa hlæfdian **eadmodlice**
> *Archbishop Wulfstan greets king Cnut his lord*
> *and Ælfgyfu the lady humbly.*

Often in the protocol of the king's writ, the adverb used with the verb **gret** *greets* is **freondlice**, as seen below:

Cnut cyngc gret Eadsige biscop and Ælfstan abbot and Ægelric and ealle mine þegnas on Cent **freondlice**

The meaning should be clear enough when you are reading the Old English, but it presents problems for the translator, since although **freondlice** corresponds to *friendly*, this word in modern English is not an adverb but an adjective. Normally modern adverbs end in -*ly* (which of course derives from -**lice**), the exceptions being a few words like *friendly* and *likely*; so we can send *friendly greetings* but we cannot say, for example, *she greeted him friendly*. To try and solve the problem some scholars translate **freondlice** as *amicably* while others use the phrase *in a friendly way*. Others translate the sentence:

King Cnut sends friendly greetings to bishop Eadsige, and abbot Ælfstan, and Ægelric, and all my thegns in Kent.

Expressing the idea *of deeds, of men* **etc. (genitive plural)**

As was pointed out in the presentation of numerals in Unit 5, the genitive plural ends regularly in -**a**:

tyn tid<u>a</u> *ten of hours*, i.e. *ten hours*

Other examples are:

> twelf hund heafd**a** *twelve hundred heads*
> sid**a** twa *two sides* (see **Test Yourself** (2) below)
> dæd**a** demend *judge of deeds* (see Unit 2)

When an adjective describes and occurs with the genitive plural noun, it will usually take the strong ending -ra:

> on maneg**ra** godd**ra** manna gewitnysse
> *in the presence of many good men*
> eall cristen folc min**ra** gewealda
> *all Christian people of my domains*

For now, and to speed up the process of learning to recognize the form and meaning, we will follow a general rule of thumb: look out for the -a ending; in an appropriate context, it probably indicates genitive plural.

More ways of recognizing the genitive singular

For the genitive singular, the endings can vary a lot, depending on the category of noun and its gender. The masculine and neuter ending of the common type of 'strong' noun is usually -s:

> uppan Crist**es** agen weofod
> *on Christ's own altar*
> on þæs arcebiscop**es** gewitnysse and on Þurkilles eorl**es**
> *in the presence of the archbishop and of earl Thorkell*

Note here the ending -s also on the definite article **þæs** *of the*. Looking at the definite article is another way of recognizing a genitive, especially with nouns for which the genitive ending is not particularly distinctive. Where the articles **se** and **þæt** change to **þæs** *of the* in the genitive, the feminine article **seo** goes to **þære** *of the*. So in the religious formula **on þære halgan þrinnesse naman** *in the name of the holy Trinity*, the base form **seo þrinnes** *the Trinity* is in the nominative case. This becomes **þære þrinnesse** *of the Trinity* in the genitive.

Reading

The use of the king's writ

The king usually sent his writ to the shire court in order that its instructions might be put into force. An account of how this might happen is found in a declaration (S 1456) of the year 995 concerning a dispute over an estate at Snodland in Kent. As the text tells us, the new bishop of Rochester discovers his right to the land when he reads the **swutelunga** (i.e. *declarations*) in the cathedral to which he has been appointed. He immediately begins to lay claim to the estate against a man called Leofwine Ælfheahson. When the king hears about the claim (termed **seo spræc** or **seo talu**; both words also mean *speech, telling*), he sends his writ and *seal* **þæt insegl**, with instructions on how they should hear both **ontalu** *claim* and **oftalu** *counterclaim.*

Ongan ða to specenne on ðæt land, and elles for Godes ege ne dorste, oððæt seo spræc wearð þam cynge cuð. Þa ða him seo talu cuð wæs, þa sende he gewrit and his insegl to þam arcebisceope Ælfrice, and bead him þæt he and hys þegenas on East Cent and on West Cent hy onriht gesemdon, be ontale and be oftale.

onginnan to begin (**onginnð, ongan, ongunnon, ongunnen**)
specan, sprecan to speak (**specan on** to lay claim to; **seo spræc** claim)
elles otherwise, else
oððæt until
cuð known
bead commanded (**beodan** to command)
ge-seman reconcile

QUICK VOCAB

He began to lay claim to the land, and did not dare do otherwise for fear of God, until the claim became known to

(Contd)

the king. When the claim was known to him, then he sent
writ and seal to archbishop Ælfric and commanded him that
he and his thegns in East Kent and in West Kent should justly
reconcile them, according to the claim and counter-claim.

The particular writ mentioned in the above was probably destroyed
after it had served its ephemeral purpose, although other more
important messages have survived, either in their original format or
as later copies. One problem for historians has been distinguishing
authentic writs from later forgeries or ascertaining which of
the writs have been tampered with to make their wording more
favourable to later users of the document.

Insight

The noun **spræc** and the verb **sprecan** – similar to German
Sprache and **sprechen** – gradually lost their r in the late
Old English period, thus **spræc** became **spæc**, pronounced
roughly as 'spaych'.

Cultural contexts

The archaeology of the seal

A good example of a contemporary royal seal is preserved in a
French library. The seal, from the reign of Edward the Confessor,
is a wax disc about two inches in diameter and looks rather like a
large coin depicting the figure of a seated king; on one side the king
holds an orb and sceptre, on the other a sword and sceptre.
A legend running round the rim reads in Latin:

+ SIGILLUM EADVVARDI ANGLORUM BASILEI *SEAL OF
EDWARD RULER OF THE ENGLISH.* The writ was attached to
the seal by a thin strip of vellum cut parallel to the bottom of the
document.

Few other seals have survived in good condition, but an ivory seal matrix (the die used to imprint the wax seal) has been found near Wallingford. Dated to about 1040, it has a similar Latin inscription round the rim: + **SIGILLUM GODWINI MINISTRI** *SEAL OF GODWINE THE THEGN.*

The image shows a cloaked and bearded nobleman holding a sword; it has been suggested that this figure represents Godwine, the port reeve or town sheriff of Oxford. The reeve was the king's appointee, an idea underlined by the carving on the ivory handle depicting two figures in a scene from Psalm 110 on the theme of royal power given by God.

TEST YOURSELF (1)

1 **Plurals** Look again at Cnut's proclamation of 1020 and find examples of plural nouns.

2 **Style** Identify any words or phrases that alliterate in the text.

3 **Antonyms** In the text, find and translate as many words or phrases as you can that form antonyms, paired opposites on the pattern *short/long, true/false, amateur/professional, public/private* etc.

TEST YOURSELF (2)

1 **The ranks of society, from high to low**
Arrange the following social ranks into order of seniority, starting with the highest and finishing with the lowest in the hierarchy: aþeling, burh-mann, casere, ceorl, cypa, cyning, ealdorman, eorl, hlaford, hlæfdige, scir-gerefa, þegn, þeowa, wita.

2 **Positions in the church**
In the following list of religious ranks, is it possible to say which is the highest? How are the other offices in the list related to each other? Are there any anomalies that do not fit into the standard hierarchy?

abbod, abbodesse, ancor, arcebiscop, biscop, capellan, mæssepreost, munuc, mynecen, mynstermann, preost.

3 **Noun declension** Take the strong noun **se biscop** *the bishop* and write out its full declension in all four cases, singular and plural, with a translation; use as a model the declension of **eorl** in the **grammar** section above.

4 **Comprehension** Reread the extract from Cnut's writ to archbishop Lyfing.
   a What was the archbishop's grievance?
   b What was Cnut's initial response?
   c How did he finally resolve the situation?

8

He promised her the land at Orleton

This unit will cover:

texts
- *a Worcestershire marriage agreement*
- *an extract from* The Life of Euphrosyne

grammar and usage
- *declension of personal pronouns: the third person*
- *more on the dative case*

◀♪ TR 23

He behet hyre þæt land æt Ealretune
He promised her the land at Orleton

Marriage in Anglo-Saxon England

On the whole, marriage in Anglo-Saxon England seems to have been designed to protect equally the property rights of both man and wife. Each was separately accountable under the law: if a man was found guilty of a crime, for instance, his wife could only be charged if she had been a willing accomplice. In order for a marriage actually to take place, the suitor had to meet with the woman's kinsmen, whose job it was to represent her best interests.

The suitor was required to make a pledge (**wedd**) of money, the so-called *bride price*, expressed in terms of a **ceap** or *purchase,* but the woman was free to accept or reject the man's offer. In addition, on the day after the marriage she received her **morgengifu** or *morning gift*, which was her personal property, and according to the ancient law code of king Æthelberht of Kent, the morning gift could pass eventually to the wife's kindred if she were childless. Primarily, then, the laws of marriage were concerned with pledges and gift giving.

Grammar

Declension of personal pronouns: the third person

Personal pronouns are classified according to first person (*I, we-two, we*), second person (forms of *you*), and third person (*she, he, it, they*). The following table summarizes the case endings for the third person:

	masculine	neuter	feminine	plural
nominative	he	hit	heo	hi
accusative	hine	hit	hi	hi
genitive	his	his	hire	hira, heora
dative	him	him	hire	him, heom

Among the third person pronouns, the basic word for *he* is **he** (pronounced 'hay'). This is its form in the nominative case, when it functions as the subject of the sentence. But when the pronoun takes other functions, such as the object of the sentence, it changes its form. A comparison with modern English may be useful here, as the vestiges of the case system have survived in our modern pronouns. In the sentence *his father loved him*, the pronoun *he* has changed to *him* because it is the grammatical object, i.e. the person or thing directly affected by the action. For native speakers it would be clearly wrong, i.e. grammatically unacceptable, to say or write *his father loved he* (where *he* is the object of the action *loved*). Similarly in Old English, the nominative **he** changes to accusative **hine** in a similar context:

> hys fæder <u>hyne</u> swiðor lufode þonne his oðre suna (see Unit 6)
> *his father loved <u>him</u> more than his other sons*

Another example concerns the feminine pronoun. Basically, the word for *she* is **heo**. But when the context requires the idea of *benefit, giving to*, the pronoun switches to the dative **hire**, meaning *to her*, as a sentence from a marriage agreement shows:

> he behet <u>hyre</u> þæt land æt Ealretune.
> *he promised <u>her</u> the land at Orleton*

Insight

The verb **behatan** *to promise*, past tense **behet** *promised*, is related to the modern English word *behest*. For the various meanings and uses of the verb **hatan** without the prefix, see Unit 6.

A note on spelling variants

Note alternative spellings with the letter y used for the vowel i: **hyne, hys, hym, hyre, hy**. This may be puzzling at first, but it is well to remember that absolute uniformity in spelling is a modern concept. It is generally true to say that almost all early English writers from king Alfred to William Shakespeare were liberal but not anarchic about their attitude to spelling. Shakespeare himself apparently spelled his name differently on different occasions and, even today, a few words allow of different vowels, such as *shown* and *shewn* or *grey* and *gray*, and they even allow different consonants in *realize* and *realise*. In the past, variant spellings of the same word were regarded as normal or perhaps even useful as a way of adding interest and variety to a written text. You will have noticed already that the Old English consonants þ and ð alternate freely. Sometimes the scribe alternates the spelling purely for variety, but also for reasons of local dialect or house style (in a monastery *scriptorium* or writing hall).

Pronunciation of the personal pronouns

On pronunciation matters, remember that **he** is pronounced with a long close vowel as (roughly) 'hay', **heo** is also pronounced long, and as one syllable, rather like 'Héo'. Note also that the pronoun **hi** for the feminine accusative singular and the nominative and accusative plural is pronounced 'hee', likewise with a long vowel. As we have seen already in the language of Byrhtferth (Unit 5), the alternative spelling of plural **hi** was **hig**, pronounced 'hee', just as the -ig was pronounced 'ee' in adjectives such as **blodig** *bloody* 'bloh-dee'.

Changes in the system of English pronouns

Many of the Old English pronouns have survived into modern English, sometimes with little change, as in **he, his, him**; or with some changes in spelling, as in the change from **hire** to modern English *her*.

Although language is never strictly logical in all its forms, nevertheless, from the point of view of convenience, there were some flaws in the Old English pronoun system. A glance at the table above will elucidate. Several of the forms have a multiple function and meaning: **his, him, hit, hi, hire**. Although the context usually made the message clear, when Old English began to lose its inflectional endings in the 11th and 12th centuries it became difficult to distinguish the meaning that was intended. The possibility of confusion was particularly acute for nominative **hi**, which could mean *she* or *they*, for **him**, which could mean *to him, to it* or *to them*, and for **hire**, which came to be pronounced and then spelt the same whether it meant *her* in the singular, or *their* in the plural. To solve the problem, speakers in the north, who were in daily contact with Danish settlers, began to imitate forms in the language of the Danes, Old Norse. As we shall see in Unit 20, Old English and Old Norse were similar enough as cognate languages for people from the two speech communities to understand each other, and this facilitated borrowing between the two languages. The northern speakers of Old English borrowed *they, their* and *them* from Old Norse and the new pronouns spread slowly southwards. Chaucer, in the fourteenth century, still used *her* to mean *their*, but the change had reached most forms of English by the time of Malory in the 15th century.

Uses of the dative

Basic meaning of the dative (he gave the land to her)

The basic meaning of the **dative** is *to* or *for*, as in the sentence *he promised the land to her* or *he promised her the land at Knightwick*. In modern English, the structure of this sentence consists of a **subject**, i.e. the doer, a **verb**, i.e. the action, a **direct object** of the action and **an indirect object**, who benefits from the action. This can be represented as follows:

subject	verb	object	indirect object
he	promised	the land	to her

subject	verb	indirect object	object	complement
he	promised	her	the land	at Knightwick

In the Old English equivalent, **he behet hire þæt land æt Cnihtewican**, the structure is similar, but because this is an inflected language with inflectional endings, it makes sense to represent the structure in terms of the cases used, so that the subject is in the **nominative** case, the indirect object in the **dative**, and the direct object in the **accusative**:

nominative	verb	dative	accusative	complement
he	behet	hire	þæt land	æt Cnihtewican

Dative after prepositions

Many Old English prepositions such as **æt** (*at* or *from*), **mid** (*with*), **on** (*on*), **to** (*to* or *as*) are followed by a word or words in the dative case. It may help to picture the case endings as a useful way of knitting the words together to form a **prepositional phrase**, in various combinations such as:

preposition + noun *in town*
or preposition + the + noun *from the community*
or preposition + proper noun (i.e. a name) *at Knightwick*

There are several examples in the study text below:

nominative	dative
se dæg *day, lifetime*	**on dæge** and **æfter dæge** *in (her) lifetime* and *after (her) lifetime*
se hired *the community*	**æt ðam hirede** *from the community*
Eanulfintun (place name; masculine)	**æt Eanulfintune** *at Alton*
se arcebiscop *the archbishop*	**mid ðam arcebiscope** *with the archbishop*
ða forwerda *the terms* (feminine plural)	**to ðysum forwordan** *for these terms*

The dative in idiomatic expressions
Various idiomatic uses of the dative can be derived from the basic meaning of *to* or *for*:

<u>ðam</u> ðe hire leofest wære
to whoever was dearest to her i.e. *to whoever she wished*

he begeat ðæs arcebisceopes swuster <u>him</u> to wife
he acquired the archbishop's sister as his wife
  (literally *for himself as wife*)

A Worcestershire marriage agreement (S 1459)

In the eleventh century, Worcester (**Wigoreceaster**) was an important ecclesiastical and administrative centre. By a traditional arrangement, the man appointed to the archbishopric of York also held in plurality the bishopric of Worcester, probably for political and economic reasons. Worcester was a more prosperous diocese than York, and the double office promoted easier relations between the south and the politically more independent regions of the north. From 1002 the office was held by the capable figure of Wulfstan, sometimes known as Wulfstan the Homilist to distinguish him from others of the same name. Originally bishop of London, Wulfstan gained a reputation for rhetoric and eloquence. But as well as a composer of homilies and sermons and a church administrator, archbishop Wulfstan was also a politician and lawyer, who composed sets of laws implemented at great assemblies of king, nobility and clergy. A solid figure of continuity in a changing world, Wulfstan wrote these law codes for both king Æthelred and his successor king Cnut.

Insight

Wulfstan the Homilist was a charismatic speaker with a characteristic rhetorical style, rhythmical and alliterative, for example **bisceopas syndon bydelas and Godes lage lareowas** where he refers to bishops as beadles (i.e. messengers) and lecturers of God's law: (*Homilies of Wulfstan* ed. Bethurum, no. XVII). For mention of Wulfstan in the Chronicle, see Unit 4; for more on his style, see Unit 14.

It is only rarely that we glimpse anything at all of Wulfstan's family life or domestic arrangements. The following document (S 1459 in Sawyer's catalogue) outlines the terms of agreement reached by archbishop Wulfstan when he finalized the betrothal of his sister ðæs **arcebisceopes swuster** to a certain Wulfric, who promised (**behet**) to the young woman a rich array of gifts.

◀» TR 23 00:09

Her swutelað on ðysum gewrite ymbe ða forwerda ðe Wulfric and se arcebisceop geworhtan ða he begeat ðæs arcebisceopes swuster him to wife;

ða forwerda *the terms, assurances*
from **seo foreweard** *agreement in advance* (cf. adj. **foreweard**
forward, future)
begeat *received* (past tense of **begytan** *acquire, receive*)
him to wife *as his wife* (more literally *to him as wife*)

◀) TR 24

þæt is þæt he behet hyre þæt land æt Ealretune and æt
Ribbedforda hire dæg, and he behet hire þæt land æt
Cnihtewican – þæt he wolde hit hire begytan ðreora manna
dæg æt ðam hirede on Wincelcumbe –

---

hyre, hire *her, to her, for her* (dative of **heo** *she*)
hyre dæge *in her day,* i.e. *in her lifetime*
wolde... begytan *would acquire*
se hired *community*

◀) TR 25

and sealde hyre þæt land æt Eanulfintune to gyfene and to
syllenne ðam ðe hire leofest wære, on dæge and æfter dæge,
ðær hire leofest wære, and behet hire fiftig mances goldes and
þritig manna and þritig horsa.

ðam ðe hire leofest wære *to whoever was dearest to her*
i.e. *to whoever she wished*
mances from **mancus** *thirty silver pence, one eighth of a pound*

◀) TR 26

Nu wæs ðyses to gewitnesse – Wulfstan arcebisceop, and
Leofwine ealdorman and Aeþelstan bisceop and Aelfword
abbod and Brihteh munuc, and manig god man toeacan

heom, ægðer ge gehadode ge leawede – þæt ðas forewerda
ðus geworhte wæran.

toeacan *in addition to*
ægðer ge... ge *both ... and* pronounced 'either yay... yay'
ðas *these* (the demonstrative – see Unit 11)
ðus *thus*
ge-worht *made* (past participle of **wyrcean**)

QUICK VOCAB

◀) **TR 27**

Nu syndon to ðysum forwordan twa gewrita, oðer mid ðam
arcebisceope on Wigereceastre and oðer mid Aeþelstane
bisceope on Herforda.

oðer... oðer *the one... the other*

QV

*Here is declared in this document the agreement which
Wulfric and the archbishop made when he received the
archbishop's sister as his wife. That is that he promised her
the land at Orleton and Ribbesford for her lifetime, and he
promised her the land at Knightwick, that he would obtain
it for her for three people's lifetimes from the community
at Winchcombe, and gave her the land at Alton to give
and donate – to whoever she liked, in her lifetime or after
her lifetime – wherever she liked, and he promised her fifty
mancusses of gold and thirty men and thirty horses.*

*Now as witness to this were archbishop Wulfstan and
ealdorman Leofwine and bishop Æthelstan and abbot
Ælfweard and Brihtheah the monk, and many a good man
in addition to them, both clergy and laity, that these terms
were agreed thus. Now there are two copies of this, the one
with the archbishop at Worcester and the other with bishop
Æthelstan at Hereford.*

From *The Life of Euphrosyne*

The following extract from the life of a female saint gives further insights into the process of wooing a maiden and securing a betrothal. The text was copied in a manuscript of the early 11th century. As you read, pay attention to the precise use of the forms of the personal pronoun heo *she*, as used in various grammatical cases to describe the process of gift giving and promising that accompanied the act of betrothal. Then see the analysis below.

Þa asprang hire hlisa and wisdom and gelærednys geond ealle þa ceastre, forþam heo wæs on þeawum gefrætwod. And manige wurdon atihte þæt hi gyrndan hire to rihtan gesynscipe, and hit to hire fæder spræcon, ac he symle ongen cwæð, 'Gewurþe Godes willa.'

Þa æt nyxtan com him an þegen to, se wæs weligra and wurþra þonne ealle þa oþre and hire to him gyrnde. Þa onfeng se fæder his wedd, and hi him behet.

aspringan *to spread, spring forth*
se hlisa *sound, fame* 'hleeza'
seo gelærednys *learning, skill*
þeawas *virtues* (masculine nominative plural)
gefrætwod *adorned* (past participle of **gefrætwan**)

atiht *drawn* (past participle of **ateon**)
gyrnan *to seek for, yearn for* (takes the genitive case)
se gesynscipe *marriage*
gewurþe Godes willa *may God's will be done*
æt nyxstan, æt niehstan *at last*
weligra *wealthier* (from **welig**)
wurþra *richer, more worth* (from **wurþ**, also spelt **weorþ**)
þæt wedd *pledge* (cf. modern English wedding)

Analysis of the feminine personal pronoun in the passage

1 The nominative: <u>heo</u> wæs on þeawum gefrætwod *<u>she</u> was adorned with virtues.*
2 The accusative: se fæder... <u>hi</u> him behet *the father promised <u>her</u> to him.*
3 Genitive as possessive: <u>hire</u> hlisa *<u>her</u> fame*; manige... hit to <u>hire</u> fæder spræcon *many spoke about it to <u>her</u> father.*
4 Genitive used after the verb *gyrnan*: gyrnan belongs to a group of verbs which take an object in the genitive, where we would expect an accusative:

an þegen... <u>hire</u> to him gyrnde	*a thegn yearned <u>for her</u> for himself*
hi gyrndan <u>hire</u> to rihtan gesynscipe	*they yearned <u>for her</u> in lawful marriage*

5 The dative pronoun *hire*: for several uses of the feminine pronoun in the dative, see the above text of the Worcestershire marriage agreement; the examples include:

and he behet <u>hire</u> þæt land æt Cnihtewican
and he promised <u>her</u> the land at Knightwick

þæt he wolde hit <u>hire</u> begytan ðreora manna dæg æt þam hirede on Wincelcumbe
that he would obtain it <u>for her</u> for three people's lifetimes from the community at Winchcombe

and sealde <u>hyre</u> þæt land æt Eanulfintune
and gave <u>her</u> the land at Alton

to gyfene and to syllenne ðam ðe <u>hire</u> leofest wære
to give and donate to whoever was most pleasing <u>to her</u>

Reading

The Old English laws

Three hundred years before the tenth-century unification of England, Æthelberht, king of Kent, became the first of the English kings to convert to Christianity. He began a tradition that English rulers would compile sets of their laws in the vernacular language, rather than in Latin as was the norm on the Continent. His law code, written down originally by the new missionaries from Rome and hence the oldest document in the English language, was copied and preserved over the centuries and indeed many of the practices so recorded seem to have been remarkably long lasting. The only surviving text occurs in the famous *Textus Roffensis*, a large anthology of Old English laws made at Rochester in the twelfth century.

From *The laws of Æthelberht* **(paras 77–81)**

77 Gif mon mægð gebigeð, ceap geceapod sy, gif hit unfacne is.
77.1 Gif hit þonne facne is, eft þær æt ham gebrenge, and him man his scæt agefe.
78 Gif hio cwic bearn gebyreþ, healfne scæt age, gif ceorl ær swylteþ.
79 Gif mid bearnum bugan will, healfne scæt age.
80 Gif ceorl agan wile, swa an bearn.
77 *If a man buys a maiden, the transaction will stand, if there is no deceit.* **77.1** *But if there is deceit, she should be brought back*

to her home and his money should be returned to him. **78** *If she bears a living child, let her have half the money, if the husband dies before.* **79** *If (she) wants to depart with the children, let her have half the money.* **80** *If the husband wants to have (them), then (let her have) one child [i.e. one child's share of the property].*

From the Exeter Book poem *Maxims I*

In a very similar style to *Maxims II* from the C version of the Chronicle, this poem deals with the connections between the microcosm and the macrocosm, the human sphere and the natural world.

Cyning sceal mid ceape   cwene gebicgan
bunum ond beagum: bu sceolon ærest
geofum god wesan.

A king must buy a queen with a transaction,
with goblets and with rings: both must above all
be generous with gifts.

From the story of Thamar (Genesis 38)

In Genesis the *Joseph* narrative is interrupted by a long digression concerning his half-brother Judah. There are a number of ways in which the Old English version can be seen as addressing contemporary cultural issues. First, the story itself highlights the anxieties many women must have felt about providing an heir for the dynasty or household into which they had married. In addition, the version in the Old English Hexateuch provides an illustration of how the artist of the manuscript understood the 'purchase with rings', the negotiation with a woman for a suitable *pledge*, or **underwedd** as it is called here. The **beah** illustrated in this picture is clearly large, and the image resembles the arm-rings found in Viking treasure hoards of the period.

The word **beah** is connected with the verb **bugan** *to bend or to bow*; its etymology points to the process of manufacture. In the 12th century, the adjective **buhsum** is recorded, meaning *pliant*, and hence also *compliant* (Dutch **buchsam** and German **biegsam**); this later developed into the modern word *buxom*, and there exists also a nautical term *bee*, a kind of pulley, which derives from **beah**.

Þa cwæð heo, 'Hwæt sylstu me wið ðam þe ðu mines gemanan bruce?'
Ða cwæð he, 'Ic sende ðe an ticcen of minre heorde.'
And heo eft cwæð, 'Ic ðolige locahwæt ðu wylle, gyf ðu me sylst underwedd oð þæt ðu me sende þæt ðu me behætst.'
Þa cwæð Iudas, 'Hwæt wylt ðu to underwedde nyman?'
Ða cwæð heo, 'Ðinne hring and ðinne beah and þinne stæf, ðe þu on handa hæfst.'

Then she said, 'What will you give me in return that you should enjoy my companionship?'
Then he said, 'I will send you a goat kid from my herd.'
And she said in reply, 'I will allow whatever you will, if you give me a pledge until you send me what you promise.'
Then Judah said, 'What will you take as a pledge?'
Then she said, 'Your ring and your arm-ring and the staff which you have in your hand.'

From *Beowulf*

The following passage shows how a wife could become important as a pledge of peace between nations, a diplomatic presence at great feasts in the meadhall:

Hwilum mæru cwen,
friðusibb folca flet eall geondhwearf,
bædde byre geonge, oft hio beahwriðan
secge sealde, ær hie to setle geong.

At times the great queen, peace-pledge of nations, processed
all through the hall, encouraged the young men, often she
gave a ring to a warrior, before she returned to her seat.
(*Beowulf*, lines 2016b–2019)

A royal wedding in 1017

As we saw in Unit 4, the young king Cnut was able to bolster his position on the throne of England by marrying Æthelred's widow Emma, daughter of Richard duke of Normandy; she soon gave him a son. The annal D 1023 tells that **Imma seo hlæfdie mid hire cynelican bearne Hardacnute** *Emma the Lady with her royal heir Harthacnut* appeared at a great ceremony in honour of St Alphege. In the brief account of her marriage six years before, note the use of the verb **het** *ordered*:

From C 1017 þa toforan *Kalendas Agusti* het se cynigc fetian him þæs cyniges lafe Æþelrædes him to wife Ricardes dohtor.

Then before the kalends of August, the king ordered king
Æthelred's widow – Richard's daughter – to be brought to
him as wife.

TEST YOURSELF

1 Provide the correct form of the pronoun in the following sentences.

Ða his broðru þæt gesawon, þæt hys fæder (**a**) _____ swiðor lufode þonne his oðre suna, ða onscunodon (**b**) _____ (**c**) _____.

When his brothers saw this, that his father loved him more than his other sons, then they shunned him.

Witodlice hyt gelamp þæt (**d**) _____ mætte, and he rehte þæt his gebroþrum; þurh þæt (**e**) _____ hyne hatodon þe swiþor.

So it happened that he had a dream, and he told that to his brothers; because of that [literally through that] they hated him the more.

2 Reread the passage from *The Life of Euphrosyne*, then answer the comprehension questions.

Þa asprang hire hlisa and wisdom and gelærednys geond ealle þa ceastre, forþam heo wæs on þeawum gefrætwod. And manige wurdon atihte þæt hi gyrndan hire to rihtan gesynscipe, and hit to hire fæder spræcon, ac he symle ongen cwæð, 'Gewurþe Godes willa.' Þa æt nyxtan com him an þegen to, se wæs weligra and wurþra þonne ealle þa oþre and hire to him gyrnde. Þa onfeng se fæder his wedd, and hi him behet.

    a Why was Euphrosyne so well known in the town?
    b What did the father imply by the words he spoke to the young men seeking his daughter's hand in marriage?
    c Why did the father change his mind?

9

I seek my brothers, where they are keeping their herds

This unit will cover:

texts
- *a passage from the Joseph **family saga from Genesis***

grammar and usage
- *possessives*
- *the conjugation of verbs*

vocabulary
- *the meaning of **-ley** in place names*

◀) TR 28

> Ic sece mine gebroðru, hwar hig healdon heora heorda
> *I seek my brothers where they are keeping their herds*

Cultural contexts: The pastoral economy

The Old English Joseph story takes place against a background of a pastoral economy that must have been immediately recognizable to 11th-century English readers from their own experience. Throughout the period the principal farm animals were cattle, pigs and, above all, sheep. Cattle in Anglo-Saxon times were important for labour, especially for ploughing, and cultivated land was measured by the number of plough teams. Interestingly, the word **feoh** originally meant *cattle*, but its meaning gradually evolved through *moveable goods* and *property* to *money*; from this last use is derived the modern word *fee*, perhaps influenced also by the French **fee** meaning a *fief*.

Pigs or swine were **swin** (pronounced 'sween'). As manuscript illustrations and archaeology reveal, Anglo-Saxon pigs were dark and hairy and looked rather like small wild boar. They were often pastured in areas of open woodland, especially in the autumn when the ground was covered with acorns and beech mast.

Sheep (**scep**, pronounced like 'shape') had multiple uses, for milk and meat (**meolc**, **flæsc-mete**), but, above all, for wool. The increasing quantities of sheep bones, sheep shears and spindles in archaeological sites of late Anglo-Saxon England point to the great importance of sheep in the economy

of the time, when England began to develop its highly lucrative trade in wool and textiles.

Several common types of place name contain the element *shep-*, or *ship-*, both usually deriving from Old English **sceap** or **scep**; examples include:

Sheppey: **sceap** or **scep** + **iege** *island*

Shipley: **sceap** + **leah** *glade* or *clearing*. For the name **leah**, see **wordhoard** below.

Shipton: **sceap** + **tun** *settlement, estate*

Shifford: **sceap** + **ford** The crossing-place or ford was crucial on large rivers such as the Thames and Severn. The name Oxford illustrates this well: the *ford of the oxen*, first recorded in a document of 900 in the oblique case form of **Oxnaforda**; further upstream to the west of Oxford is Swinford, near Eynsham and several miles further up the Thames again is Shifford, near Kingston Bagpuize.

Grammar

The possessive *(his, her, their)*

The Old English personal pronoun had a genitive form, e.g. **án heora** and **heora án** *one of them*. This form also served as the possessive pronoun (i.e. *their*). The possessives resemble their modern English equivalents, although the pronunciation of the vowels has changed over time:

ic *I*	'itch'		**min** *my*	'meen'
þu *thou*	'thoo'		**þin** *thy, your*	'theen'
he *he*	'hay'		**his** *his*	'hiss'
heo *she*	'HÉo'		**hire** *her*	'HIRReh'
hit *it*	'hit'		**his** *its*	'hiss'
we *we*	'way'		**ure** *our*	'OO-reh'
wit *we-two*	'wit'		**uncer** *our*	'un-ker'
ge *you*	'yay'		**eower** *your*	'Éo-wer'
git *you-two*	'yit'		**incer** *your*	'incher'
hig *they*	'hee'		**heora** *their*	'HÉora'
			hira *their*	'HIRRa'

Examples of the possessive have occurred in the **reading** texts: **to heora clericum** *to their clerics* (Unit 5), **he gewregde his broðru to hira fæder** *he accused his brothers to their father* (Unit 6). In such contexts the possessives **min, þin, ure, eower** take endings when used with a noun; these strong adjective endings will be covered in Unit 14. They usually do not hinder recognition of the possessive and its meanings, e.g. **þine gebroðru healdað scep on Sichima** *your brothers are keeping the sheep at Sichim* and **ic sece mine gebroðru** *I seek my brothers* (see text below).

> ## Insight
> The plural of **broðor** *brother* in Old English was either **broðru** *brothers*, or **gebroðru** – with its suggestion of *brothers together*, or *group of brothers*, expressed by the prefix **ge-**.

Joseph follows his brothers

We left the Joseph story in Unit 6 with the brothers' emotions turning to hatred as their upstart brother recounts his dreams. Joseph has now remained at home for some time. But the plot takes a new twist as his father Israel (i.e. Jacob) sends Joseph out to look for his brothers after they have been away too long with the herds on the pastures at Shechem.

> ◀) TR 28, 00:12
>
> **Þa hys gebroðru wæron to lange on Sichem**
> *When his brothers were too long in Shechem*
>
> Þa hys gebroðru wæron to lange on Sichem mid heora fæder heordum on læswum, ða cwæð Israel to him, 'Þine gebroðru healdað scep on Sichima. Far to him and loca hwæðer hyt wel sy mid him and mid heora heordum, and cum to me and cyð me hu hyt sy.'

on læswum *on the pastures* (dative plural of **seo læs** *pasture*)
far *go* (imperative of **faran**)
loca *look* (imperative of **locian**)
sy *is* (subjunctive mood of **is** and **bið**; for explanation see Unit 13)

QV

••

◄)) TR 29

He com ða to Sichem *He came then to Shechem*

He com ða to Sichem fram Ebron dene. And hyne gemitte
ðær an man, þa he eode on gedwolan, and axode hyne hwæt
he sohte. He andswarode and cwæð, 'Ic sece mine gebroðru,
hwar hig healdon heora heorda.'

Ða cwæð se man to him, 'Hi ferdon of ðisse stowe.
Ic gehyrde ðæt hi cwædon þæt hig woldon to Dothaim.'

Iosep ferde to Dothaim æfter his gebroðrum.

••

gemitte *met* (**gemittan** *to meet, find*)
se gedwola *error, wandering*
sohte *sought* (**secan** *to seek* 'sé-chan')

QV

Grammar

Introduction to the conjugation of verbs

As we saw in Unit 4, the two basic types of verb in Old English are the weak and strong **conjugations**. In the grammars of languages like Latin and Old English, verbs **conjugate**; in other words, they take a set of inflections or endings to indicate the **person** doing the action (e.g. I, thou, she) or to indicate **number**, i.e. to distinguish singular and plural (thou or you, she or they etc.). Modern English only uses endings to show such distinctions in the third person of the present tense: *she plays* (-s ending) but *they play* (no ending).

The past tense, however, does not distinguish singular and plural: *she played* and *they played.*

Various patterns of Old English conjugation have already been observed in the study texts. In Units 4 and 6 it was seen that the inflectional ending **-on** marks the plural for the past tense:

wunode *(he or she) remained*   **wunodon** (they) *remained*
fór *(he or she) travelled*   **fóron** *(they) travelled*

In Unit 5 we saw that the present tense of most verbs has some form of 'th' ending in the third person. This is true of both singular and plural, though the exact forms may differ, the present singular usually having **-ð** contracted from **-eð**, while the plural has **-að**:

> **singeð sumeres weard**
> *summer's guardian sings* (*The Seafarer*, line 54a)

> **We wyllað cyðan iungum preostum ma þinga**
> *we want to tell young priests more things* (Byrhtferth of Ramsey)

The two conjugations form their past tenses differently: weak verbs have a consonant **-d-** as part of the ending (e.g. **wunode** *remained*) while strong verbs change the internal vowel (e.g. **faran** *to travel* – **fōr** *travelled*).

Since the grammar books list three classes of weak verbs (numbered I to III) and seven classes of strong verbs (I to VII), it is not practical or even useful to learn them all at once. It is best to learn some basic patterns first and then slowly but surely assimilate the others as they arise. This unit will focus on the conjugation of two common verbs: the class II weak verb **lufian** *to love* and the class III strong verb **singan** *to sing*.

The weak verb *lufian*
The verb **lufian** 'LU-vian' is related to the noun **seo lufu** 'LU-vu'. For the present tense there are separate endings according to **number** (singular or plural). In the singular it changes its inflection according to person, but in the plural there is simply one inflectional ending:

present singular	**ic lufige**	I love
	þu lufast	*you* (sg.) *love* (cf. Shakespeare *thou lovest*)
	heo lufað	*she loves*
plural	**we lufiað**	we love (similarly for **ge, hi** *you, they*)
participle	**lufiende, lufigende**	*loving*

In the past tense, the ending is the same for **ic** and **heo** (first and third person singular) and there is again a common inflection for the plural:

past singular	**ic lufode**	*I loved* (also **he, heo, lufode**)
	þu lufodest	*you loved*
plural	**we lufodon**	*we loved* etc.
participle	**gelufod**	

Other weak verbs which follow the pattern of **lufian** are:

andswarian *answer*, **áscian** *ask*, **blissian** *rejoice*, **bodian** *preach*, **geearnian** *earn*, **ferian** *carry*, **folgian** *follow*, **fremian** *benefit*, **gaderian** *gather*, **leornian** *learn*, **locian** *look*, **ge-nerian** *save*, **swutelian** *declare*, **ge-þáfian** *allow*, **ge-utlagian** *outlaw*, **wacian** *wake*, *keep watch*, **wunian** *dwell*, *remain*

Insight

A verb related to **faran** *to go* is **ferian** *to carry*, past tense **ferode** *carried*. A cognate Old Norse word from the same root **far-** was **ferja**, which reached the English language through Viking settlers and gave rise to the modern word *ferry*.

The strong verb *singan*

The verb **singan** has a corresponding noun **se sang** *song, singing, poem* with related compounds **blisse-sang** *song of joy* and **lof-sang** *song of praise*. Its present and past tenses are given in the table:

present singular	**ic singe**	*I sing*
	þu singst	*you* (sg.) *sing* (thou singst)
	heo singð	*she sings*
plural	**we singað**	*we sing* (similarly for **ge, hi** *you, they*)
participle	**singende**	*singing*
past singular	**ic sang**	*I sang* (also **he, heo sang**)
	þu sunge	*you sang*

| plural | we sungon | we sang etc. |
| participle | gesungen | (e.g. have sung, was sung, a hymn sung well) |

In the past tense of strong verbs there is a change of vowel to mark off the past from the present and another vowel change within the past tense itself, so that:

| ic sang *I sang* | differs from | þu sunge *you* (sg.) *sang* |
| he, heo sang *he, she sang* | differs from | we, ge, hi sungon *we, you, they sang.* |

Verbs on the same pattern as **singan** include:

byrnan *burn*, **climban** *climb*, **drincan** *drink*, **hlimman** *resound*, **gelimpan** *happen*, **springan** *sprout*, **swimman** *swim*, **swincan** *toil*, **winnan** *strive*, **yrnan** *run*

Sometimes in strong verbs the present tense drops or alters its final 'th' ending for phonetic reasons, so that **bindan** *bind* or **findan** *find* have present tenses **bint** and **fint**. Other patterns are:

helpan *help* with present tense	**hilpð** *helps*
delfan *dig*	**dilfð** *digs*
meltan *melt*	**milt** *melts*
gyldan *pay*	**gylt** *pays*

Therefore, when learning a new verb as a vocabulary item, it is best to note down the **four principal parts** with changeable vowels, i.e. its present tense (3rd person singular i.e. **he** or **heo**), its two past tense forms in the singular (1st and 3rd person i.e. **ic** and **he** or **heo**) and in the past and, finally, the past participle:

	3rd singular present	singular past	plural past	past participle
singan	**singð**	**sang**	**sungon**	**sungen**
byrnan	**byrnð**	**barn**	**burnon**	**geburnen**

Wordhoard

The place name element -ley

The name **leah** ('léah') is one of the most common topographical names in Old English, originally signifying *ancient woodland*, but gradually developing to mean *glade* or *clearing*. Sometimes it occurs with the name of a man such as Beorn in Barnsley, Becca in Beckley, Blecca in Bletchley, Ceolmund in Cholmondeley and Chumleigh, Cyneheard in Kinnerley, Eardulf in Ardley; or with the name of a woman Ælfgyð in Alveley or Aldgyð in Audley. These are probably the names of the original holders of the land. As in the case of Farnley in Yorkshire (from **fearn** *fern*), the **leah** element could be combined with many other kinds of natural and agricultural elements, such as:

Trees: seo ac *oak* (Oakley), **se æsc** *ash* (Ashley), **seo beorc** *birch* (Berkeley), **seo lind** *lime* (Lindley), **seo plume** *plum* (Plumley), **se þorn** *thorn* (Thornley), **se wiðig** *withy, willow* (Weethley, Widley).

Crops and plants: seo æte, seo ate *oats* (Oatley), **se hæþ** *heath* (Hadley), **þæt hiege** *hay* (Hailey), **se hwæte** *wheat* (Wheatley), **þæt lin** *flax, linseed* (Linley); another kind of crop is the sticks or staves that were cut and gathered at Staveley, from Old English **stæf** *staff*, plural **stafas** ('sta-vas').

Physical features: brad *broad* (Bradley), **efen** *even, smooth* (Evenley), **lang** *long* (Langley), **ðæt (ge)mære** *boundary* (Marley), **se mor** *marsh* (Morley), **roh** *rough* (Rowley), **se stan** *stone* (Stanley).

TEST YOURSELF (1)

Questions on the study text

1 What was Joseph supposed to do when he found his brothers?

2 What was Joseph doing when the man spoke to him?

3 How did the man know where Joseph's brothers had gone?

TEST YOURSELF (2)

1 On the model of the verb table for **lufian** *to love*, write out a paradigm for the weak verb **blissian** *to rejoice*. Include the personal pronouns and show all the forms of the present tense, present participle, past tense and past participle.

2 Translate into Old English, using the correct form of the strong verb: (**a**) it happened (**b**) we toiled (**c**) they strove (**d**) I swam (**e**) she ran (**f**) we drank (**g**) you found it.

3 Using an Ordnance Survey map of an English town and countryside that you know well, see if you can identify any names in the region which use place name elements beginning with Ox-, Swin-, Shep-, Ship-, or Shiff-. Check their etymology in a book on the place names of the area (e.g. the publications of the Place Name Society). Try a similar task tracing the *-ley* or *-ford* place names in your chosen area.

10

These are the bounds of the pasture at Hazelhurst

This unit will cover:

texts
- **the Hazelhurst charter written by the Canterbury scribe Eadui Basan**

grammar and usage
- **the definite article**
- **more uses of the dative**
- **the weak declension**

vocabulary
- **charter bounds and descriptions of the landscape**
- **place names**

◀) TR 30

Ðis syndan ðæs dennes landgemæru to hæsel ersc
These are the bounds of the pasture at Hazelhurst

Charters

To a considerable extent, the present-day English landscape was made and named by speakers of Old English. The fields, the boundary ditches and borders of estates and woodland – many of these landmarks were established in the Old English period. We know this from the evidence of place names still in use, and from the descriptions in documents. Land ownership in Anglo-Saxon England was recorded for posterity in numerous bilingual land charters. A charter, called a **boc** (literally a *book*) in Old English, was a title deed. Typically, it consisted of a religious preamble and record of the transaction in Latin, a description of the bounds of the property in Old English, and a list of witnesses. The Old English description of the bounds often tallies remarkably with the present-day shape of a piece of land.

Insight

The historian John Blair writes on the Old English namers of the landscape: 'Their topographical vocabulary was astonishingly rich and sensitive: the modern usages of "hill", "valley", "stream", or "wood" are blunt instruments compared with the range of lost terms which are preserved in place-names, enabling us to decode the landscape as the Anglo-Saxons saw it.'

The Hazelhurst charter

In the year 1018 king Cnut granted some land, a copse called Hæselersc, now Lower Hazelhurst near Ticehurst in Sussex, to archbishop Ælfstan Lyfing. The event was recorded in a Latin charter (S 950). The important scribe Eadwig Basan, who around the same time also wrote Cnut's writ to archbishop Lyfing in the Royal gospel book (see Unit 7), wrote the main text of this Latin charter, adding Old English bounds and a list of witnesses.

The text below gives a transcription of the Old English charter bounds in the manuscript, with the original punctuation and mostly with the original word division. The only capital letter is on the first word, marking the new section; for the modern reader, the question of capitalization becomes an issue when identifying the names of places or landmarks that occur in the charter. Most names in Old English are descriptive and informative rather than mere labels: the name Thornhill, for instance, would mean literally *thorn hill*, a hill with a thorn tree. The charter bounds encompass a piece of land at Hazelhurst known as a **denn**. The name **denn** developed only in the Weald of Kent and Sussex to designate a woodland pasture, usually a swine pasture, at some distance from the parent estate. An example is the modern place Tenterden, meaning originally the **denn** of the people of Thanet, in fact 45 miles away.

Insight

Over time the **denn** developed into an independent settlement in its own right, sometimes with the name of an original owner or inhabitant attached to it: **Beaduric** in Bethersden, **Bidda** in Biddenden, **Ciolla** in Chillenden (note the newer *ch* spelling that preserves the old pronunciation).

QUICK VOCAB

ðæt wig *sacred place, shrine* (also spelt **weoh**)
seo smiþðe *forge, smithy*
þæt geat *gate*
se sihter, seohter *drain, ditch*
se fearn *fern* + **se leah** *glade, clearing* (cf. the modern name Farnley in Yorkshire)
se burna *burn, brook, stream*
runanleages *of ?rough glade*, i.e. Rowley

◀ **TR 30**

Ðis syndan ðæs dennes landgemæru to hæsel ersc *These are the bounds of the pasture at Hazelhurst*

Ðis syndan ðæs dennes landgemæru to hæsel ersc. ærest andlang fearnleges burnan. oð runan leages mearce. of runan leages mearce be holan beames mearce. of holan beames mearce swa on geriht to wiglege bufan ðære smiþðan to þam geate. of þam geate innan þæne sihter. andland sihtres innan þæne bradan burnan. niðer andland bradan burnan. be þæs arcebiscopes mearce eft innan fearnleages burnan.

These are the estate boundaries of the denn at Hazelhurst.
First along Fern Glade Brook to the border of Rough Glade,
from the border of Rough Glade by Hollow Tree Border;
from Hollow Tree Border thus straight ahead to Sacred
Glade, above the smithy to the gate; from the gate into the
ditch, along the ditch into the broad brook, down along
Broad Brook, by the archbishop's border back into Fern
Glade Brook.

Grammar

The definite article

The text illustrates various cases of the masculine definite article **se**; in the accusative, genitive and dative cases the forms are **þæne**, **þæs**, and **þam**. There is also an example of the feminine form **þære**. This kind of information can be presented usefully in a table:

	masculine	neuter	feminine
nominative	**se**	**þæt**	**seo**
accusative	**þæne**	**þæt**	**þa**
genitive	**þæs**	**þæs**	**þære**
dative	**þam**	**þam**	**þære**

The plural does not distinguish gender; in the four cases (nominative, accusative, genitive, dative) the forms are: **þa**, **þa**, **þara** and **þæm**.

Other spellings of the above forms do occur, notably **þone** for **þæne** and **þan** for **þam**.

The dative is often used after a preposition: **to þam geate** *to the gate*, **bufan þære smiþðan** *above the smithy*.

The strong noun

The basic kind of noun in Old English, the strong declension, varies its case endings depending on its gender. The following table illustrates three basic strong nouns in the singular (to aid pronunciation, length is marked by a macron over the vowel, e.g. **bēam**):

	singular		
nominative	**se bēam** *the tree*	**þæt land** *the land*	**sēo mearc** *the border*
accusative	**þæne bēam**	**þæt land**	**þā mearce**
genitive	**þæs bēames** *of the tree*	**þæs landes**	**þære mearce**
dative	**þǣm bēame** *to the tree*	**þǣm lande**	**þære mearce**

Insight

The three nouns declined in the above table illustrate yet again the phenomenon of grammatical gender, which is best understood as a system of grouping nouns so that they can be made more distinctive, for there is no obvious naturalistic reason why these three nouns should be assigned different genders. For those who know German it will be seen that the three cognate nouns **der Baum**, **das Land**, and **die Mark** belong to the same gender groups as their Old English equivalents.

Introduction to the weak (-an) declension

The so-called 'weak declension' is a term used for a characteristic set of endings. The typical weak ending is **-an** and it appears in the oblique cases, i.e. all the cases except the nominative case. An example of a weak noun is **seo smiþðe** *the smithy, forge*. In the dative case we have **bufan ðære smiþðan** *above the smithy*. Similarly, the neutral or nominative form of *the broad stream* would be **se brada burna** but, as we can see in the above text, the preposition **innan** *into* takes the accusative, which gives the **-an** endings 'innan þæne bradan burnan' *into the broad stream*.

The weak ending on adjectives

Usually after the definite article (*the*), adjectives take the weak (**-an**) endings, for example the common phrase in the Chronicle, **on þam ilcan geare**. In the nominative the phrase would be **þæt ilce gear**, but – as stated above – in the oblique cases (accusative, genitive, dative) the adjective takes **-an**. So the basic rule is that the weak ending is **-an** except in the nominative. The masculine nominative takes **-a** while the neuter and feminine ending is **-e**.

Other examples of the nominative include **se ilca lencten, se grena weg, seo greate dic, seo mæste wroht**; in the oblique cases these adjective endings appear as:

accusative	on þæne **grenan** weg *onto the green way* (accusative after **on**)
genitive	ðære **mæstan** wrohte (Unit 6) (*accused*) *of the greatest wrong*
dative	æfter þan **grenan** wege *after the green way* (dative after **æfter**)
	to þære **greatan** dic *to the great ditch* (dative after **to**)

The preposition **on** takes an accusative when it means *onto* (i.e. movement) and takes a dative when it means *on* (i.e. static location). Note the different cases used in the following two phrases:

on þæne **grenan** weg *onto the green way* (accusative after **on** expressing movement *onto* something)

on ðam ilcan lentene (ASC C 1002) *in the same spring* (dative after **on** expressing location in time).

Other uses of the weak ending

The weak ending is met in other 'definite' contexts, i.e. phrases where the meaning is definite and specific, even if the definite article is not present:

accusative: þurh Godes miltsiendan gife (Unit 5) *through God's merciful grace*

dative: æt Niwantune i.e. æt niwan tune *at Newton*
be holan beames mearce *by Holbeam's boundary, by the boundary of Hollow Tree*

(Note that, in this instance, the original name persisted long after its meaning became obscure, so that a modern place name near Hazelhurst is Holbeanwood.)

Cultural contexts

The witness list of the Hazelhurst charter

The witness list of the charter contains some familiar names: Cnut, Wulfstan, Ælfgyfu, earl Thorkell and earl Godwine. Thorkell is the earl of East Anglia, exiled by Cnut in 1021 but restored to power in 1022. The other earl is to be identified as the father of the famous Harold II, who ruled England in 1066. This is one of the first appearances in the historical record of earl Godwine, a nobleman who was to become head of the most powerful family in the England of Cnut and Edward the Confessor. In the Latin text, Ælfgyfu is entitled **regina**, Latin for *queen*, although the consort of the king was normally termed **ðæs cyninges wif** *the king's wife*. But Cnut's new wife – Emma of Normandy, whom Cnut had married in 1017 – was the most politically active of royal women since Eadgifu in the mid-tenth century, and she came to be called **seo hlæfdige** ('HLÆF-di-yuh') *the Lady*. The strength of her influence is indeed discernible even here in this document. As the Latin of the main text reveals, Cnut had given the grant at his queen's instigation. Emma was not, of course, new to England, having been the wife of the previous king Æthelred Unræd from 1002. On that first marriage, when she was a very young woman, her foreign name had been changed to Ælfgyfu (also spelt Ælfgifu), pronounced 'Ælf-yivu'. But like Godwine, Emma rose to much greater power and prominence during the reign of Cnut.

The scribe Eadwig Basan

The rather stately handwriting of the Hazelhurst charter has been recognized as that of a Christ Church monk called Eadwig Basan. During his career, Eadwig (pronounced 'Éa-dwi' and also spelt Eadui) produced a number of fine illustrated manuscripts, including Latin gospel books and a book of psalms. In this period the style of Latin script was known as Anglo-Caroline minuscule, but Eadwig developed a new variant on the style, which was widely imitated and became the dominant form of Anglo-Latin handwriting before the Norman Conquest.

Fawler

There were older features in the landscape than the hedges and ditches of tenth-century estates. Roman remains still existed, remembered in the Chester place names (see Unit 2) and evoked splendidly in the Exeter Book poem *The Ruin*, probably about **Akemannesceastre**, i.e. Bath:

Hryre wong gecrong
gebrocen to beorgum þær iu beorn monig
glædmod and gold beorht gleoma gefrætwed
wlonc and wingal wighyrstum scan,
seah on sinc, on sylfor, on searogimmas,
on ead, on æht, on eorcanstan,
on þas beorhtan burg bradan rices.
Stanhofu stodan, stream hate wearp
widan wylme; weal eall befeng
beorhtan bosme þær þa baþu wæron,
hat on hreðre.

(Contd)

*The site is fallen into ruin, reduced to heaps, where once
many a man blithe of mood and bright with gold, clothed
in splendours, proud and flown with wine, gleamed in his
war-trappings, and gazed upon treasure, on silver, on chased
gems, on wealth, on property, on the precious stone and on
this bright citadel of the broad kingdom; and the stone courts
were standing and the steam warmly spouted its ample surge
and a wall embraced all in its bright bosom where the baths
were, hot at its heart.*

(lines 31B–41A; translated by S.A.J. Bradley)

The Roman roads were still in use, marked often by the name
stræt, e.g. Akeman Street, the road that ends at Akemanchester
i.e. Bath. Further afield, the ruins of old Roman villas still dotted
the countryside, and their mosaic floors were known as **fag flor**
the coloured floor, **fag** (or **fah**) being an adjective with various
connotations from *variegated* and *dappled* to the more negative
stained.

Insight

Fawler in Oxfordshire is a modern place name derived
from **fag flor**, the fricative **g** becoming **w** (as in the change
from Old English **boga** to modern *bow*). Archaeology has
confirmed the origin of the name: a Roman villa has been
found on the site. It seems that sometimes the local hall or
even church was built on or near these older sites.

Strikingly, given that the poem is set in Denmark, *Beowulf* has
a variegated floor, in the hall of king Hrothgar. The detail is
mentioned in the description of the monster Grendel breaking
down the door and advancing onto the floor to attack the sleeping
Geats (724b–727):

Raþe æfter þon
on fagne flor feond treddode,
eode yrremod; him of eagum stod
ligge gelicost leoht unfæger.

> *Quickly after that*
> *onto the decorated floor the enemy stepped,*
> *advanced angrily; from his eyes stood*
> *most like a flame an ugly light.*

Wordhoard

Place names

Some common elements in place names are:

se **æcer** *field, acre*
se **beorg** *barrow*; also means *mountain*
se **broc** *brook* 'broak'
seo **brycg** *bridge*
se **croft** *croft, small field*
seo **denu** *valley* (not to be confused with **dun** *hill* or **denn** *swine pasture*)
seo **dic** *ditch, dike* 'deetch'
seo **eorðbyrig, eorðburh** *earthwork*
þæt **fenn** *fen, marsh*
se **geard** *enclosure* 'YÉard' (cf. the O.E. name for the world **middangeard**)
se **graf** *grove* 'graaf'
se **hege** *hedge, fence* 'haya'
seo **hegeræw** *hedgerow*
seo **hid** *hide* 'heed' (land supporting one household; a unit of tax assessment)
se **hlæw** *mound, burial-mound* (-*low* in names, e.g. Wenslow *Woden's Low*)
seo **hyð** *landing-place on a river* (cf. the place-name Hythe)
se **port** *town* (esp. with market or harbour; from Latin **porta**)
seo **stow** *place, site* (e.g. Stow-on-the-Wold; cf. Chepstow = *market town*; and Bristol = Brycgstow: **brycg** *bridge* + **stow** *place*)
seo **stræt** *road, high road* (from Latin **strata via**)
se **weg** *path*
se **wic** *place, settlement, trading centre* 'weetch' (e.g. Sandwich)
seo **wylle, wælle** *spring, well, stream*

TEST YOURSELF

1 In the following extract from the bounds of a Worcester charter (S *1393*), fill in the correct form of the definite article:

Ofer (**a**) _____ weg west riht to (**b**) _____ ealdan dic; æfter (**c**) _____dic to (**d**) _____ bradan stræt. Of (**e**) _____ bradan stræt be (**f**) _____ grafe innan (**g**) _____ port stræt; æfter stræte innan Dillameres dic.

Over the way westwards to the old ditch; after the ditch to the broad road. From the broad road by the grave into the town road; after the road into Dillamere ditch.

2 Translate this extract from the same charter (S*1393*):

Of þære dice ende innan þa wællan. Of þære wællan in þa sandihte stræt; æfter stræte norð on bisceopes scirlett, ofer bisceopes scirlett in lin aceran wege þam innmæstan. Of lin aceran innan ðone hege, æfter þam hege on brocc holes weg. Of brocc holes wege innan þone croft. Of þam crofte be þam gearde innan leofesunes croft.

3 **Revision** Without looking back to the original text, see if you can fill in the missing words or phrases of the Hazelhurst charter bounds

Ðis syndan (**a**) _____ dennes landgemæru to Hæselersc. Ærest andlang (**b**) _____ _____ oð runan leages mearce. Of runan leages mearce be (**c**) _____ _____ mearce. Of (**d**) _____ _____ mearce swa on geriht to Wiglege, bufan (**e**) _____smiþðan to (**f**) ____ geate. Of (**g**) _____ geate innan (**h**) _____ sihter, andland sihtres, innan (**i**) _____ bradan burnan. Niðer andland bradan burnan, be (**j**) ____ arcebiscopes mearce, eft innan fearnleages burnan.

11

Here is declared in this document

This unit will cover:

texts
- **the role of the** swutelung *declaration* **in the governance of Anglo-Saxon England**

grammar and usage
- **the demonstrative þes** *this*

vocabulary
- **formulaic phrases**
- **rhythmical language**

◀) **TR 31**

> **Her swutelað on ðysum gewrite**
> *Here is declared in this document*

The declaration

The following document (S 1220), known as a declaration, or **swutelung**, records the grant of a Kentish **dænn** *swine pasture* (like Hazelhurst in Unit 10) to Leofwine the Red some time between the years 1013 and 1020. Paying the original price (Old English **sceatt** coin, price), Leofwine receives the pasture as an **éce yrfe** *eternal* i.e. *permanent inheritance*, then attaches it to his land at Boughton (Boughton Malherbe, Kent).

Insight

Note the text's insistence that Godwine *grants* the land to Leofwine, the completion of the action being emphasized with the (optional) perfective prefix **ge-** on the verb **geann**. In the second sentence, however, where the later recipient of the grant is still unknown, the form used is **ann**. For more on the **ge-** prefix, look back to Unit 4.

◆) TR 31, 00:10

Leofwine reada *Leofwine the Red*

Her swutelað on ðysan gewrite þæt Godwine geánn Leofwine readan ðæs dænnes æt Swiðrædingdænne on ece yrfe, to habbanne and to sellanne, on dæge and æfter dæge, ðam ðe him leofost sy, æt þon sceatte ðe Leofsunu him geldan scolde: þæt is feowertig penega and twa pund and eahta ambra cornes. Nu ann Leofwine þæs dænnes ðon ðe Boctun to handa gega æfter his dæge.

Here is declared in this document that Godwine grants to Leofwine the Red the swine pasture at Southernden as a permanent inheritance, to keep and to give, in his day and after his day, to whoever is dearest to him, for the price which Leofsunu had to pay him, that is: forty pence and two pounds and eight ambers of corn. Now Leofwine grants the pasture into the hands of whoever Boughton may pass after his day.

◆) TR 32

Nu is þyses to gewittnesse: Lyfingc bisceop and Ælfmær abbud, and se hired æt Cristescyrcean and se híred æt sancte Augustine, and Síred, and Ælfsige cild, and Æþelric, and manig oþer god man binnan byrig and butan.

Now as witness of this are bishop Lyfing and abbot Ælfmær, and the community at Christ Church, and the community at Saint Augustine's, and Sired, and Ælfsige Child, and Æthelric, and many other good man within the city and without.

swutelian	*to declare* (**swutelað, swutelode, swutelodon, geswutelod**)
geunnan	*grant* (present **ánn, unnon,** past **uðe, uðon,** past participle **geunnen**)
Godwine geánn... ðæs dænnes	*G. grants the swine pasture* (**geunnan** takes a genitive object rather than accusative – see grammar in Unit 13)
Leofwine readan	*to Leofwine the Red* (dative; weak adjective; see Unit 10)
ece	*eternal* (see formulaic phrases below)
seo yrfe	*inheritance, bequest* (also spelled **ierfe**)
sellan	*to give, sell* (also spelled **syllan**)
ðam ðe	literally *to-that-one who*
leof	*dear*
se sceatt	*coin, price:* **æt þon sceatte** *at the price* (dative; spelling **þon** for **þam**)
geldan	*pay*
feowertig	*forty*
se peneg	*penny* (also **peaneg, pening**)
þæt pund	*pound*
amber	*pitcher, measure, amber*
nu	*now*
ðon ðe =	**ðam ðe**
gega	*should go* 'yuh-GAH' (subjunctive)
cild	*child, youth of aristocratic birth* (hence the title Childe in later ballads)
manig	*many a*
binnan	*within*
byrig	*city, stronghold* (dative form of **seo burh,** also spelled **burg**)
butan	*without*

Cultural contexts

Canterbury

Ecclesiastical Canterbury in the year 1000 centred on the cathedral of Christ Church and the monastery of St Augustine's, both established around the year 600 after Pope Gregory the Great sent a mission to Æthelberht king of Kent. The leader of this mission was an Italian with the same name as the fifth-century patristic writer Augustine of Hippo. This other Augustine became the first archbishop of Canterbury and eventually gave his name to the monastery. As the seat of the archbishopric, urban Canterbury flourished in the early middle ages. By the reign of Cnut, Christ Church had followed in the wake of tenth-century reforms and installed monks to run the cathedral rather than the normal secular clergy, so that there were now two monastic communities in the city. Usually they acted as partners, as in the present document here, although on occasions rivalry did break out between the two institutions.

Language and style

Formulaic phrases

The vocabulary of the text typifies many of the formulaic phrases commonly found in charters and writs.

Her swutelað on ðysan/ðyssum gewrite (lit. *here declareth in this writing*) is the standard formula for opening this type of **swutulung**, *declaration, notification;* the verb **swutelian** *to explain,* which occurred in Unit 5, derives from an adjective **swutol** or **sweotol** meaning *clear.* As with the definite article **þam** and **þan**, there are different ways of spelling **ðysan** and **ðyssum** (see **grammar** below).

On ece yrfe *as a perpetual inheritance*, the common adverb and adjective **ece** usually means *eternal*.

To habbanne and to sellanne *to keep or to give, to have or to sell* is expressed in the form of **to** + the inflected infinitive, which had a regular ending normally spelled **-nne**. A similar formula in the marriage agreement in Unit 8 is **to gyfene and to syllenne** (note the spelling variant **syllenne** for **sellanne**). **To + infinitive** was often used to express cause or purpose.

On dæge and æfter dæge *in his day and after his day*. Here the word **dæg** is used metaphorically to signify *lifetime*. Another common expression is **þreora manna dæg** to signify *for three people's lifetimes*, after which the leased property would revert to the original owner, such as a cathedral. Also connected with this usage is a phrase such as **on Æþelrædes dæge cyninges** *during the reign of king Æthelred*.

The relative clause **ðam ðe him leofost sy** depends on the preceding formula **to sellanne** and implies that the recipient is free to give the land to whoever he please, *to whom it may be dearest to him*. The final word **sy** (here translated *may be*) is the subjunctive form of the verb **is**. Another form of the subjunctive **wære** *would be* occurs in the formula **ðam ðe hire leofest wære** *to whom it would be dearest to her*, in other words, *to whoever she please* (see Unit 8). A similar linguistic pattern recurs in the next sentence of our passage in the relative clause **ðon ðe Boctun to handa gega** literally *to whom Boughton may pass into the hands*, with **ge-ga** here being the subjunctive of the verb **gan** or **ge-gan**. For the forms of the subjunctive, see **grammar** in Unit 13.

··

Insight

Formulas are not stock epithets or clichés but variable pieces of language that follow recognisable patterns. They function as identifying markers that tell the listener what genre or type of discourse he or she is listening to; the formulas serve the structural purpose of marking the beginning and end of a piece of language; they make the text more accessible and memorable, so it becomes easier to listen to the declaration as it is read out loud in a formal situation.

··

Nu is þyses to gewittnesse literally *now is of-this* (genitive) *as witness* or in more natural word order *now as witness of this is...* serves as a formula to introduce the list of witnesses to the transaction. As with many such formulas the wording or tense can vary slightly, so that we also find: **nu wæs ðyses to gewitnesse** in the past tense. Another grammatically more complex formulation is to say *this was spoken... with the witness of X, and of Y and of Z...* Here each of the male names of witnesses that follow in the list is given an **-es** ending for the genitive case:

Ðis wæs gespecen... on Lyfinges arcebiscopes gewitnesse, and Ælfmeres abbodes, and Æþelwines sciregerefan, and Siredes ealdan, and Godwines Wulfeages sunu...

This was said... with the witness of archbishop Lyfing... and abbot Ælfmer... and Æþelwine the sheriff, and Sired the Old, and Godwin Wulfeah's son...

Not all of those present at a meeting were necessarily named and sometimes the list of witnesses ends conventionally with a disclaimer such as **and manig oþer god men** *and many other good people*, or **mænig god cniht toeacan ðysan** *many a good retainer as well as these*. In the latter phrase, it is worth noticing incidentally the process of semantic change. The word **cniht**, which originally meant *young man*, was by the 11th century beginning to develop its later meaning of *knight*.

Rhythmical language

The language of the administrative documents draws on the traditional forms of oral parley and debate for some of its stylistic effects. One popular feature of style in all genres of Old English discourse is the two-stress phrase, an example in modern English being *hands and feet*. The latter phrase has one weak syllable between two strong or stressed syllables, and its pronunciation could be represented 'HANDS and FEET' or by a notation that marks the pattern:

hands and feet / x / (strong–weak–strong),

where / is a stressed or emphatic syllable and x is a weak or unstressed syllable.

A two-stress phrase can vary in length, because the number of weak syllables can range from one to four or more:

LONdon TOWN	/ x /
CIty of OXford	/ x x / x
saint DAvid's caTHEdral	x / x x / x

The two-stress phrase can also combine with other effects like rhyme, half-rhyme, assonance (similar vowel sounds) or alliteration; examples are *kith and kin* (alliteration and assonance), *hearth and home* (alliteration), *sticks and stones* (alliteration).

Insight

A series of two-stress phrases can form a memorable saying:

Sticks and stones may break my bones but words will never hurt me.

This proverb could be analysed as three two-stress phrases each highlighted by memorable alliteration, rhyme and half-rhyme.

Phonetically speaking, modern English word stress does not normally depend on the accent or dialect of a particular native speaker. There are exceptions, such as 'GArage' and 'gaRAGE', but normally we all follow the pattern 'MInister', 'PRINcess' or 'SHEPherd'. And whether you are from Pembrokeshire, Belfast or Ohio, you will nevertheless still place the stress on the second syllable of the word *caTHEdral*. Word stress may be different in other languages however, even for related words; so for example the French say *cathéDRALE*. Although the stressed syllable in a particular modern English word is usually fixed, it can occasionally shift when two similar words are contrasted, such as *inhale* and *exhale*. Normally we say *inHALE*, but when the two words come together we may well say *INhale and EXhale*.

Bearing these principles in mind, it is worth reading the Old English **swutulung** documents out loud, since the style of their language seems to draw heavily on the patterns and rhythms of speech. These are formal declarations made before witnesses in which the words must be weighed, and form must balance content.

Prominent in their language is the two-stress phrase made up of two nouns, adjectives, verbs or adverbs each with a stress on its most prominent syllable. In the above document for instance, listen to the chiming effects of the ending on the two-stress phrase made up of two infinitives (analysis of rhythm in brackets):

to HABB<u>anne</u> and to SELL<u>anne</u>

the similar rhetorical contrast of the formula

on <u>dæge</u> and æfter <u>dæge</u>

perhaps pronounced contrastively as 'ON dæge and ÆFter dæge', or the alliterative rhythm of the final phrase:

binnan BYrig and BUtan.

Other examples include the alliteration of **swa full and swa forð** *as fully and completely*, rhyme in **unforboden and unbesacan** *unforbidden and uncontested* and **ægðer ge gehadode ge leawede** *both clergy and laity*. Parallelism (where the two elements of the phrase have the same structure or parallel pattern) highlights the antithesis in the formula **on wuda and on felde** *in wood and in field*.

Some formulas are a kind of shorthand and require further explanation. A grant of land **mid mete and mid mannum** means literally *with food and with men* and relates to the food provision and labour that went with the estate. The term **mid sake and mid socne**, sometimes called *sake and soke*, means *jurisdiction* and probably refers to the right to hold a court in the area and/or to profit from any fines exacted.

One final point to note is that many of the terms and formulas used in declarations are also used in other legal documents (for examples, look back to the king's writ in Unit 7 and the marriage agreement in Unit 8).

Grammar

The demonstrative þes (this)

singular	masculine	neuter	feminine	
nominative	þes	þys	þēos	this
accusative	þysne	þys	þās	this
genitive	þyses	þysses	þysse	of this
dative	þyssum	þyssum	þysse	to this

The plural forms are þās, þās, þyssa, þyssum *these, these, of these, to these*, the first two being pronounced with a long 'ah' vowel (marked ā with a macron over the vowel to show length, a convention used in grammars of Old English).

Insight

The endings on **þes, þysne, þyses, þyssum** are similar to those of the definite article **se, þæne, þæs, þæm** (see Unit 10) and of the personal pronoun **he, hine, his, him** (see Unit 8); the **-ne** ending is a sure sign of a masculine accusative while the **-s** identifies the genitive of the masculine and neuter pronouns.

Many of the forms of þes have been met already in previous units. In riddle 66 (Unit 3), the speaker begins:

ic eom mare þonne þes middangeard
I am greater than this middle world

where **middangeard** is a masculine noun, while a neuter nominative occurred in Jacob's question to his son Joseph (see Unit 6):

Hwæt sceal ðis swefn beon?
What is this dream supposed to be?

An example of the genitive is:

nu is þyses to gewittnesse
now as witness of this is

while various uses of the dative include:

her swutelað on ðysum gewrite *here declareth in this document*
her on þyssum geare *here in this year*
hi ferdon of ðisse stowe *they went from this place* (Unit 9).

Insight

A common variant of **þyssum** is **þysan** or (with the letter eth)
ðysan, so that we find **her swutelað on ðysan gewrite** *here
declareth in this document* instead of **on ðysum gewrite.** The
explanation is phonetic: in late Old English the ending **-um**
was weakly stressed with a reduced vowel and difficult to
distinguish from **-an**; both endings may well have sounded as
[an] in þhonetic script.

In the following sentence, describing a gift to Bury St Edmunds, the
neuter singular functions as a general *this* and is followed by the
plural **syndon**; in modern English grammar, of course, only *these*
would combine with *are*:

**Þis sendan þa land þe Þurkytel gean Gode and sancte Marian
and sancte Eadmunde**
*These are the lands that Thorketel grants to God and saint Mary
and saint Edmund.*

Similarly in the charter bounds for Hazelhurst (Unit 10):

Ðis syndan ðæs dennes landgemæru to Hæselersc
These are the bounds of the pasture at Hazelhurst

As far as plural forms of the demonstrative are concerned, we saw
Byrhtferth's reason for writing about the calendar in Unit 5:

þæt hig magon þe ranclicor **þas þing** heora clericum geswutelian
so that they [the priests] may explain these things the more boldly to their clerics

And in the dative plural we have the following use:

nu syndon **to ðysum forwordan** twa gewrita
now for these terms of agreement there are two documents.

TEST YOURSELF

1 Cnut gives the archbishop more land *(S 988; Harmer no. 30)*

In the following royal writ, fill in the gaps with the most likely word as suggested by the context.

> Cnut cyngc **(a)** _____ Eadsige bisceop and Ælfstan abbod and Ægelric and ealle **(b)** _____ þegenas on Cent **(c)** _____. And ic **(d)** _____ eow þæt ic hæbbe geunnan Æþelnoðe arcebisceope ealre þare landare þe Ælfmær hæfde and mid rihte into Cristes cyricean gebyrað, binnan **(e)** _____ and butan, on **(f)** _____ and on felda, swa full and swa **(g)** _____ , swa Ælfric arcebiscop hyre weold oþþe ænig his forgengena.

2 Translate the following document (S 1222)

Ic þored geann þæt land æt Horslege þam hirede æt Cristes cyrcean for mine sawle swa full and swa forð swa ic sylf hit ahte.

3 Translate (S 1225)

> Þis sendan þa land þe Þurkytel gean Gode and sancte Marian and sancte Eadmunde: þæt is þæt land æt Culeforde þæt his agen wæs, swa hit stænt, mid mete and mid mannum, and mid sake and mid socne, and eal þæt land æt Wridewellan; and þæt land æt Gyxeweorðe swa hit stent mid mete and mid mannum.

4 Replace the definite article with the appropriate form of the demonstrative *this*; for examples: se wer: þes wer; heo lufað þone wer: heo lufað þisne wer

  a se ceorl   **e** he hit geaf þam ceorle

  b he hatað þone cyning   **f** þa eorlas

  c he lufað þa cwen   **g** he hit geaf þam eorlum

  d þæs cynges land

12

I saw a creature travel
on the wave

This unit will cover:

texts
- **riddles**
- **short extracts from Byrhtferth's** *Handbook*
- **a passage from the Exeter Book poem** *The Seafarer*
- **an extract from the Chronicle narrative** *Cynewulf and Cyneheard*

grammar and usage
- **more on the declension of nouns**

vocabulary
- **parts of the body**
- **numbers**
- **the names of animals and birds**

◀ TR 33

Ic wiht geseah on wege feran
I saw a creature travel on the wave

The five senses

Image

The famous ninth-century Fuller brooch, a disc brooch used for fastening the cloak at the shoulder, is an ornate piece of silver metalwork with an elaborate allegorical decoration. In the main frame, four figures are grouped around the image of a man who holds plant stems in his hands and stares straight out from the centre of the brooch. Each figure mimes a clear and unmistakable action:

one puts hand to open mouth in a gesture of taste, another – with hands behind his back – smells a piece of vegetation, a third touches hand to hand and foot to foot, a fourth puts right hand to ear in a gesture of hearing. Like the central figure of the Alfred jewel, which represents Wisdom, the central figure here is Sight, or Spiritual Vision, with large round eyes that gaze out at the viewer like a Greek icon.

For a conveniently accessible image of this brooch, in colour, see the front cover of *The Cambridge Companion to Old English Literature*. In the next section, we will consider the Old English words that these images represent.

eye **ēage** pronounce 'Éa-yuh' (*eyes* **ēagan**)
ear **ēare** (*ears* **ēaran**)
nose **nosu** pronounce 'nozzu' (medial **-s-** is pronounced as 'z')
mouth **mēð** 'mooth'
tongue **tunge**
hand **hand** (*hands* **handa**)
foot **fōt** 'foat' (*feet* **fēt** 'fate')

As *eyes, ears, nose, mouth, hands* and *feet* testify, many basic Old English words have changed very little in the course of history. These fundamental words have informed the English speaker's experience and perception of the world for the last 1,500 years.

The living body

The difference between the old and new forms of the words often lies in the vowel sounds. To help to remember the following list and to make the right old–modern connections, say or chant the words out loud. The occasional long vowels are worth highlighting; they are marked here with an editorial macron (e.g. the ē in fēt feet) to emphasise their length, so that fēt sounds like modern 'fate'.

body	**bodig** pronounce as in modern English 'body'
head	**heafod** cf. German cognates *Haupt* and Latin *caput* (pronounce -f- as 'v': in Middle English the 'v' sound eventually dropped, leaving 'head')
eye	**ēage** pronounce 'Éa-yuh' (*eyes* **ēagan**)
nose	**nosu** pronounce 'nozzu' (medial -s- is pronounced as 'z')
mouth	**mūð** 'mooth'
ear	**ēare** (ears **ēaran**)
neck	**swēora** or **hnecca**
back	**hrycg** pronounce 'hrüdge' (modern English *ridge*) or **bæc**
shoulder	**eaxl** (cf. modern English *axle*) or **sculdor**
arm	**earm**
elbow	**elnboga**
hand	**hand**
finger	**finger**
thumb	**þūma**
index finger	**scytefinger** (from **scyte** shooting, e.g. a bow and arrow)
side	**sīde**
stomach	**wamb** or **womb**
leg	**scanca** (cf. *Edward Longshanks* or *shank's pony*)
foot	**fēt** 'foat' (feet **fēt** 'fate')

As well as the everyday words for the body such as **bodig** and **lic**, there are many poetic expressions for the living body. These include **feorhus** *life-house*, **feorhbold** *life-mansion*, **feorhhord** *life treasury* and **bānhus** *bone-house*. The last is the poet Seamus Heaney's favourite: it occurs in *Beowulf* and is echoed in Heaney's poem 'Bone Dreams'. For more examples, see the thesaurus section of Stephen Pollington's *Wordcraft* (1993).

Noun declension

As Old English nouns, our six words for the main organs of sense – *eyes*, *ears*, *nose*, *mouth*, *hands* and *feet* – are classified grammatically according to their **declension**, the type of endings which accrue to them in sentences. Where **muð** belongs to the strong masculine declension, **eage** and **eare** are weak neuter nouns, while the other three are irregular, **fot** being irregular masculine and **hand** and **nosu** irregular feminine nouns:

	strong masc.	weak neuter		irregular masc.	feminine	
				singular		
nom.	mūð	ēage	ēare	fōt	hand	nosu
acc.	mūð	ēage	ēare	fōt	hand	nosu
gen.	mūðes	ēagan	ēaran	fētes	handa	nosa
dat.	mūðe	ēagan	ēaran	fēt	handa	nosa
				plural		
nom.	mūðas	ēagan	ēaran	fēt	handa	
acc.	mūðas	ēagan	ēaran	fēt	handa	
gen.	mūða	ēagena	ēarena	fōta	handa	
dat.	mūðum	ēagum	ēarum	fōtum	handum	

Insight

In the above table, observe the patterns of inflection in the system of noun declension. For instance, apart from the irregular noun **hand**, most nouns have a recognizable genitive and dative plural.

Numbers one to 12

It is worth learning Old English numbers alongside Latin numerals in the form in which they were written in Old English manuscripts and as they appear in many printed editions. The Latin notation was the only one used until the arrival of Arabic numerals in the twelfth century. Long vowels are marked for convenience (e.g. ān, pronounce 'ahn').

- .i.   **ān**'ahn'
- .ii.   **twegen** 'twayen' also **twā** 'twah' (fem.) and **tu** 'two' (neuter)
- .iii.   **þrȳ** (also spelt **þrīe;** masculine) **þrēo** (feminine and neuter)
- .iv.   **fēower**
- .v.   **fīf**
- .vi.   **syx** (also spelt **siex**)
- .vii.   **seofon** (two syllables 'SEHuh'+'vun')
- .viii.   **eahta** (pronounce **h** as the ch in Loch Ness); rarely also **ehtuwe**
- .viiii.   **nigon** 'ni' + 'gon'
- .x.   **tȳn**
- .xi.   **endlufon** or **endleofon** (pronounce **-f-** between vowels as 'v')
- .xii.   **twelf**

More numerals

The *-teen* numerals end in **tȳne**: 13 þrēotȳne, 14 fēowertȳne, 15 fiftȳne, 16 syxtȳne, 17 seofontȳne, 18 eahtatȳne, 19 nigontȳne.

The number **twentig** sounds almost exactly the same as modern English *twenty*, since the combination of letters -ig was regularly pronounced as a short 'ee' sound. The same is true of 30 þritig, 40 fēowertig, 50 fīftig, and 60 sȳxtig. Thereafter up to 120 an ancient and original system of counting takes over in which the names for 7, 8, 9, 10, 11, 12 end with the suffix -tig and each is preceded by **hund**, even though **hund** normally means *hundred*:

70	**hundseofontig**
80	**hundeahtatig**
90	**hundnigontig**
100	**hundteontig**
110	**hundendleofantig**
120	**hundtwelftig**

Roman numerals

It is worth recalling the basic principles of the Roman system of numerals that is often used in Old English manuscripts and printed editions. Based on the letters M, D, C, L, X, V and I representing the hierarchy *thousand, five hundred, hundred, fifty, ten, five,* and *one*, the main principle is cumulative: the most senior letter comes first and any junior letters that appear to its right are simply added to it. So we have:

VI	six	VII	seven	VIII	eight
XI	eleven	XII	twelve	XIII	thirteen
XV	fifteen	XVI	sixteen	XVII	seventeen
XX	twenty	XXI	twenty-one		
LI	fifty-one	LVI	fifty-six		
LXXII	seventy-two				
CLXXXVII	one hundred and eighty-seven				

(C is Latin *centum* = 100)

If, however, a junior letter precedes a senior, then its value is subtracted. This gives the following numbers:

IV	four (sometimes written by scribes as IIII)
IX	nine
XL	forty
XC	ninety (etc.)

Reading

Byrhtferth of Ramsey on numbers

The following is Byrhtferth's passage on **getæle** *counting*, i.e. his explanation of Roman numerals. There is perhaps one error or confusion in his list, namely the symbol for *six*: probably he meant to write **V and I getacnað syx** *V and I signify six*.

> Þas stafas synt on Ledenum getæle: I getacnað an, V getacnað fif, X getacnað tyn, L fiftig, C *centum* hundred, M þusend, I and V syx, X and I endlufon, X and L feowertig, L and X syxtig, X and C hundnigontig, D and C syx hundred, *duo* CC twa hundred, CCC þreo hundred, CCCC feower hundred, D and CCCC nigon hundred, M þusend.

Further details

To express the figure XXIV, Old English said **feower and twentig** in the style of the nursery rhyme 'four and twenty blackbirds'. Often the following noun was put into the genitive plural (ending in **-a**) so that the idea is expressed as 'four and twenty of blackbirds': examples are, **dæg** *day*, **tyn dag-a** *ten of-days*, **þrittig daga and tyn tida**, *thirty days and ten hours*. With large numbers the noun may be repeated: **þreo hund daga and feower and fiftig daga** *three hundred and fifty-four days*.

For multiplication, Byrhtferth uses **siðon** *times*:

> **Nim twelf siðon þrittig; do togædere; þonne hæfast ðu þreo hund daga and syxtig.**

*Take twelve times thirty; add together; then you have three
hundred and sixty days.*

Like many medieval writers Byrhtferth is fascinated by the
symmetry and interconnections of numbers. In his **handboc** he
writes about:

> þa feower timan *the four seasons*: **lengtentima, sumor,
> hærfest, winter**
> þa feower gesceaft *the four elements*: **lyft, fyr, wæter, eorðe**
> and their related adjectives: **ceald** *cold*, **wearm** *warm*, **wæt**
> *wet*, **drigge** *dry*
> þa feower mægna *the four virtues* (literally *the four powers*):
> **rihtwisnys** *righteousness*, **snoternys** *wisdom*, **ge-metgung**
> *moderation* and **strengð** *strength*

(For more on Byrhtferth, look back to Unit 5.)

Learning vocabulary

The study of vocabulary serves two purposes. Practically
speaking, a wide knowledge of the lexical patterns of the language
accelerates the process of learning to read the language. More
theoretically, the systematic study of the Old English lexicon throws
light on the way the speakers viewed the world, on the things and
phenomena they thought necessary to name and label. It is part of
the study of Old English culture, equally relevant to both literature
and history.

The lexical fields studied so far in Units 1–11 include the
language of riddles, kingship, family and marriage, education,
time and the seasons, lordship and land use. For the rest of this
unit, several ways of studying, recording and learning vocabulary
will be explored. The area of lexis chosen is the animal world,
but the methods and exercises presented here can easily be adapted

and applied to other areas of vocabulary, depending on your interests.

Names of birds and animals

Basic word lists
To activate connections in your mind, list words in different ways:

1a English–Old English:
adder seo **næddre**, *bear* se **bera**, *beaver* se **befor**, *badger* se **brocc**, *boar* se **bar** or se **eofor**, *deer* or *stag* se **heorot** or **heort**, *horse* þæt **hors**

1b Old English–English:
se **cran** *crane*, se **crawe** *crow*, se **earn** *eagle*, seo **gos** *goose*, se **hafoc** *hawk*, se **higera** *jay*, se **hræfn** *raven*, se **hremn** *raven*, se **swan** *swan*

1c Old English synonyms:
[HORS] eoh, hengest, hors, mearh, wicg

Insight
The basic distinction between the poetic lexicon and the everyday usage is worth bearing in mind. Where **hors** for example is the everyday term, archaic words such as **eoh**, **mearh** and **wicg** are confined to verse, and **hengest** *horse, stallion* is mostly poetic. Two almost legendary figures in the early years of the Anglo-Saxon Chronicle are the brothers Hengest and Horsa.

2 Learning words in context: *The Seafarer*

Relate the words you learn to the text in which you first read them. For example, some well-known lines in the Exeter Book poem *The Seafarer* enumerate the many seabirds that the protagonist encounters on his long winter pilgrimage. The birds are solitary creatures, tokens of his isolation, but at the same time emblems of his determination and resolve. Because he is resolved to travel, he prefers the gannet's cry and the curlew's song to the laughter of men and he prefers the singing of the gull to the drinking of mead in the hall. The following are the birds named in the passage:

seo ilfetu *swan*
se hwilpe *curlew*
se ganet *gannet*
se mæw *mew, seagull*
se stearn *tern*
se or þæt earn *eagle*

In this context it makes sense to learn the words in the order in which they appear in the poem (lines 18–26):

Þær ic ne gehyrde butan hlimman sæ,
iscaldne wæg. Hwilum ylfete song
dyde ic me to gomene, ganetes hleoþor
and huilpan sweg fore hleahtor wera,
mæw singende fore medo drince.
Stormas þær stanclifu beotan, þær him stearn oncwæð
isigfeþera; ful oft þæt earn bigeal
urigfeþra. Nænig hleomæga
feasceaftig ferð frefran meahte.

There I heard nothing but the sea resounding,
the ice-cold wave. At times the song of the swan
I made my joy, the gannet's cry
and the curlew's melody for the laughter of men,
the gull singing rather than the drinking of mead.
Storms beat stone cliffs there, where the tern replied
icy-feathered; very often the eagle called back
dewy-feathered. No protecting kinsmen
could comfort the desolate spirit.

Remembering items in a list

When listing vocabulary for the purpose of memorization it is useful to record any relevant information on grammar, usage or pronunciation. For verbs, especially strong verbs, you could list the forms of the past tense. For the names of people, things and concepts, it is suggested that you record each noun with its gender and (if you wish) its plural. Learn the gender of the noun by marking it with the definite article:

> **se gat** *the goat*
> **þæt hors** *the horse*
> **seo culfre** *the dove*

Alternatively, follow the policy of Old English dictionaries and mark the gender by an abbreviation for masculine, neuter, and feminine:

> **gāt** (m.) *goat*
> **hors** (n.) *horse*
> **culfre** (f.) *dove*

Note also any particularities of pronunciation, such as the medial -f- of **culfre**, pronounced 'v', which may help to connect the word with its modern equivalent *culver dove*. Although the original texts do not usually indicate long vowels, you may wish to mark (with a macron) the long vowel of **gāt** to show that is pronounced 'gaht'. Often this long 'ah' vowel appears in words which in modern English have a long 'o' sound; examples are **drāf** *drove*, **stān** *stone*, **tāde** *toad*. Similarly, the long **ū** of **mūs** points to the later *ou* of *mouse* and the long **ō** of **gōs** looks ahead to the *oo* of the modern word *goose*. The sounds of the words are thus set to work usefully; the pronunciation establishes connections by which the lexical items can be remembered.

Old–modern correspondences

Attention to changes in meaning brings life to the history of vocabulary. The process of semantic change sometimes preserves old words in the language with new, specialized meanings. Generally **fugol** meant *bird*, rather than the specific meaning that *fowl* has assumed in more recent times. Similarly, the general word for *animal* is **se dēor** (cognate with Modern German *Tier*); again in later times this word has taken on the more particular meaning of *deer*.

Occasionally also the reverse process takes place and a word with a specific meaning has become more general: thus the modern word *bird* was originally **bridd**, which designated *a young bird* or *fledgeling*.

Wordhoard

One potentially useful way of acquiring a set of vocabulary items, such as names of animals, is to organize the items into a semantic field, a set of words associated by meaning. One such group could be studied under the heading *herd*, Old English **heord**. In making such an arrangement, you will immediately see that Old English had more synonyms for the concept *cattle* than does modern English, and that wealth, money and livestock were more closely associated than they are in the present-day language.

HERD	HEORD
herd	**seo heord;** → *oxherd* **se oxanhyrde;** *shepherd* **se sceaphyrde**
cattle	**se ceap** (also means purchase, trade)
	þæt feoh (also means money, cf. fee)
	þæt neat, þæt nyten, þæt orf
cow	**seo cu** or **þæt hriðer**
ox	**se oxa** or **þæt hriðer**
cattleshed	**seo scipen** (cf. German **Schuppen;** modern English **shippen**)
sheep	**se scēap,** or **se scēp,** or **se scîp**
sheepfold	**þæt scēapwîc** 'SHÉap-weech'

Connections with place names

Many Old English words are preserved in the names of places. Focusing on the natural world, you can learn new vocabulary and also study evidence about which animals were considered important in Old English land use and agriculture. So **se oxa** *the ox* is associated with a dairy farm (**wic**) at Oxwich (Nf), with

an enclosure **hæg** at Oxhey (Hrt), with a **ford** or river crossing
for the oxen at Oxford – originally **Oxenaford** *ford of the oxen*
(genitive plural), and with an island (ēg) *of the oxen* at Oxney (K).
A variety of creatures are associated with **mere**, the word for *pond*
or *lake*: **se bridd** *young bird*, **se bula** *bull*, **se catt** *wild cat*, **se cran**
crane or *heron*, **se crawa** *crow*, **se frosc** *frog*, and **se wulf** *wolf*.
The equivalent modern place names are Bridgemere (Ch), Boulmer
(Nb), Catmore (Brk), Cranmere (Ha), Cromer (Hrt), Frogmore (D,
Do, Hrt) and Woolmer (Ha) – the missing **f** in the latter name is
reflected also in later spellings of the personal name **Wulfstan** as
Wulstan. From a literary point of view, the most famous creature
associated with a **mere** is Grendel, the monster in *Beowulf*.

Insight

A special case is the name of the type Merton, Marten,
Marton, deriving from Old English **mere** *pond* combined
with **tun** *estate*. As Kenneth Cameron in *English Place Names*
points out, the ponds indicated by these names are often
situated on frequently-used land routes and Roman roads.
They provided water and refreshment for travellers (who
presumably travelled on horseback if they could afford it)
as well as water, fish, waterfowl and reeds for the local
economy.

As an element in place names, the Old English **tun** (pronounced
'toon'), the word for *estate*, often combines with a word denoting
agricultural or economic use. This can include crops in Flaxton,
Linton, Ryton and trees such as Pirton or Appleton (see Unit 2).
Other **tun** names reflect the animal husbandry or farming practised
at the location or associate the estate with a particular species of
bird or animal, such as Everton, associated with the boar, **se eofor**
(pronounced as two syllables 'Éo-vor'):

Shepton (So), Shipton (O)	**se scēp** or se **scīp** *sheep*
Rampton (C)	**se ramm** *ram*
Natton (Gl), Netton (W)	**þæt neat** *cattle*
Calton (WRY), Kelton (Cu)	**þæt cealf** *calf*
Calverton (Bk, Nt)	**cealfa** *of the calves* (genitive plural)

Butterton (St)	**seo butere** *butter*
Honiton (D)	**þæt hunig** *honey*
Everton (Bd, La, Nt)	**se eofor** *boar, wild boar*

Note: the abbreviations in this section refer to the traditional pre-1974 counties in which the places occur, thus Bd is Bedfordshire, Bk Berkshire, C Cambridgeshire, Ch Cheshire, Cu Cumberland, D Devon, Do Dorset, Du Durham, Gl Gloucestershire, Ha Hampshire, Hrt Hertfordshire, K Kent, La Lancashire, Nb Northumberland, Nf Norfolk, Nt Nottinghamshire, Nth Northamptonshire, O Oxfordshire, So Somerset, St Staffordshire, W Wiltshire and WRY is the West Riding of Yorkshire.

Most of the **shires** and counties of England were administrative units based on the West Saxon system of administration and founded at various times in the Old English period. For the **scirgemot** or *shire court* in action, see Units 19 and 20.

Reading

A place name of the Merton type occurs in the famous short saga of Cynewulf and Cyneheard interpolated into manuscript A of the Anglo-Saxon Chronicle (A 755). At this point in the narrative Cyneheard decides to attack the king, who is visiting a woman **on Merantune** *at Merton*:

> Ond þa geascode he þone cyning lytle werode on wifcyþþe on Merantune, ond hine þær berad, ond þone bur utan beeode, ær hine þa men onfunden þe mid þam kyninge wærun.
>
> *And then he discovered the king with a small troop visiting a woman at Merton, and overtook him there and surrounded the sleeping-hall on the outside, before the men who were with the king were aware of him.*

TEST YOURSELF (1)

Numerals and parts of the body in riddles

In the two riddles below, the main figure is a strange **wiht** (*wight, being, creature*) with an unusual physical appearance. In riddle 36, for instance, the wight is described as having **siex heafdu** *six heads*. Read or listen to each text and note the numbers used, then suggest a solution to the riddle.

QUICK VOCAB

on wege *on the wave*
wrætlice *marvellously*
wundrum gegierwed *girded with wonders*
cwom *came*
on mæðle *at their talk*
mode snottre *with a prudent mind*

◀》 **TR 33, 00:09**

(a) From riddle 36

Ic wiht geseah on wege feran,
seo wæs wrætlice wundrum gegierwed.
Hæfde feowere fet under wombe
ond ehtuwe ufon on hrycge;
hæfde tu fiþru ond twelf eagan
ond siex heafdu. Saga hwæt hio wære.

◀》 **TR 34**

(b) Riddle 86

Wiht cwom gongan þær weras sæton
monige on mæðle, mode snottre;
hæfde an eage ond earan twa,
ond twegen fet, twelf hund heafda,
hrycg ond eaxle, anne sweoran
ond sida twa. Saga hwæt ic hatte.

TEST YOURSELF (2)

1 Translate the following text:

Annus solaris (the solar year)

Annus solaris hæfð þreo hund daga and fif and syxtig, and twa and fiftig wucena, and twelf monðas. And soðlice ðæt ger hæfð eahta þusend tida and syx and syxtig. (Byrhtferth, *Enchiridion*, ed. Baker and Lapidge, II.3, lines 178–80)

2 Fill in the missing numbers of hours:

On anum dæge and þære nihte beoð (a)_____ tida, and on twam dagum beoð (b)_____ tida, and on þrim dagum beoð (c) _____. On feower dagum syx and hundnigontig. On fif dagum beoð (d) _____ tida and _____ tida.

TEST YOURSELF (3)

Give the etymology of the following place names and identify the Old English birds or animals referred to (example: Crawley 'Crow Glade' from **se crawa** *crow*):

1 Cowden (K)   **2** Shapwick (Do)   **3** Gateford (Nt)
4 Earnley (Sx)   **5** Carnforth (La)   **6** Horsforth (Nf)
7 Shipley (frequent)   **8** Hartburn (Du)   **9** Woolley (Brk)
10 Hardwick (frequent)   **11** Chalvey (Bk)   **12** Hunton (Ha)
13 Eversholt (Bd)   **14** Shiplake (O)

13

And they put him into the waterless well

This unit will cover:

texts
- *the betrayal into slavery in Joseph*

grammar
- *the inflected infinitive*
- *introduction to the subjunctive*
- *the prefixes be- and a-*

vocabulary
- *metaphorical language*
- *trade*

🔊 **TR 35**

And dydon hyne on þone wæterleasan pytt
And they put him into the waterless well

Grammar

The inflected infinitive after *þencan*

Almost any narrative thrives on exploring the purposes and intentions of its characters. Readers of stories are fascinated by the uncertainty and are impelled to read further to find out what happens next. In the following extract from *Joseph*, the verb **þencan** (*to think, intend*) describes the conflicting intentions of Joseph's brothers and Ruben: on the one hand, we have **hi ðohton hyne to ofsleane** *they thought to slay him* and, on the other hand, there is Ruben's intention **he ðohte hyne to generienne of heora handum** *he thought to rescue him from their hands*. Here, as we saw in 11, the inflected infinitive (**to + infinitive + ending**) is used to express purpose and adds considerable interest and tension to the narrative.

þa hi hyne feorran gesawon
When they saw him from afar

The brothers discuss what they should do with their brother Joseph when he falls into their hands. The words in **bold** are examples of the subjunctive mood of the verb, which expresses conjecture and anticipation (further explanations follow).

🔊 **TR 35, 00:10**

Þa hi hyne feorran gesawon *When they saw him from afar*

Þa hi hyne feorran gesawon, ær ðam þe he him to come, hi ðohton hyne to ofsleane, and cwædon him betwynan, 'Her gæð se swefniend. Uton hyne ofslean and don on þone ealdan pytt and secgan þæt wildeor hyne fræton. Ðonne byð gesyne hwæt him hys swefen fremion!'

*When they saw him from afar, before he **had reached** them, they thought to slay him, and said among themselves, 'Here goes the dreamer. **Let us** slay him and put him in the old well-pit and say that wild animals have eaten him. Then it will be seen how his dreams **may benefit** him!'*

QUICK VOCAB

gesawon *they saw* 'yuh-SAH-won' (Note long vowel in **sawon**)
(cf. **seah** *he saw*, **seon** *to see*)
feorran *from afar*
ær ðam þe *before* (conjunction)
hi ðohton *they thought* (Note long vowel **ðohton**)
(cf. **he ðohte** *he thought*)
to ofsleane *to kill* (inflected infinitive)
cwædon *they said* (Note long -**æ**- vowel)
(but **he cwæð** *he said*, with short vowel)
se swefniend *dreamer* (cf. **swefn, swefen** *dream*; see Unit 6)
ofslean *to kill* (standard infinitive)
don *to put* (the long vowel **don** rhymes with 'Doane')
(NB **don** literally means *to do*)
se pytt *well-pit* (from Latin **puteus***)
wildeor *wild animals* (**wild + deor**)

fræton *they ate* (used to describe animals)
gesyne *seen* 'yuh-SEE-nuh' (past participle)
fremian *to benefit*

Cultural contexts

Rivalry between half-brothers was a perennial problem of tenth- and eleventh-century royal politics. The problem became acute on two occasions after the unexpected departure of a strong and forceful ruler; the first such occasion being the death of Edgar the Peaceable in 975, the second that of Cnut in 1035. In 975 opinion was sharply divided over which of Edgars's two sons should succeed him; even the great monastic reformers St Dunstan and St Æthelwold could not agree. In the end the older half-brother Edward succeeded, but three years later, on a journey to visit his stepmother in Dorset, he was ambushed and killed near Corfe Castle by unknown assailants. Immediately his half-brother Æthelred (later called **Unræd** *the Ill-advised*) succeeded him; he was young enough to be innocent of blame, but it was an unhappy start to his reign.

Insight

Looking back a generation later, the writer Wulfstan called this treachery **hlafordswice** *betrayal of a lord*, from the verb **beswican** *to betray*, connected with the noun **swicolnes** *deceit*. In the successive versions of the Anglo-Saxon Chronicle, the level of shock and indignation at the treachery – possibly by members of Edward's own kindred – rose with each retelling of the events (see **reading** below).

It is a measure of the awe with which the sacred office of kingship was regarded that, like his nephew Edward the Confessor after 1066, this king too was popularly considered a saint and came to be known as Edward the Martyr.

Grammar

Introduction to the subjunctive

The subjunctive expresses the idea of conjecture. It can appear after a conjunction of time; the following is an example from the *Joseph* story in the study text of this unit:

ær ðam þe he him **to come** *before he reached them*

Here the conjectural subjunctive **com-e** (instead of indicative **com**) is used to talk about an event that was being anticipated in the future. A further example of anticipation from the same text is the brothers' speech as they plot to kill Joseph:

'Ðonne byð gesyne hwæt him hys swefen **fremion!**'
*'Then it will be seen how his dreams **may benefit** him!'*

A protracted sense of anticipation runs through the whole passage, from the moment when the possibility of Joseph's arrival is first aired (and marked by the **subjunctive**) to the moment when he actually does arrive (marked by the *indicative*), whereupon he is seized by the brothers and thrown into the pit:

Sona swa he to hys broðrum <u>com</u>, swa bereafodon hi hyne hys tunecan and dydon hyne on ðone wæterleasan pytt
As soon as he <u>came</u> to his brothers, they deprived him of his tunic and put him into the waterless well

Between these two moments marked by **come** (subjunctive) and <u>com</u> (indicative) is the debate between the brothers, during which Joseph's fate hangs in the balance. A similar period of anticipation then follows as Joseph's brothers Ruben and Judah discuss with the other brothers what is to be done with Joseph now that he has been taken prisoner.

Soðlice þa Ruben ðis gehyrde, he ðohte hyne to generienne
Truly when Ruben heard this he thought to save him

Soðlice þa Ruben ðis gehyrde, he ðohte hyne to generienne
of heora handum, and cwæð, 'Ne ofslea we hyne, ne we hys
blod ne **ageotan**, ac wurþað hyne on ðone pytt, and healdað
eowre handa unbesmitene.' Þæt he sæde, for þam ðe he
wolde hyne generian of heora handum and hys fæder 'agyfan.

ge-nerian to save
ageotan to spill
unbesmiten untarnished
agyfan to deliver, give over to

Grammar

The *be-* prefix on verbs

As well as the perfective *ge-* prefix with its emphasis on the idea of
completed action, there are other prefixes before verbs; the study
text has **ā-**, **be-** and **of-**. Like *ge-*, these prefixes are weakly stressed,
the main stress falling on the stem or root syllable of the verb:

ageotan to spill, shed	'ah-YÉotan'
bereafodon they deprived	'be-RÉa-vo-don'

The **ā-** prefix (pronounced long as 'ah') can intensify the meaning,
as in the case of **geofan** *give* becoming **āgeofan** *deliver*, but often
ā- behaves rather like *ge-* in that it adds perfective force, a sense of
completion:

fysan to drive	**afysan** to drive away
geotan to pour	**ageotan** to pour out

Similarly, **of-** (pronounced 'off-') has perfective force:

ofgyfan *to give up*
ofsendan *to send for*
ofslean *to strike down*, i.e. *slay, kill*
ofsniðan *to cut down, kill*

Prefixes are described in linguistic terms as **productive** if they can be readily used to form new words, as in the case of **be-**, which is still used in modern English. The Old English prefix **be-** was likewise productive and had several meanings. A basic meaning is *round about* as in the following:

lucan *to lock*	**belucan** *to enclose, lock up*
settan *to put*	**besettan** *to beset, surround*
sittan *to sit*	**besittan** *to besiege*
standan *to stand*	**bestandan** *to stand round* cf. Unit 21, *Maldon*, line 68
windan *to wind*	**bewindan** *to wind round, encircle*

A similar meaning for **be-** is found in modern English words such as *besiege, benight, betake, bestraddle*, all of which seem to have come into existence after the Old English period – sometimes, as in the case of *besiege*, the older English prefix combining with a newer word imported from French.

Another use of **be-**, corresponding to the modern *be-* in *bewail*, is to convert an intransitive verb into a transitive one, i.e. the **be-** converts a verb which normally stands on its own into one which requires an object: *the monk was wailing* as opposed to *the monk* *was bewailing his wicked deeds*. Some Old English examples show how this works:

wēpan *to weep*	**bewēpan** *to bewail*
delfan *to dig*	**bedelfan** *to dig round, bury*
scīnan *to shine*	**bescīnan** *to illuminate*
þencan *to think*	**beþencan** *to think about something, ponder*

A third meaning of be- adds a sense of *depriving* to the verb, as in the modern English *bereft*. For example, recall the proverb **cyning sceal beagas dælan** in Unit 2. If the prefix is added it alters the meaning pejoratively:

dǽlan *to distribute*	**bedǽlan** *deprive*
niman *take*	**beniman** *take away*.

The example **berēafodon** *they deprived* in the *Joseph* passage is particularly apt, as **rēaf** also means *garment*, and it is this which the brothers remove, literally *be-reave*, from their brother:

Sona swa he to hys broðrum com, swa **bereafodon** hi hyne hys tunecan
As soon as he reached his brothers, they deprived him of his coat

---

◀) **TR 37**

Sona swa he to hys broðrum com
As soon as he came to his brothers

Sona swa he to hys broðrum com, swa bereafodon hi hyne hys tunecan, and dydon hyne on ðone wæterleasan pytt. And þa hi woldon etan, hi gesawon twegen Ismahelitisce wegfarende men cuman of Galaad, and læddon wyrtgemang on heora olfendon, and tyrwan and stacten, on Egypta land.

---

berēafian *to deprive* (cf. **se rēaf** *garment, booty*)
twegen *two*
Ismahelitisc *Ismaelite*
wegfarend *wayfaring*
seo wyrtgemang *mixture of spices*
olfendon *camels* (**se olfenda**; false etymology from Latin *elephantem*)
se tyrwa *resin*
stacten *myrrh*

Language and style

Metaphorical language

As books like *Metaphors we Live by* (Lakoff and Johnson, 2003)
show, languages employ many metaphors so completely assimilated
into the structure of our vocabulary that we barely notice them.
It is interesting to consider how Old English metaphors construe
the world when compared and contrasted with the language of the
present. As already suggested in Unit 11, **on dæge** *in his lifetime* is
an obvious metaphorical use of the word *day*, as is the phrase **to
handa gan** *to come into the hands of* or the description of the act
of giving **unnendre handa** *with a giving hand* or **unnendre heortan**
with a giving heart. In these phrases, the act of giving, taking
and receiving derives from a metaphor of the body. They may be
compared with similar expressions in the biblical passage, where
the *hands* metaphor is used to denote ideas firstly of captivity and
then of innocence and guilt:

> he wolde hyne generian **of heora handum** and hys fæder agyfan
> *he wanted to rescue him from their hands and deliver him to
> his father*

> selre ys þæt we hyne syllon to ceape Ismaelitum þæt **ure handa**
> beon unbesmitene
> *it is better that we sell him to the Ismaelites so that our hands
> may be untarnished*

Hwæt fremað us? *What will it benefit us?*

Þa cwæð Iudas to hys gebroðrum, 'Hwæt fremað us ðeah we urne broðor ofslean? Selre ys þæt we hyne syllon to ceape Ismaelitum þæt ure handa beon unbesmitene; he ys ure broðor and ure flæsc.' Þa cwædon hys gebroðru þæt hyt swa mihte beon. And þa þær forun Madianisce cypan, hi tugon hyne up of þam pytte and sealdon hyne Ismaelitum wið ðrittigum penegum. And hi hyne læddon on Egypta land.

QUICK VOCAB

selre *better*
se cēap *price, transaction* (cf. place name **Ceapstow** Chepstow, i.e. *market town*)
mihte *it could* (past tense of **magan**)
þæt flæsc *flesh* (pronounce with long vowel)
cypan *merchants* (se **cȳpa**; cf. archaic *chapman*)
tēon *to pull, drag* (**tȳhð, tēah, tugon, getogen**)
lǣdan *to lead, carry*

Wordhoard

Ceap *trade*

The verb *to buy* comes from the Old English **bycgan** *to pay for*. In the same semantic field belongs the noun **se cēap** ('chéap'), which like **feoh** *fee, money* could also mean *cattle* but usually denoted *trade* and related ideas, with a verb **cēapian** *to bargain, trade, buy* (derived like German **kaufen** *to buy* from Latin **caupo**). A series of related concepts are found as compounds. A wordlist in a manuscript records **cēap-dæg** *market-day*; elsewhere we find **cēapland** *purchased land*, **cēapman** *trader* (cf. the now archaic word *chapman*), **cēapscip** *trading vessel*, **cēapsetl** *toll-booth* and **cēapstræt** *market*. Another word for a market is **seo cēapstow** which combines **cēap** with the general word for a *place* **seo stow**, as in the town Stow-on-the-Wold and, of course, Chepstow. Similarly **seo cēapung** *trade* is the origin of place names like Chipping Norton and Chipping Camden.

Insight

The phrase **butan cēape** *without price*, i.e. *gratis*, has given us *cheap* in modern English.

Grammar

More on the subjunctive

In grammatical terms the **subjunctive** (e.g. *so be it*) is a mood of the verb that expresses an idea of wish or conjecture; it contrasts with the regular mood of the verb, the indicative, used for assertions (e.g. *so it is*). Sometimes the same idea or mood can be expressed by the auxiliary *may, might,* as in *long may it prosper*, or perhaps in a prayer or petition *may the situation remain stable*. Generally, however, the subjunctive in modern English is rare; it exists in a few fixed and formal expressions like *long **live** the king* (cf. the indicative *the king **lives** long*) or in certain formal contexts such as *the king required that each town **render** tribute*.

In Old English the subjunctive mood was found more widely. In form the present subjunctive can often be recognized by its lack of the *-th* ending associated with the present indicative *he maketh*. So in the declaration in Unit 11 by Leofwine, the normal present tense **gæð** (*goes*) becomes subjunctive **ga** or **ge-ga**, and in the plural the present subjunctive would be **gan**. The past subjunctive is harder to spot, particularly in late Old English spellings. One example is **com, comon** *came,* which in the subjunctive would have the endings **-e** and **-en** as **come, comen**. For irregular verbs there are anomalous forms. The indicative **bið** (*is*) from **beon** *to be* becomes **beo** in the subjunctive, e.g. the closing remark in one of Cnut's writs (Harmer no. 29) **beo gerefa se þe beo** *be the reeve whoever* *he may be.* A second alternative form of the present subjunctive of *to be* is **sy**, while yet another form is the past subjunctive **wære**; they occur in the formula ðam ðe him leofost sy in the Leofwine document and ðam ðe hire leofest wære and ðær him leofost wære in the Worcestershire marriage agreement seen in Unit 8.

Reading

Versions of the Chronicle

The story of Edward the Martyr's murder is given further significance with each successive version of the Chronicle. The earliest version, manuscript A, gives bare facts, C mentions the martryrdom, while D publishes a prose poem, a kind of homily in rhythmical prose on the saintliness of the king and the futility of earthly endeavour.

A 978 Her wearð Eadweard cyning ofslegen. On þis ylcan feng Æðelred æðeling his broðor to rice.

Here king Edward was slain. In the same year prince Æthelred his brother succeeded to the kingdom.

C 978 Her on þysum geare wearð Eadweard cyning gemartyrad, and Æþelred æþeling his broðor feng to þam rice, and he wæs on þam ylcan geare to cinge gehalgod. On þam geare forðferde Alfwold, se wæs bisceop on Dorsætum, and his lic lið on þam mynstre æt Scireburnan.

Here in this year king Edward was martyred and prince Æthelred his brother succeeded to the kingdom, and he was in the same year consecrated as king. In that year Alfwold passed away, who was bishop in Dorset, and his body lies in the minster at Sherbourne.

D 979 Her wæs Eadweard cyning ofslægen on æfentide æt Corfes geate on .xv. Kalentas Aprilis, and hine mon þa gebyrigde

on Werhamme, butan ælcum cynelicum wurðscipe. Ne wearð
Angelcynne nan wyrse dæd gedon, þonne þeos wæs, syþþan hi
ærest Britenland gesohton. Menn hine ofmyrþredon, ac God hine
mærsode. He wæs on life eorðlic cyning, he is nu æfter deaððe
heofonlic sanct. Hyne noldon his eorðlican magas wrecan, ac hine
hafað his heofonlic fæder swyðe gewrecan. Þa eorðlican banan
woldon his gemynd on eorðan adilgian, ac se uplica wrecend hafað
his gemynd on heofonum and on eorþan tobræd. Þa ðe noldon
ær to his libbendan lichaman onbugan, þa nu eadmodlice on
cneowum gebugað to his deada banum. Nu we magan ongytan þæt
manna wisdom, and heora smeagunga, and heora rædas syndon
nahtlice ongean Godes geðeaht. Her feng Æðelred to rice, and he
wæs æfter þæm swyðe hrædlice mid micclum gefean Angelcynnes
witan gehalgod to cyninge æt Cyngestune.

*Here in this year king Edward was slain in the evening at Corfe
gate on the fifteenth of the kalends of April, and they buried him
then at Wareham without any royal honour. No worse deed had
been done in the English nation than this was, since they settled
the land of Britain. Men murdered him but God glorified him; in
life he was an earthly king: now after death he is a heavenly saint.
His earthly kinsmen would not avenge him, but his heavenly Father
has very much avenged him. The earthly killers wished to purge his
memory on earth, but the heavenly Avenger has spread his memory
in heaven and earth. The men who would not bow to his earthly
body now humbly bend their knees to his mortal remains. Now we
can see that the wisdom of men and their thoughts and plans are
as nothing to God's providence. Here Æthelred succeeded to the
kingdom, and thereafter very quickly, to the great joy of England's
Assembly, he was consecrated king at Kingston.*

TEST YOURSELF

Comprehension questions

Reread the study text and answer the following questions.

1 What did the brothers do before they put Joseph in the waterless well?

2 What were they about to do when they saw the two Ismaelite wayfarers?

3 Compare Ruben's and Judah's actions and motivations.

4 For a medieval Christian audience, what might be the significance of the price for which the brothers sell Joseph?

14

The boy is not here

This unit will cover:

texts
- *Joseph*
- **from Wulfstan's** *Sermo Lupi*

grammar
- *the negative*

vocabulary
- *rhetorical style*

◄» **TR 39**

> **Nys se cnapa her**
> *The boy is not here*

Grammar (1)

The negative

The basic way of forming a negative in many European languages is to place a negative particle before the verb. In Latin the negative is **non,** in French **ne... pas,** in Russian **nye.** Old English also places a particle **ne** before the verb, so that **hi ne mihton** means *they could not*. Before the verb *to be* when it begins with a vowel or **w**, and before the verbs **habban** or **willan**, the negative **ne** is contracted. It drops its vowel -e and blends with the following word:

ic eom *I am*	**ic neom** *I am not*
heo ys *she is*	**heo nys** *she is not*
hit wæs *it was*	**hit næs** *it was not*
we wæron *we were*	**we næron** *we were not*
ic hæbbe *I have*	**ic næbbe** *I do not have*
heo hæfð *she has*	**heo næfð** *she does not have*
ic hæfde *I had*	**ic næfde** *I did not have*
ic wylle *I want*	**ic nylle** *I do not want*
ic wolde *I wanted*	**ic nolde** *I did not want to*

The contrastive pairs **wylle nylle** and **hæbbe næbbe** have survived into modern English in disguised spellings. *Will I nill I*, or *will he nill he*, became *willy nilly*, i.e. *whether one likes it or not*.

Insight

In the expression *hob nob*, from *hab nab*, the pair **hæbbe næbbe** has changed its meaning more drastically: from *have it or don't have it* to *give and take*; eventually this meant two friends giving and taking drinks and proposing toasts to each other, i.e. *hob-nobbing* or being on familiar terms with each other.

Other words such as **æfre** *ever* and **an** *one* can also be preceded by the particle **ne** to make them negative. Again the two words are written together as one word **næfre** and **nan** and these survive as *never* and *none*. For an example in context see *Joseph* in Unit 6, on the brothers' animosity:

ða onscunodon hi hine and **ne** mihton **nane** freondrædene wið hine habban
then they shunned him and could not have any friendship with him

Notice here that the negative particle **ne** is repeated twice, once before **mihton** and once in the determiner **nan** (= ne + an).

Insight

Multiple negation is also found in Russian and other languages, as well as in some varieties of modern spoken English; there is a striking Old English example in the Herefordshire law dispute from the reign of Cnut (see Unit 20).

Two further examples are found in the next section of *Joseph*. In the absence of Ruben, who had hoped to rescue his brother from the dry well and return him to his father, the brothers have sold Joseph to the Midianite traders. Ruben returns only to find the well empty:

Þa Ruben eft com to þam pytte and þone cnapan þær **ne funde**, ða tær he hys claðas and cwæð to hys broðrum, '**Nys** se cnapa her! hwyder ga ic?'
When Ruben came back to the well and could not find the boy there, he tore his clothes and said to his brothers, 'The boy is not here! Where will I go?'

Later the brothers hypocritically try to console their father, but to no avail:

he **n**olde **n**ane frefrunge underfon
he would not receive any consolation

Joseph: the father's grief

The illustrations

The Old English Hexateuch narrates the story of Jacob's loss of Joseph in a series of four illustrations interspersed with short lines of text. The effect is to highlight the grieving figure, who always stands or sits on the right of the picture, in broadly the same position. In three of the pictures, the grieving figure points to his eyes, a medieval convention used to indicate tears, for instance in the figure of Edith weeping for Edward in the Bayeux tapestry.

A published facsimile of the Hexateuch exists and reproductions from the book often appear in books on Anglo-Saxon England; for full references see **bibliography** at the end of the book. It is worth noting that references to manuscripts are usually given by folio number rather than page number; a folio number refers to the full page, both front (recto) and back (verso). For example, the pictures of Jacob and Joseph weeping are found on facing pages on folios 54*v* and 55*r* of the Hexateuch manuscript (where *r* means *recto* and *v* means *verso*).

Language and style

The text, which is given below, recounts the deception the brothers practise on their father; it centres on the image of the coat of many colours, **seo tunece**, a feminine noun referred to later by the accusative pronoun **hi** (*it, her*) – in the crucial phrase **ða ða he hi gecneow** *when he recognized it*. Before studying the passage any further, consider the following points:

▶ **Hwyder** means *whither* in the directional sense of *where to*; the corresponding word for *where* expressing stationary location is **hwær** (also spelt **hwar**).

184

- As in modern English, but more frequently and consistently, it is possible to emphasize the object of a sentence by placing it first, so that **þas tunecen we fundon** (where **þas** marks the accusative, see Unit 11) means literally _this tunic we found_. To capture the meaning in translation, use a paraphrase: _look at this tunic we have found_. The illustrator of the Hexateuch read the text closely. The emphasis on the 'pointing word' _this_ is brought out very strongly in the gestures of the brothers and in the prominent position of **seo tunece** in the middle of the picture.

- Note the use of **sy**, the subjunctive of **beon** _to be_, in the next part of the brothers' speech: **sceawa hwæðer hyt sy ðines suna þe ne sy** _see whether it may-be your son's or not_.

- Check past tenses: **tær** tore, **namon** _took_, **ofsniðon** _killed_, **bedypton** _dipped_, **brohton** _brought_, **cwædon** _said_, **fræton** _devoured_, **scrydde hyne** _clothed himself_, **weop** _wept_, **gesamnodon** _assembled_, **gefrefrodon** consoled, **sealdon** _sold_.

◆ TR 39, 00:07

Þa Ruben eft com to þam pytte
When Ruben came back to the well

Þa Ruben eft com to þam pytte and þone cnapan ðær ne funde, ða tær he hys claðas and cwæð to hys broðrum, 'Nys se cnapa her! hwyder ga ic?'

Þa namon hi an ticcen and ofsniðon hyt and bedypton hys
tunecan on þam blode, and brohton to heora fæder, and
cwædon, 'Þas tunecan we fundon; sceawa hwæðer hyt sy
ðines suna þe ne sy. Ða cwæð se fæder ða ða he hi gecneow,
'Hyt ys mines suna tunece.' Þa cwædon hi, 'Wildeor fræton
Iosep.' He totær hys reaf and scrydde hyne mid hæran and
weop hys sunu lange tide.

Soðlice hys bearn hi gesamnodon to þam þæt hi heora fæder
gefrefrodon: he nolde nane frefrunge underfon, ac cwæð
wepende, 'Ic fare to minum suna to helle.'

◀ TR 42

Ða Madianiscean sealdon Iosep on Egypta land Putifare, þam
afyredan, Faraones cempena ealdre.

claðas *clothes* (**se cla**ð *garment* 'klahth')
se cnapa *boy*, lad (also spelt **cnafa** 'kna-va', cf. *knave*)
þæt ticcen *goat kid*
þæt blod *blood*
þæt reaf *garment*
seo frefrung *consolation*
seo hære *sackcloth* (the garment is thought of as a hairshirt)
hell *Gehenna, Hades, hell*
se afyreda *eunuch*
se cempa *warrior* (**cempena** *of warriors*)
ealdor *chief, captain, prince*

QUICK VOCAB

Cultural contexts

Manuscripts

The *Joseph* story appears in four manuscripts:

- London British Library Cotton Claudius B iv (the Illustrated Hexateuch), a bible translation from Genesis to Joshua; contains about four hundred illustrations (see inside front cover of this book and Unit 20)
- Oxford Bodleian Library, Laud Misc. 509 (Hexateuch, Judges); the manuscript once concluded with the Old English *Life of St Guthlac* now in London British Library Cotton Vespasian D. xxi (for *Guthlac* see unit 17)
- London British Library Cotton Otho B. x (an anthology of saints' lives); the manuscript was destroyed in a disastrous fire at the Cotton library in the 18th century.
- Cambridge Corpus Christi College 201 (the Corpus Wulfstan anthology)

> ## Insight
> Each of these manuscripts has its particular context and purpose. What they have in common is an insistence on the exemplary and hagiographic nature of the *Joseph* story – in two of the above manuscripts the story is juxtaposed with legends of the saints as though it is regarded as another story from the same genre.

The Corpus anthology is obviously intended to bring together archbishop Wulfstan's religious and legal writings. But the presence of *Apollonius of Tyre* and *Joseph* at the end of the anthology suggests a further purpose, namely that the story of Joseph was intended to be read as an exemplum, as a model of behaviour. The life of the biblical Joseph, or for that matter the life of the Greek prince Apollonius, can be used as a concrete illustration of how the archbishop's legal precepts should be put into practice in the real world, in a moral world where people feel jealousy and hate, love and loyalty, and in the end have to learn through bitter experience how to do right and make right decisions.

Grammar (2)

Strong adjective endings

When an adjective appears on its own without a definite determiner such as **se** *the, that* or **þes** *this*, then it is given a set of prominent endings to indicate case, gender and number:

masculine accusative
I ... fill all middle earth (Unit 2)

ic ... gefylle eal<u>ne</u> middangeard

neuter genitive
with ten pounds of red gold
(Unit 11)

mid ten pundan reod<u>es</u> goldes

feminine dative
with a generous heart (Unit 8)

unnend<u>re</u> heortan

nominative plural
all his earls (Unit 7)

eall<u>e</u> his eorlas

genitive plural
for the lifetime of three people
(Unit 8)

ðreo<u>ra</u> manna dæg

dative plural
to relatives or strangers (Unit 8)

sibb<u>an</u> oððe fremd**an** (for -**um**)

The so-called strong endings also occur in the predicative use, i.e. when an adjective comes after the verb *to be, is, are, was, were, remained* etc. Examples are:

þrymmas syndan Cristes myccl<u>e</u>
Christ's glories are great (Unit 4)

þæt ðas forewerda ðus geworht<u>e</u> wæran
that these terms were made thus (Unit 11)

From your reading so far, many of these inflectional endings will already be familiar, especially the masculine accusative **-ne** and the nominative plural **-e**. There are also parallels with the genitive **-s** of the demonstrative *this* and of strong nouns (e.g. the genitive **eorles** or **goldes**). For the purposes of reading, which after all is the primary purpose of many learners of Old English, it is often enough simply to be aware of the possible endings when meeting an unfamiliar adjective for the first time, for it is the base form of the adjective that is found in the wordlists. When you consult a dictionary, therefore, mentally subtract the ending of the adjective first, before proceeding further.

Language and style

Rhythm

As we saw when examining the style of the writs and declarations in Unit 11, in order to appreciate the rhythm of a language, you need to learn how to divide words into their constituent syllables. The pattern of stressed syllables in a sentence gives the rhythm.

A syllable is made up of a vowel with its preceding and following consonants; in linguistic terminology, the syllable can be described as having an onset, vowel and coda. So a one-syllable word such as the past tense **com** (here given with its long vowel marked as **cōm** 'kohm') is made up of:

onset	+	vowel	+	coda
c	+	ō	+	m

But in the past subjunctive, the verb becomes **cōme**, which has two syllables:

onset	+	vowel	+	coda	and	onset	+	vowel	+	coda
c	+	ō		–		m	+	e		–

The two syllables are not equally stressed, since the emphasis falls on the first syllable as it does in the words *roamer* or *comber* (in *beachcomber*). To represent the rhythm of cō-me we can use capital letters **CO-me** or the symbols / x. Returning to some of the rhythmical formulas from Unit 11, we can represent their rhythm as follows:

to habbanne and to sellanne   to HAB-ban-ne and to SEL-lan-ne,
binnan byrig and butan   bin-nan BY-rig and BU-tan
swa full and swa forð   swa FULL and swa FORÐ
unforboden and unbesacan   un-for-BO-den and un-be-SA-can

The point of the last example here is that the main stress tends to be on the root or stem of the word rather than on any weaker prefixes.

From Wulfstan's *Sermo Lupi*

Wulfstan's most famous sermon was delivered originally in 1014 as a call to the nation to repent of its sins, which he believed had led to the military disasters that had befallen them. Note the rhythmical two-stress phrases (marked here by the punctuation):

And eac we witan ful georne hwar seo yrmð gewearð, þæt fæder gesealde: his bearn wið wurðe, and bearn his modor, and broðor sealde oþerne, fremdum to gewealde; and eal þæt sindon micele – and egeslice dæda, understande se ðe wille. And git hit is mare and mænigfealdre, þæt derað þisse þeode: manige sind forsworene, and swiðe forlogone, and wed synd tobrocene, oft and gelome.

And also, we know very well where that crime occurred: that a father sold his son for profit, and a son his mother, and one brother sold another, into the power of strangers, and all these are great – and terrible deeds, may he understand who will. And yet there is a greater and more numerous one that harms this nation: many are perjured, and greatly forsworn, and pledges are broken, again and again.

seo yrmð *misery*, *crime* (also spelt **iermð**, cf **earm** *poor*, *miserable*)
þæt wurð *price*
mænigfeald *manifold*, *numerous*
derian *damage*, *harm* (verb with dative object)
oft *often*
gelome *frequently*

TEST YOURSELF (1)

Comprehension and interpretation

Reread the passages from the *Joseph* story in this unit.
1 What did the brothers do with Joseph's tunic?
2 How do both Ruben and Jacob react to Joseph's disappearance? What parallels can be drawn between the two passages and their illustrations?
3 What happened to Joseph when he arrived in Egypt?

TEST YOURSELF (2)

Exploring Wulfstan's style

Reviewing the section on the oral-formulaic style of the declaration in Unit 11, find the following stylistic devices and linguistic features in the passage from *Sermo Lupi*.
1 In the first sentence, find: (a) words that alliterate on initial w- (ignore the unstressed ge- prefix when looking for alliteration) (b) an example of full rhyme (c) a two-stress phrase with the verb in the subjunctive.
2 In the second sentence, find (a) alliteration on m- and sw- (b) three words that rhyme (c) two adverbs forming a two-stress phrase.
3 Marking stress and rhythm

The first part of the second sentence could be written using capitals to mark the heavily stressed syllables:
And git hit is MAre and MÆnigfealdre, þæt DErað þisse þEOde:
Write out the second half of this sentence, marking stressed syllables in the same way.
4 Strong adjectives
Reread the Wulfstan passage and list any adjectives with strong inflectional endings.

15

I always wanted to convert to the monastic life

This unit will cover:

texts
- **monastic sign language**
- **extract from** The Life of Euphrosyne
- **riddles 47 and 48**

grammar
- **the use of** mon, man
- **word order in** if **clauses**
- **the verbs** don, willan, gan
- **the verb with object in the genitive**

vocabulary
- **home and everyday life**

◀ **TR 43**

Ic symle wilnode to munuclicum life gecyrran
I always wanted to convert to the monastic life

The daily round

The monasteries were an important bulwark of education and literary activity in the Old English period. Monks led an extremely regulated life, summoned by the ringing of a bell to the frequent monastic **hours**, i.e. church services and communal prayer, and to intervening periods of manual labour and reading. For those brothers who possessed particular skills, the work periods involved teaching in the monastic school, perhaps composing literary works of various kinds or, more likely, copying other people's compositions in the monastery scriptorium. Periods of silence were built into the working pattern at certain times of the day, including special mealtimes when a reader was employed to read a devotional work while the monks ate in the dining hall.

The monks' sign language

The following extracts from the sign language (ed. Banham, 1991, see **bibliography**) describe hand signals for use during periods of silence. As these are signs (**tacen**), unreal representations, the verbs used to describe them are often in the subjunctive.

◄) TR 43, 00:11

Huniges tacen is þæt þu sette þinne finger on þine tungan.

The sign of honey is that you set your finger on your tongue.

þæt tacen *sign* 'tahkun' (cf. *token*)
þu sette subjunctive of **þu settest**
seo tunge *tongue*

av

◀) TR 44

Ðonne þu fisc habban wylle
þonne wege þu þyne hand
þam gemete þe he deþ his tægl
þonne he swymð.

When you may want to have fish,
then wave your hand
in the way which it does its tail
when it swims.

QV

wylle subjunctive of **þu wyllt** (see **willan** in **grammar** below)
wegan *to move* (cf. **se wæg** also spelled **weg** *wave, motion*)

◀) TR 45

Ðæs diacanes tacen is
þæt mon mid hangiendre hande do
swilce he gehwæde bellan cnyllan wille.

The sign of the deacon is
that one should do with hanging hand
as if one would ring a little bell.

QV

se diacen *deacon* (or *dean*, see D. Banham, *Monasteriales Indicia*, p. 57)
do subjunctive of **deþ** *does* (see **grammar**)
gehwæde *little* (**ge-hwæ- de**)
swilce *as if* (conjectural **swilce** is followed by the subjunctive)

Grammar

Comparing regular and irregular verbs

Review the forms of the regular verbs **deman** *judge* (weak verb) and **cuman** *come* (strong verb) and compare them with the paradigm for three frequent but irregular verbs **don** *do*, **willan** *want* and **gán** *go* (note long vowels marked ā, ē, ō, ǣ-):

| | regular | | irregular | | |
| | weak | strong | | | |
	deman	cuman	don	willan	gan
present indicative					
1 singular	dēme	cume	dō	wille	gā
2	dēmst	cymst	dēst	wilt	gǣst
3	dēmð	cymð	dēð	wile	gǣð
1, 2, 3 plural	dēmað	cumað	dōð	willað	gāð
present subjunctive					
1, 2, 3	dēme	cume	dō	wille	gā
1, 2, 3	dēmen	cumen	dōn	willen	gān
past indicative					
1, 3 singular	dēmde	cōm	dyde	wolde	ēode
2	dēmdest	cōme	dydest	woldest	ēodest
1, 2, 3 plural	dēmdon	cōmon	dydon	woldon	ēodon
past subjunctive					
1, 2, 3	dēmde	cōme	dyde	wolde	ēode
1, 2, 3	dēmden	cōmen	dyden	wolden	ēoden

The pronoun *man* or *mon*

The useful impersonal pronoun **man**, or in its alternative spelling and pronunciation **mon**, has appeared in various texts so far, usually translated as *they*. Recall the passage from the Chronicle in Unit 4:

And Cnut cyning com eft to Englalande, and þa on Eastron wæs mycel gemot æt Cyringceastre, þa geutlagode **man** Æþelweard ealdorman and Eadwig 'ceorla cyngc'. (ASC C 1020)

Although the nearest modern equivalent might be the pronoun *one*, used in such expressions as *one should not do that*, this does not cover all the contexts in which **man** is used and it is better to compare it with the German word **man**, e.g. in the common notice **man spricht deutsch** *German spoken*. As a general rule Old English **man** can be translated either with *they* or a passive:

> þa geutlagode man Æþelweard ealdorman

either then they outlawed ealdorman Æthelweard (*they* is rather general)

or then ealdorman Æthelweard was outlawed (passive)

Notes on *if*, *when* and the subjunctive mood

In Old English the verb dependent on **gif** or **þonne** goes to the end of the clause:

> ðonne þu fisc habban wylle...
> *When you want to have fish...*

Because it expresses a hypothesis, the verb is put in the subjunctive as **wylle** or **wille** rather than indicative **wile**. In this case, you could also translate *whenever you may want to have fish* or, possibly, *if you wanted to have fish, then...* but often a simple translation such as *when you want to have fish* is the best modern equivalent, even if it does not retain all the connotations of the original Old English.

Insight

While the verb following **swilce** *as if* is almost always subjunctive because it expresses a hypothesis, the verb following **gif** or **þonne** can be either subjunctive or indicative depending on the context.

In the opening lines of the Exeter Book poem *Wulf and Eadwacer*, there is a clear example of a contrast between *subjunctive* and indicative:

> Leodum is minum swylce him mon lac **gife**.
> **Willað** hy hine aþecgan, gif he on þreat **cymeð**
> *To my people it's as if they were given a present*
> *They want to consume him if he comes in a troop*

Although the speaker and situation are not stated, the choice of verbs here is nevertheless precise, employing subjunctive and indicative to make distinctions of mood between the **swilce** and the **gif** clauses. There is conjecture in the subjunctive clause **swylce him mon lac gife** where the subjunctive is dependent on **swylce** *as if*. This is followed by the declarative meaning of the indicative **gif he on þreat cymeð** *if he comes in a troop*, which implies that this is the expected course of events. Nevertheless, the subjunctive mood sets the tone for the whole lyric, which is strong on feeling but enigmatic and riddle-like in meaning. (For this text see the anthologies by Richard Hamer or Elaine Treharne in the **bibliography**.)

Verbs with a genitive object

Some verbs take an object in the genitive case. In other words, where you would expect the accusative case, the object of the sentence has genitive endings. An example is found in Unit 11, after the verb **geunnan** *to grant*:

> Godwine geánn Leofwine readan **ðæs dænnes** æt
>   Swiðrædingdænne
> *Godwine grants to Leofwine the Red the pasture at*
>   *Southernden*

Although it seems to mean literally *Godwine grants of the pasture*, the intended meaning is *Godwine **grants** the pasture*. It may be useful in understanding this idiomatic usage to consider some phrasal verbs in modern English such as *look for a monastery*, he will *petition for an audience*, he *is desirous of a hearing*. These phrases, which consist of verb + preposition, or be + adjective + preposition, are the nearest modern equivalents. In each case the verb does not take a direct object; it needs the preposition to make a well-formed verb phrase. In the same way the genitive follows verbs such as **beþurfan** *need*, **brūcan** *enjoy*, **gyrnan** *desire*, **neodian** *require*, **þyrstan** *thirst for*, **wēnan** *expect*. An example from the monastic signs is the word **disc** *dish*, put into the genitive as object of the verb **beþurfan** *to need*:

> Gif þe disces beþurfe, þonne hefe þu up þine oþre hand
>   and tospræd þine fingras
> *If you need a dish, then raise up your other hand and*
>   *spread your fingers*

Insight

Another verb that would substitute for **beþurfe** is **geneodian**, also spelt **genyodigan** *need* in the *Monastic Signs*; the above phrase would then be **gif þe disces genyodige...** *If you have need of a dish.*

The verb **wilnian** *to desire, seek* is used in a similar way; in the story of Euphrosyne, for instance, the gate-keeper of the monastery reports to the abbot the arrival of a mysterious young stranger:

> Þa eode se geatweard to þam abbode, and cwæð him to,
>   'Fæder, her is cumen an eunuchus of cinges hirede, wilnað
>   þinre spræce.'
> *Then the gate-keeper went to the abbot and said to him,*
>   *'Father, a eunuch has come here from the king's court and*
>   *seeks an audience with you' [literally, desires of your speech]*

Euphrosyne

A key to this passage from *The Life of Euphrosyne* is the following set of antonyms or opposites: **wiflic–werlic, fæmne–wer, bryd–brydguma, æfentid–mergen** (see **word index** at back).

Eufrosina þa þohte þus *Euphrosyne then thought thus*

Eufrosina þa þohte þus cweðende, 'Gif ic nu fare to fæmnena
mynstre, þonne secð min fæder me þær, and me þær findað,
þonne nimð he me neadunga ðanon for mines brydguman
þingan. Ac ic wille faran to wera mynstre þær nan man min
ne wene.' Heo þa þone wiflican gegyrlan ofdyde, and hi
gescrydde mid werlicum. And on æfentíd gewát of hire healle,
and nam mid hire fiftig mancsas, and þa niht hi gehydde on
digelre stowe.

Þa eode se geatweard to þam abbode
Then the gate-keeper went to the abbot

Þa þæs on mergen com Pafnutius to þære ceastre, and þa
æfter Godes willan eode he into cyrcan. Eufrosina betwux
þysum com to þam mynstre, þe hire fæder tó sohte. Þa eode
(Contd)

se geatweard to þam abbode, and cwæð him to, 'Fæder, her is cumen an eunuchus of cinges hirede, wilnað þinre spræce.'

Se abbod þa ut eode, and heo sona feoll to his fotum, and onfangenre bletsunge hí togædere gesæton.

QUICK VOCAB

se mergen *morning* (also **morgen** *morn*)
se geatweard *gate-keeper*
seo spræc *speech* 'spræ ch'
tó *towards*
feoll *fell* (**feallan**)
onfangenre bletsunge *having received a blessing* (imitates Latin construction)
gesæton *sat* (**sittan**)

◀)) TR 48

For hwilcum þingum come þu hider?
For *what reasons did you come here?*

Þa cwæð se abbod, 'Bearn, for hwilcum þingum come þu hider?'

Ða cwæð heo, 'Ic wæs on cinges hirede, and ic eom eunuchus, and ic symle wilnode to munuclicum life gecyrran. Ac þyllic lif nis nu gewunelic on ure ceastre. Nu geaxode ic eowre mæran drohtnunge, and min willa is ðæt ic mid eow eardian mote, gif eower willa þæt bið'.

QUICK VOCAB

for hwilcum þingum *for what reason[s]*
gecyrran *to convert, turn*
þyllic *such*
gewunelic *usual*
geaxian, geacsian *to hear of* (perfective **ge-** + **ascian** see Unit 4)

mære *great, famous*
seo drohtnung *way of life*
eardian *to live, dwell*

Old–modern correspondences

In a study on the etymology of the word *girl*, Fred Robinson has argued that Middle English **gerle** does not, as is sometimes stated, derive from the medieval influence of a Low German word **gör** *child*. Instead, he argues by analogy with Old English **bratt**. The word **bratt** originally meant *over-garment*, *apron*, and then later denoted a *pinafore* as worn by a child. Eventually the child was referred to by the garment they wore, the *brat*. Similarly with **gegierla**. With its optional **ge-** prefix omitted, this is **gierla**, a garment worn by a young woman, which came to be associated with the *girl* herself.

Cultural contexts

The great age of the Old English monastery began in the middle of the tenth century, particularly during the reign of Edgar the Peaceable, father of Æthelred the Unready. This king was able to encourage the Continental monastic reform movement promoted by his reforming bishops Æthelwold and Dunstan, who were later honoured as saints.

At the beginning of the century, there were many secular minsters but only a few regular monasteries, an example being Glastonbury in the Somerset Levels, but by the year 1000 substantial numbers had been founded or re-founded. From 964, when Æthelwold replaced the secular clergy at the Old Minster in Winchester with his Abingdon monks, it became common for abbots to be appointed as bishops. By the eleventh century, England was unusual for having monastic cathedrals in three of its important cities: at Winchester, Worcester and Canterbury.

Reading (1)

More extracts from the Old English *Monastic Signs*

The Old English *Monastic Signs* occur in an eleventh-century compendium of Benedictine monastic texts in London British Library Cotton Tiberius A. iii.

Ærest þæs abbudes tacen is þæt mon his twegen fingras to heafde asette, and his feax mid genime.

First the abbot's sign is that you put your two fingers to your head and take hold of your hair.

Ðonne is þæs horderes tacen þæt mon wrænce mid is hand swilce he wille loc hunlucan.

Then the cellarer's sign is that one turns with one's hand as if one wanted to open a lock.

Gyf þu mete-rædere fyldstol habban wille, oþþe oþrum men, þonne clæm þu þine handa togædere and wege hi, þam gemete þe þu dest þonne þu hine fyldan wylt.

If you want to have the mealtime reader's folding stool, then put your hands together and move them in the way that you do when you want to fold it.

Gyf þu sceat habban wille oððe wapan, þonne sete þu þine twa handa ofer þinum bearme and tobræd hi swillce sceat astrecce.

If you want to have a sheet or a napkin, then place your two hands over your lap and spread them as if you were stretching out a sheet.

Wordhoard

The monastic dining hall at mealtimes

People

se **abbud** *abbot* (head of the **hired** *community, household*)

se **profost** *provost, second-in-command* (pronounce medial -f- as 'v')

se **diacan** *deacon, dean* (see D. Banham 1991, p. 57)

se **hordere** *cellarer* (in charge of food, drink and provisions)

se **cyricweard** *sacrist* (looks after sacred vessels and shrines in the church)

se **magister** *master, teacher*

se **mete-rædere** *mealtime reader* (reads out loud to the monks at meals)

Table	**Food**
fyldstol *folding chair*	**mete** *food*
sceat *sheet, cloth*	**briw** *soup*
wapan *towel, napkin*	**hunig** *honey*
syx *knife*	**laf, hlaf** *loaf*
disc *dish*	**sealt** *salt* (**seltan** *to salt*)
sticca *skewer*	**pipor** *pepper*

Dairy	**Vegetables**
meolc *milk*	**beana** *beans*
cyse *cheese*	**grene wyrta** *green vegetables*
butere *butter*	**læc, leac** *leek*

(For more monastic words, see **bibliography**, especially D. Banham, 1991.)

Reading (2)

From the Exeter Book

The Exeter Book was certainly owned by bishop Leofric in Exeter from the mid-eleventh century, but by then the book had already been in use for several generations. Scholars agree that the handwriting indicates a date of origin of about 975, although opinions differ as to who wrote the book and who owned it before Leofric. While some have made a case for Exeter as the actual origin of the manuscript, others argue for a large writing workshop from southwest England that had connections with Canterbury. One possibility is the great abbey at Glastonbury.

A striking feature of the Exeter Book is the variety of poems it contains and the following two poems illustrate this range. Both suggest a monastic context, of work and worship, but in different moods, one making fun of the incessant reader, the other celebrating the mysteries of the faith.

Riddle 47 (The bookworm)

Moððe word fræt: me þæt þuhte
wrætlicu wyrd, þa ic þæt wundor gefrægn,
þæt se wyrm forswealg wera gide sumes,
þeof in þystro, þrymfæstne cwide
ond þæs strangan staþol. Stælgiest ne wæs
wihte þy gleawra, þe he þam wordum swealg.

A moth ate words: that seemed to me
a wondrous fate, when I heard of that wonder,
that the worm swallowed a man's song,
a thief in the dark (swallowed) a glorious saying
and its strong foundation. The stealing guest was
not one bit the wiser when he swallowed the words.

The word **þrymfæst** is a compound, made up of **þrymm** *glory* and **fæst** *firm*, forming a poetic adjective *glorious*. Similar compound adjectives include: **tirfæst** *glorious*, **arfæst** *gracious*, **stedefæst** *steadfast*, **gemetfæst** *moderate*. When the adjective **fæst** is used as an adverb it becomes **fæstlice** (see Unit 21 for an example in *The Battle of Maldon* line 82).

Riddle 48 (The chalice)

Ic gefrægn for hæleþum hring endean,
torhtne butan tungan, tila (þeah he hlude
stefne ne cirmde) strongum wordum.
Sinc for secgum swigende cwæð:
'Gehæle mec, helpend gæstra.'
Ryne ongietan readan goldes
guman galdorcwide, gleawe beþencan
hyra hælo to Gode, swa se hring gecwæð.

I heard a ring speaking before men,
bright, tongueless, prosperously (though with a loud
voice it did not speak) with strong words.
The treasure before men silently spoke:
'Save me, helper of souls.'
May men understand the mysteries of the red gold,
the magical speech, may they wisely ponder
their salvation in God, as the ring said.

TEST YOURSELF (1)

Re-read the passage from *The Life of Euphrosyne* and answer these comprehension questions.

1 Why does Euphrosyne avoid the women's convent?
2 What does Euphrosyne do before departing from the hall?
3 What happens when the abbot comes out to see the visitor?
4 Why does the stranger want to join the monastery?

TEST YOURSELF (2)

Look through the list of persons and objects in **wordhoard** and identify the missing Old English word and its translation in the following descriptions from the monastic sign language:

Đæs (**1a**) _____ taccen is þe þa cild bewat þæt man set his twegen fingras on his twa eagan and hebbe up his litlan finger. The (**1b**) _____'s sign who guides the children is that one places his fingers on his two eyes and raises up his little finger.

Gyf þe (**2a**) _____ genyodige þonne snid þu mid þinum fingre ofer þonne oþerne swylce þu cyrfan wille. If you need a (**2b**) _____ you cut with your finger over the other as if you wanted to carve.

(**3a**) _____ tacan is þæt þu wecge þine fyst swilce þu (**3b**) _____ hrere. The sign of (**3c**) _____ is that you move your fist as if you were stirring (**3d**) _____ .

Đonne þu (**4a**) _____ habban wylle, þonne geþeoddum þinum þrim fingerum hryse þine hand swylce þu hwæt (**4b**) _____ wylle. When you want to have (**4c**) _____ then with your three fingers joined drop your hand as if you want (**4d**) _____ something.

16

It happened one night

This unit will cover:

texts
- *from the Old English prose* Life of St Guthlac
- *extracts from the Old English Bede and the Chronicle*

grammar
- *the indefinite pronoun* sum
- *revision of the definite article*

vocabulary
- *the Old English hermit: way of life and spirituality*

◀) TR 49

Ðæt gelamp on sumere nihte
It happened one night

Se halga wer *The holy man*

The hermit or anchorite, the spiritual warrior who spends his time
in solitude and meditation; the holy man who lives apart but acts
as guide and adviser to people who take the trouble to seek him out
in his wilderness home: this ideal seems to have gone out of fashion

in tenth-century England. The reasons are not hard to see. First, the world had become a more dangerous place, with Viking attacks putting an end to the solitary life from a practical point of view. Second, the Benedictine revival – as we saw in Unit 15 – had made the communal monastic life the ideal to which people aspired.

However, in the 11th century a number of Old English texts appear that are variously concerned with hermits and anchorites; they suggest that an interest in the way of the hermit was reviving. One of these texts is a recopying of the ninth-century Old English *Life of St Guthlac*, a story with a long history going back to the early 700s (see reading below). In the story the hermit Guthlac is presented as having qualities of spiritual fortitude, closeness to nature and (more unusually) good humour – as seen, for instance, in the episode of the thieving raven from chapter 9 of the story. This begins as follows:

◆ TR 49, 00:07

Ðæt gelamp on sumere nihte þæt þær com sum man to þæs halgan weres spræce. Mid þy he þær dagas wunode, þa gelamp hit, þæt he sum gewrit awrat on cartan. Ða he hæfde þæt gewrit awriten, þa eode he ut. Ða com þær sum hrefn inn; sona swá he þa cartan geseah, þa genam he hig sona and gewat mid on þæne fenn. Sona swa se foresæda cuma ongean com, þa geseah he þone hrefen þa cartan beran, þa wæs he sona swyðe unbliþe.

It happened one night that there came a certain man for talk with the holy man. While he was staying there a few days, it happened that he wrote out a document on a piece of parchment. When he had written the document he went out. Then a raven came in; as soon as he saw the parchment he immediately took it and departed with it into the fen. As soon as the aforesaid guest came back again, then he saw the raven carrying the parchment, [and] then he was immediately very distraught.

gelamp *it happened* 'hüt yuh-LAMP' (a set phrase; present tense
  gelimpeð)
mid þy *while*
dagas *(a few) days* (irregular plural of **dæg** *day*)
wunode *remained* (from **wunian**, cf. German)
wohnen *to live, inhabit*
awrat *wrote* (past tense of **awritan**)
awriten *written* (past participle of **awritan**)
ut *out*
inn *in*
se hrefn *raven*
sona swa *as soon as*
ongean *back again*
sona *immediately*
-unbliþe un *un* + **bliþe** *happy* (cf. *blithe*)

Insight

Although grammar books use the term *rules*, these can usefully
be seen as *patterns* of language observable within a text. Before
you read the grammar section below, look through the above
text for examples of the third person pronoun and phrases
containing the definite article. Observe any patterns of usage.

Grammar

Comparing definite article and personal pronoun

	masculine		
	article	*pronoun*	
nominative	**se** halga wer ***the*** holy man	**hé**	*he*
accusative	**þone** hrefn ***the*** raven	**hine**	*him, it* (direct object)

masculine			
	article		*pronoun*
genitive	**þæs** halgan weres *the* holy man's	**his**	*his*
dative	on **þam** ylcan timan *at the* same time	**him**	*it* (dative after on)

neuter			
	article		*pronoun*
nominative	**þæt** gewrit ***the*** document	**hit**	*it*
accusative	**þæt** gewrit ***the*** document	**hit**	*it* (direct object)
genitive	**þæs** huses ***of the*** house	**his**	*its*
dative	to **þam** yglande ***to the*** island	**him**	*to it*

feminine			
	article		*pronoun*
nominative	**seo** carta ***the*** parchment	**héo**	*it*
accusative	**þa** cartan ***the*** parchment	**hig**	*it* (direct object)
genitive	**þære** cartan ***of the*** parchment	**hire**	*its*
dative	to **þære** cartan ***to the*** parchment	**hire**	*to it*

Determiners

Determiners are words like *a, the, this, that, few*. A modern speaker of English will choose between determiners such as the articles (*a* or *the*), demonstrative pronouns (*this* or *that*) and quantifiers (*no, few, some, five* etc.). In modern English we make a distinction between the indefinite article *a* and the definite article *the*. Although Old English did have a way of signalling definiteness using se, seo, þæt (see above), the language did not as yet have an indefinite article. The adjectives **an** *one* and **sum** *a certain* were used instead.

Use of *sum*

The phrase **sum man** often appears in Old English narratives as a way of introducing a new character at the beginning of a new episode. A strictly literal translation would be *a certain man* but quite often the phrase simply means *a man*. Frequently, then, **sum** corresponds to the modern English indefinite article *a, an*, although in some contexts its meaning can be more specific than simply *a*. The use of **sum** is illustrated here with extracts from the first of the two 'raven episodes' in the Old English prose *Life of St Guthlac*.

In the *Life of St Guthlac*, the first raven episode begins with the words:

Ðæt gelamp **on sumere nihte** þæt þær com **sum man** to þæs halgan weres spræce.
*It happened **one night** that there came a **certain man** for the holy man's conversation [i.e. for talk with the holy man].*

The storytelling formula *one night* is here given as **on sumere niht,** literally *on a certain night.* The man's name is not given, he remains identified simply as **sum man,** but the implication is that he will be referred to again in the rest of the episode. As in modern colloquial English *some man came to see him* the determiner is indefinite but specific. If his name were to be given here it would no doubt follow the pattern found in the second 'raven episode', which names *a certain nobleman* þæs **nama wæs Æþelbald** *whose name was Æthelbald.*

While he is staying a few days at Guthlac's fenland hermitage the man copies out a **gewrit** or *document* on a leaf of parchment; then, having completed his task, he goes out:

Mid þy he þær dagas wunode, þa gelamp hit, þæt he **sum gewrit** awrat on cartan. Þa he hæfde **þæt gewrit** awriten, þa eode he ut.
*While he was staying there a few days, it happened that he wrote **a document** on a piece of parchment. When he had written **the document** he went out.*

Notice the change from the first mention of **sum gewrit** (*a certain indefinite but specific* document) to the second mention, **þæt gewrit** (any subsequent reference can refer to *the* document using the definite article).

Having introduced his human and inanimate protagonists, *some man* and *some document*, the narrator now introduces his third, an animate protagonist *some raven*:

> Ða com þær **sum** hrefn inn; sona swá he þa cartan geseah, þa genam he hig sona and gewat mid on þæne fenn.

Two possible translations suggest themselves:

> *Then **some** raven came in; as soon as he saw the parchment he immediately took it and departed with it into the fen.*
>
> *Then there came in a raven; as soon as it saw the parchment it took it and departed with it into the fen.*

The translation affects the interpretation. It may not be correct to render the grammatical gender of **he** as *it* (on natural and grammatical gender look back to Unit 5). Arguably the best translation is *a raven*, too much emphasis being placed on the animate agency of the bird if we translate *some raven came in*. But this may in fact be the very point of the story: the bird really is wilful, and Guthlac, who can communicate with other creatures, rebukes him for his cruelty. This is how the Old English narrator tells the story and (as you will see) he uses the determiner **sum** twice more in the episode, each time introducing – however briefly – a new agent in the plot: *a lake* and *a reedbed*.

Eventually, in the development of the language, the determiner **sum** declined in use and was mostly replaced by **án**, which subsequently divided into two words: the determiner *one* as in *one night* and the indefinite article *a* and *an*.

Endings on *sum*

Many examples of the form and use of **sum** can be found by looking through a text such as the *Life of St Guthlac* and noting examples, quite often at the beginning of new chapters or, as we have seen, at new turns in the story:

ch. 9 þa com he **to sumum mere** *then he came to a certain lake*
ch. 12 wæs on Eastenglalande **sum man** æþeles cynnes þæs nama wæs Hwætred
there was in East Anglia a man of noble kin whose name was Hwætred
ch. 13 swilce eac gelamp on sumne sæl... *similarly also it happened at one time...*
ch. 19 wæs on sumre tíde þæt ... *it happened at one time that...*

These endings have been encountered before in various contexts and in various parts of speech:

▶ the common **-ne** ending marks masculine accusative
▶ the genitive **-es** is found in the masculine and neuter
▶ the dative has **-um** in the masculine and neuter
▶ the feminine genitive and dative ending is **-re**.

Insight

The importance of the notion of **æþel cynn** in Old English society is reflected in words like **cyning** *king*, **cynelic** *royal*, **Angelcynn** *the English*, **Wealhcynn** *the Welsh*. More general uses of **cynn** include **stancynn** *type of stone* (Unit 5) and **gecynd** *nature*, modern English *kind*.

Word order

The fast-paced narrative affords a good opportunity to review word order after conjunctions of time. In this passage, look out for the conjunctions **mid þy** *while* and **sona swa** *as soon as*; usually the <u>verb</u> goes to the end of the clause or towards the end of that part of the sentence (in contrast to the Modern English equivalent):

mid þy he þær dagas <u>wunode</u>, þa gelamp hit þæt...
while he <u>was staying</u> there a few days, it happened that...
sona swá he þa cartan <u>geseah</u>, þa genam he hig sona
as soon as he <u>saw</u> the parchment, then he took it at once

Another example from later in the passage – worth studying as it marks a key moment in the story – is **efne swa** *even as if*, a conjunction which (like **swilce**) takes a subjunctive and sends the verb here to the end of the clause:

> **efne swa** hig mannes hand þær <u>ahengce</u>
> *even as if a man's hand <u>had hung</u> it there*

The same pattern is usually found after the temporal phrases *then it happened that…, it was not long afterwards that…* In these contexts the verb also tends to go near the end of the sentence:

> Mid þy he þær dagas wunode, **þa gelamp hit þæt** he sum gewrit <u>awrat</u> on cartan.
> *While he was staying there a few days, **it happened that** he <u>wrote</u> out a document on a piece of parchment.*

Perhaps for reasons of emphasis the writer chose to end with the word **cartan**. In the first sentence of the story, too, it looks as if the narrator avoids putting the verb at the end by using the 'empty subject' *there* in *there came* and so allowing the sentence to conclude with a heavy emphasis on the hermit and the purpose of the visit:

> Ðæt gelamp on sumere nihte þæt **þær** com sum man to þæs halgan weres spræce.
> *It happened one night that there came a certain man for talk with the holy man.*

A final point on style, syntax and sentence structure in this passage is the way the conjunction **sona swa** is recapitulated and echoed in the main clause by the adverbs **þa** *then* and **sona** *immediately*:

> Ða com þær sum hrefn inn; **sona swá** he þa cartan geseah, **þa** genam he hig **sona** and gewat mid on þæne fenn.
> *Then there came a raven in; **as soon as** he saw the parchment **then** he took it **immediately** and departed with it into the fen.*
> **Sona swa** se foresæda cuma ongean com, **þa** geseah he þone hrefen þa cartan beran, **þa** wæs he **sona** swyðe unbliþe.

As soon as the aforesaid guest came back again, **then** *he saw the raven carrying the parchment, [and]* **then** *he was* **immediately** *very distraught.*

This is rather like the correlation of þa... þa meaning *when... then,* which also occurs in the passage (look back to Unit 6 for more discussion):

Þa he hæfde þæt gewrit awriten, **þa** eode he ut.
When *he had written the document* **then** *he went out.*

By such methods of correlation, the Old English narrative is held together and the connections between the various clauses of the sentence are made clearer and tighter.

One final example of correlation comes from the mouth of the hermit himself. This is the construction **swa... swa... þonne...** *as... so... then...* found in the advice which Guthlac gives to his guest on how to recover the stolen parchment:

'Ne beo þu broþor sarig, ac **swa** se hrefn þurh þa fennas upp afligeð, **swá** þu him æfter row; **þonne** metest þu þæt gewrit.'
'*Do not be sad, brother, but* **as** *the raven flies up through the fens,* **so** *you row after him;* **then** *you will find the document.*'

Study now the whole of the story; try reading it out loud, at a lively pace.

....

◀ TR 49

Ðæt gelamp on sumere nihte *It happened one night*

Ðæt gelamp on sumere nihte þæt þær com sum man to þæs halgan weres spræce. Mid þy he þær dagas wunode, þa gelamp hit, þæt he sum gewrit awrat on cartan. Þa he hæfde þæt gewrit awriten, þa eode he ut. Ða com þær sum hrefn inn; sona swá he þa cartan geseah, þa genam he hig sona and gewat mid on þæne fenn. Sona swa se foresæda cuma ongean
(Contd)

com, þa geseah he þone hrefen þa cartan beran, þa wæs he
sona swyðe unbliþe.

Ða wæs on þam ylcan timan, þæt se halga wer Guðlac ut of
his cyrcan eode; þa geseah he þone broþor sarig. Þa frefrode
he hine and him to cwæð, 'Ne beo þu broþor sarig, ac swa
se hrefn þurh þa fennas upp afligeð, swá þu him æfter row;
þonne metest þu þæt gewrit.'

Næs þa nænig hwil to þan, þæt he to scipe eode se ylca þe
þæt gewrit wrat. Mid þy he þurh þa fenland reow þa com he
to sumum mere, þe wel neah þam eglande wæs; þa wæs þær
on middan þam mere sum hreodbed; þa hangode seo carte on
þam hreode, efne swa hig mannes hand þær ahengce; and he
sona þa bliþe feng to þære cartan, and he wundriende to þam
Godes were brohte...

_{QV}

sarig *sad*
frēfran *to console*
mētan *meet, find* (**mētt, mētte, mētton, gemēted**)
bliþe *happy* (**unbliþe** *unhappy*)

Check your comprehension of the second half of the passage
against the translation:

*It happened one night that there came a certain man for talk
with the holy man. While he was staying there a few days,
it happened that he wrote out a document on a piece of
parchment. When he had written the document he went out.
Then a certain raven came in; as soon as he saw the parchment
he immediately took it and departed with it into the fen. As
soon as the aforesaid guest came back again, then he saw the
raven carrying the parchment, [and] then he was immediately
very distraught. Then it happened at the same time that the
holy man Guthlac came out of his church; then he saw the
brother sad. Whereupon he consoled him and said to him,*

> 'Do not be sad, brother, but as the raven flies up through the fens, so you row after him; then you will find the document.'
>
> It was not any time before he went to his ship – the same one who wrote the document. As he rowed through the fenlands he came to a certain lake, which was well near to the island; there was in the middle of the lake a certain reed-bed and there was the parchment hanging on the reed as if a man's hand had hung it there. And immediately he took the parchment, and marvelling he brought it to the man of God.

Cultural contexts

Part of the Guthlac prose narrative occurs in the form of a sermon in the tenth-century Vercelli Book, but the only full copy of the Old English *Life of Guthlac* appears in British Library manuscript Cotton Vespasian D. xxi, copied in the eleventh century. Although separated from its original binding, it looks – from the evidence of parchment and script – as if this story occurred originally as the final piece in a manuscript of the Old English Hexateuch translation, following the version of the biblical Judges by Ælfric, abbot of Eynsham, friend of Wulfstan and a prolific writer of sermons in the late Old English church.

Reading

From the Anglo-Saxon Chronicle AD 714

The first mention of Guthlac in Old English is a brief entry in the Anglo-Saxon Chronicle for the year 714; the following is the text in the D Chronicle:

AN. .dcccxi.
AN. .dcccxii.

AN. .dcccxiii.
AN. .dcccxiiii. **Her geferde Guðlac se halga.**
714 Here Guthlac the holy departed.

For the preceding three years (711–13), the chronicler had
apparently found nothing worth recording and the date of
Guthlac's passing away thus stands out prominently on the
manuscript page.

The Old English prose *Life of Guthlac*

Historically, Guthlac was a famous Mercian warrior of the late
seventh century who became profoundly dissatisfied with his
military lifestyle and converted first to the monastic life and then
to the solitary isolation of an anchorite's cell in the wild fenland
of Crowland near Peterborough. His *Life* was told first in Latin
by the Mercian writer Felix and then in Old English by two
anonymous poets (*Guthlac A* and *Guthlac B*). Probably during
the reign of king Alfred in the ninth century, when Old English
became a medium of education, the Latin life was translated into
Old English. The following is the moment when Guthlac decides to
follow his vocation:

Ða ymbe twá winter, þæs he his lif swa leofode under
munuchade, þæt he þa ongan wilnian westenes and
sundersetle. Mid þy he gehyrde secgan and he leornode be
þam ancerum, þe geara on westene and on sundorsettlum
for Godes naman wilnodon and heora life leofodon, ða wæs
his heorte innan þurh godes gifu onbryrdod, þæt he westenes
gewilnode.

*After two winters when he had lived his life in monastic
orders, he began to yearn for the wilderness and a solitary
cell. And when he heard tell and learned of the anchorites
who, for the name of God, desired the desert and lived the
life of seclusion, then his heart was inspired within by God's
grace so that he desired the wilderness.*

The story of Fursa from the Old English Bede, III.19

The events in the life of Guthlac and its various retellings were
inspired by the stories of St Antony and the other Desert Fathers,
the first hermits who had inhabited the Egyptian desert in the
early Christian centuries. The desire to live in the desert, or in
northern European terms *the wild*, was taken up by Irish pilgrims
and hermits. Felix wrote about Guthlac with the model of the
Irish hermit Fursey in mind and Bede, the greatest Latin writer of
the early Anglo-Saxon period, also wrote of Fursey and told the
story of the Irish-inspired St Cuthbert on his island hermitage near
Lindisfarne. During Alfred's reign, Bede's Latin was translated into
Old English. Compare the following description of Fursa the saint
with that of Guthlac.

Mid ðy ðe Sigeberht þa gytá rice hæfde, cwom of Hibernia
Scotta ealonde halig wer sum, þæs noma wæs Furseus. Se
wæs in wordum and dædum beorht and scinende, swelce
he wæs in æðelum mægenum mære geworden. Wilnade he,
þætte he swa hwær swa he gelimplice stowe findan meahte,
þæt he wolde for Godes noman in elþeodignisse lifian. [ed.
T. Miller, p. 210]

*While Sigeberht was still on the throne, there came from
Ireland, the island of the Scots, a holy man, Fursey by name.
He was bright and shining in words and deeds, just as he had
become famous for his noble virtues. He desired, wherever he
might find a suitable place, that he would live, for the name
of God, on pilgrimage.*

From the Anglo-Saxon Chronicle

The following is a famous story of the visit of the three Irish
pilgrims to king Alfred's court in the year 891. In the short passage
given in Old English compare Fursa's ideal of living *on pilgrimage*
with the Irishmen's desire to be **on elþeodignesse**; the same
wording is used in each case.

In this year the Viking army went to the east, and king Earnulf, with the East Franks, Saxons and Bavarians, fought against the mounted army and put them to flight before the ships had arrived. And three Scots in a boat without any oars came to king Alfred from Ireland, which they left because they wanted, for the love of God, to be on pilgrimage; and they did not care where.

[and þry Scottas comon to Ælfrede cynge on anum bate butan ælcum gereþrum of Hibernia, þanon hie bestælon for þon ðe hi woldon for Godes lufon on elþeodignesse beon, and hi ne rohton hwær.]

The boat they travelled in was made of two and half hides; they took with them enough that they had food for seven nights, and after the seven nights they came to land in Cornwall, and they went from there to king Alfred. Their names were Dublasne, Machbethu and Maelmumin. And Swifneh died, the best teacher there was among the Scots. In the same year after Easter around Rogationtide, or earlier, the star appeared that is called, in Latin, a 'cometa'. Some men say in English that it is 'the long-haired star', because long beams of light come out of it on one side or the other.

Guthlac's cell

In the Old English prose life, the great mound (**mycel hlæw**) where Guthlac takes up his abode is associated with buried treasure plundered by robbers long ago and now the haunt of demons, with which he must do spiritual battle before he can make the place habitable and fit for visitors:

Wæs þær in þam sprecenan iglande sum mycel hlæw of eorðan geworht, þone ylcan hlæw men iu geara men bræcon and dulfon for feos þingum.

There was there in the above-mentioned island a certain great hlowe made of earth, which same hlowe in former years men broke into and dug up for the sake of its treasure.

The Wife's Lament

Similarly, in the Exeter Book poem *The Wife's Lament*, the speaker appears to have been exiled into the wilderness to an old barrow or earth cave, a landscape with pagan associations (lines 27–32):

Heht mec mon wunian on wuda bearwe,
under actreo in þam eorðscræfe.
Eald is þes eorðsele, eal ic eom oflongad,
sindon dena dimme, duna uphea,
bitre burgtunas brerum beweaxne,
wic wynna leas.

They ordered me to dwell in a forest barrow,
under oak tree in the earth cave.
This earthen hall is old, I am all longing,
the valleys are dim, the hills up high,
the bitter town dwellings are grown over with briars,
the settlement joyless.

A description of Guthlac

Wæs he on ansine mycel and on lichaman clæne, wynsum on his mode and wlitig on ansyne; he wæs liðe and gemetfæst on his worde, and he wæs geþyldig and eadmod; and á seo godcunde lufu on hys heortan hat and byrnende. [ed. Gonser, p. 111]

He was in appearance large, in body clean, cheerful in his
mind and handsome of face; he was gentle and modest in his
speech, and he was patient and humble; and ever the divine
love hot and burning in his heart.

Mantat the Anchorite (S 1523)

The following declaration addressed to king Cnut and the lady Emma is one of several documents that reveal the existence of anchorites and hermits in England in the early eleventh century.

(For more discussion see Clayton in the **bibliography**.) The present text is remarkable for its friendly tone, and for the information it reveals about Cnut and Emma's spiritual concerns. It is recorded in a late copy, with the language modernized by the later scribe to fit the spelling system of his own day.

Mantat ancer godes wræcca gretet Cnut king and Emma þe læfdie swiþe bliþelike mid godes blisse, and ic cyðe þat ic habbe ure almesse criste betaht and hise allen halgan ure saule to froure and to blisse þær it lengest wunian sculen; þæt is ærest þæt land at Twywelle into Þornige þær ure ban resteð, and þat land at Cunintun. Prestes and diaknes þa þe hit at me earnodan on mine liue, and hi habbeð God behaten and me on hand eseald þat hi sculen elke ear don for us twa hundred messen and twa hundred sauters, and þerto eaken fele holye beden. Nu bidde ic inc for godes luue and for ure wreccan bene þat þis non man ne awende; þat wat god þat inc ne was non bescoran man nyccere þænne and þat inc sceal ben cuð on þan towarden liue. Gehealde inc here on liue heofan engle kinge, and gelede inc on his lihte mid him þer yt wiþuten sorhge euere wunian. Amen.

Mantat the Anchorite, God's exile, greets King Cnut and Queen Emma very joyfully with God's joy. And I make known to you that I have entrusted our charitable gift to Christ and all his saints where it shall remain longest, for the comfort and happiness of our soul. First, the estate at Twywell to Thorney, where our bones shall rest, and the estate at Conington, to priests and deacons who have deserved it of me during my life. And they have promised God and given pledge to me that each year they will recite for us two hundred masses and two hundred psalters and in addition many holy prayers. Now I pray you for the love of God and on account of an exile's entreaty, that no man may alter this. God knows that no tonsured man has been more useful to you both than [I], and that shall be known to you in the future life. May the King of the angels of heaven uphold you both in this life and lead you into his light where you may ever dwell with him without sorrow. Amen.

TEST YOURSELF

The second 'raven episode' from the *Life of St Guthlac*

Read the text and then answer the questions below.

Note the following words and usages: **begytan æt** *to acquire from*, **forlǽtan** *to leave behind*, **gesegon** *saw*, **þæt nebb** *beak*, **þæt þæc** *thatch*, **þrean** *to rebuke*, **hyrsumode** *obeyed*, **fugel** *bird*, **westen** *wilderness*, **seo gyrd** *staff*, **seo hyð** *hithe, landing place*, **þæt tacen** *signal*, **se andwlita** *face*, **feng to** *began, took to*, **smerciende** *smiling*, **seo bletsung** *blessing*.

Þa wolde he [Æþelbald] to þæs halgan weres sprace cuman, beget þa æt Wilfride, þæt he hine to þam Godes were gelædde; and hi þa sona on scipe eodon and ferdon to þam yglande þær se halga wer Guthlac on wæs.

Ða hi þa to þam halgan were comon, þa hæfde Wilfrið forleten his glofan on þam scipe; and hi þa wið þone halgan wer spræcon. He þa se eadiga wer Guthlac acsode hi hwæðer hi ænig þinc æfter heom on þam scipe forleton, swa him God ealle þa diglan þingc cuð gedyde. Þa andswarode him Wilfrið and cwæð þæt he forlete his twa glofan on þam scipe.

Næs þa nænig hwil to þan, sona swa hi ut of þam in eodon þa gesegon hi þone hræfn mid þan sweartan nebbe þa glofe teran uppe on anes huses þæce. He þa sona se halga wer Guðlac þone hrefn mid his worde þreade for his reþnysse, and he þa his worda hyrsumode; swa fleah se fugel west ofer þæt westen. He þa Wilfrið mid gyrde of þæs huses hrofe þa glofe geræhte.

Swylce næs eac nænig hwil to þam, sona comon þær þry men to þære hyðe and þær tacn slogon. Þa sona eode se halga wer Guðlac út to þam mannum mid bliðum andwlite and góde mode; he þa spæc wið þam mannum. Mid þan þe hi

(Contd)

faran woldon, þa brohton hi forð ane glofe, sædon þæt heo
of anes hrefnes muðe feolle. He se halga wer Guþlac sona to
smerciende feng, and heom his bletsunge sealde, and hi eft
ferdon; and he eft ageaf þa glofe þam þe hi ær ahte.

1 How did the nobleman Æthelbald find his way to Guthlac's
   hermitage?

2 What had Wilfrid done with his gloves? How did Guthlac
   know this?

3 What did they realize had happened when they came out of
   the house?

4 Why did the raven fly away?

5 What did the three men do as soon as they arrived at the
   landing place?

6 Why had they come to the hermitage?

7 What words or phrases are used to describe Guthlac's state of
   mind?

8 Review both raven episodes and make a list of nouns whose
   gender you can identify from the context. Pay careful attention
   to the endings of any definite articles or adjectives that occur
   with the nouns.

17

And bishop Æthelnoth travelled to Rome

This unit will cover:

texts
- *texts from the Anglo-Saxon Chronicle*
- *Old English letters and writs*

grammar
- *adverbs*
- *adverbial phrases*

language and style
- *word order*

vocabulary
- *events in the career of Æthelnoth, archbishop of Canterbury 1020–38*

◀)) **TR 50**

And Æþelnoð biscop for to Rome
And bishop Æthelnoth travelled to Rome

Archbishop Æthelnoth

Æthelnoth was archbishop of Canterbury from 1020 to 1038. Information about his career can be found in a number of charters and annals, including two entries in the D Chronicle which offer some rare biographical details about him.

The following annal, D 1020, tells of events following Cnut's return to England after spending the winter in Denmark. The account here should be compared with the corresponding text of C 1020, in Unit 4.

> D 1020 Her com Cnut cyng eft to Englalande. And þa on Eastron wæs micel gemot æt Cyrenceastre, þa geutlagade man Æþelward ealdorman. And on þisan geare for se cyng and Þurkyl eorl to Assandune, and Wulfstan arcebiscop, and oðre biscopas, and eac abbodas and manege munecas, and gehalgodan þæt mynster æt Assandune. And Æðelnoð munuc, se þe wæs decanus æt Cristes cyrcan, wearð on þam ilcan geare on Idus Nouembris to biscope gehalgod into Cristes cyrcan.

The D annal adds the phrase **and eac abbodas and manege munecas** emphasizing that *abbots and monks* were also involved in the consecration of the church at Assandun (Ashingdon). And in contrast to the C text it reports the consecration of the new archbishop, who happens also to be a monk:

> And Æðelnoð munuc, se þe wæs decanus æt Cristes cyrcan, wearð on þam ilcan geare on Idus Nouembris to biscope gehalgod into Christes cyrcan.
>
> *And the monk Æthelnoth, who was prior at Christ Church, was in the same year, on the ides of November, consecrated as bishop into Christ Church [i.e. consecrated on November 13th as archbishop of Canterbury].*

As various historians writing about the reign of Cnut have shown (see **bibliography**), the fact that Æthelnoth was **munuc** and **decanus** is significant. Following the example set by Winchester and Worcester in the tenth century, Christ Church Canterbury had recently become monastic, i.e. it was run not by cathedral clergy but by monks, on the lines of a Benedictine monastery (see Units 7 and 15).

Insight

Daily business in a monastery was conducted by meetings of the whole community in the monastic Chapter, presided over by the **abbod** *abbot*, or in his absence, by the **profost**, the *provost* or *prior*.

As usual in a Benedictine house, on the death or retirement of an abbot, it was the role of the Chapter to elect a replacement from among the members of their own community, and then to petition the king to ratify their decision. In the twelfth century, a riveting, almost novelistic account of the run-up to such an election at Bury St Edmunds is told by Joscelin of Brakelond, one of the monks of that monastery; his narrative includes the story of how the monks subsequently persuaded the king to accept the candidate of their choice (see **bibliography**).

This is what seems to have happened in 1020: the monks duly elected their new spiritual father, Æthelnoth. But the problem was that in choosing their new abbot the monks also simultaneously chose the new archbishop of Canterbury, whereas previously such an appointment had been made by the king. As revealed in the next document, a letter to Cnut and Emma from Wulfstan archbishop of York, the king agreed to the appointment, for he seems to have sent a declaration to this effect. However, on the next occasion when the see became vacant, he would take greater care to appoint his own man, as we will see.

Grammar

Adverbs

Adjectives describe a noun, whereas a major use of adverbs is to describe the verb, often giving the manner, degree, time or location of the action. Old English adverbs are formed from adjectives by adding -e, e.g. **hraðe** *quickly*; but they frequently end with -**lice** 'leecheh' instead e.g. **eadmodlice** *humbly*, **bliðelice** *happily* and sometimes also with the suffix -**unga**, e.g. **eallunga** *completely*. The -**lic** ending appears on adjectives and adds an **e** to give the adverb; originally the ending derives from a noun **þæt lic** meaning *body* (cf. modern *lychgate*); there is a corresponding adjective **gelic** *like*. The modern adverb ending -*ly*, the adverb *alike*, the adjective *like* and its noun *likeness* all derive from **lic**.

A few adverbs are formed by inflecting the noun. A genitive ending -**es** can turn some nouns into adverbs:

> **dæges and nihtes**
> *by day and by night*

Another conversion of this kind puts select nouns into the dative plural; the resulting word then functions as an adverb: **hwilum** *at times*. An adjective can also become an adverb in the same way: **miclum** ('mitch-lum') *much* or **lytlum** ('lüt-lum') *little*; there is also **furþum** *even*, from the adverb **forþ** *forth*.

Some adverbs are short monosyllabic words which behave rather like pronouns in that they can replace another word or phrase: **þa** *then*, **her** *here*, **þær** *there*.

The adverb **þa** often appears at the beginning of the clause, with the verb in second place:

> **þa geseah he þone broþor sarig**
> [literally] *then saw he the brother sad*

þa frefrode he hine and him to cwæð
[literally] *then consoled he him and said to him*

In the Anglo-Saxon Chronicle clauses starting with **her** tend to follow the same pattern:

her com Cnut cyng eft to Englalande
here came Cnut again to England

But subject–verb order also occurs as in modern English:

her Cnut kyning for ut mid his scypum to Wihtlande
[literally] *here Cnut king travelled out with his ships to Wight*

Insight

Not all adverbs describe or modify the verb; some are sentence modifiers or adjective modifiers; think of the meaning and use of **seoððan** *afterwards* or of **eac** *also*.

Some adverbs are formed from **þær** + preposition: **þæræfter** *after that*, **þærmid** *with that, immediately*.

The adverb **swiþe** from an adjective meaning *strong* is used as the intensifier *very*: **swiþe god** means *very good* while **swiþe arwurðlice** means *very honourably* (see text below).

Adverbs expressing direction or movement towards something include: **hām** *home*, **þider** *to there*, **hider** *to here*, **feorr** *far*, **ūt** *out*, **norð** *northward*, **suð** *southward*. A set of adverbs also express *direction from*: **þonan** *from there*, **heonan** *from here*, **feorran** *from afar*, **utan** *from outside*, **norðan** *from the north*, **suðan** *from the south*.

The adverbial phrase

Adverbs can be one word, as the examples above; alternatively, several words can combine into an adverbial phrase, often with a preposition. So for example in the annal D 1022 below, the adverbial **mid mycclan weorðscype** is used to show how the archbishop was received in Rome *with great honour;* the phrase is very similar in function to the single-word adverb **arwurðlice** *honourably* which occurs later in the same passage. Another adverbial of manner in the same text is **mid his agenum handum** describing how the pope performed the ceremony *with his own hands,* an adverbial phrase roughly corresponding to the modern adverb *personally.*

Because of their structure, these particular adverbials can also be described as prepositional phrases, as in the following table.

preposition	+		adjective	+	noun
mid			mycclan		weorðscype
preposition	**+ pronoun +**		**adjective**	**+**	**noun**
mid	his		agenum		handum
preposition	**+ article +**		**adjective**	**+**	**noun**
on	þam		sylfan		dæge

◄) **TR 50**

Æþelnoð biscop for to Rome
Bishop Æthelnoth travelled to Rome

D 1022 Her Cnut kyning for ut mid his scypum to Wihtlande. And Æþelnoð biscop for to Rome, and wæs þær underfangen mid mycclan weorðscype fram Benedicte þam arwurðan papan, and he mid his agenum handum him pallium on asette, and to arcebiscope swiðe arwurðlice gehalgade and gebletsade on Nonas Octobris, and se arcebiscop sona þærmid mæssan sang on þam sylfan dæge, and syððan þæræfter mid þam sylfan papan arwurðlice gereordade, and eac him seolf þone pallium genam on Sancte Petres weofode, and þa seoððan bliðelice ham to his earde ferde.

to Rome pronounced 'to Roh-meh' (dative after **to**)
wæs underfangen *was received* (**wæs** + past participle of **underfon**)
arwurð *venerable* (**seo ar** *grace, honour* + **wurð** *worthy*)
se weorðscipe *honour*
seo mæsse *mass, communion, the eucharist*
reordian *to feast*
se pallium *ceremonial scarf* (see cultural contexts)
bliðelice *happily* (cf. **blithe**)

Cultural contexts

Travels to Rome

There were many reasons for contacts between England and Rome in the Anglo-Saxon period. For religious reasons, as a city of ancient churches, as the site of St Peter's bishopric and the residence of the head of the western Church, Rome was a magnet for pilgrims, and both king Alfred in the ninth century and king Cnut in the eleventh visited the city. In the year 597 it had been the mission from Rome that had brought about the conversion of the kings of Kent and southern England, and religious, intellectual and cultural contacts continued thereafter.

Insight

From the eighth century there was a custom of paying a religious tax to Rome, called in Old English **Rom-scot** *Rome penny*, and later known as 'Peter's Pence'. This served to support the travellers' hospice especially built to accommodate the many English pilgrims, which came to be known by its Latin name **Schola Saxonum** *the Saxon School*.

Whenever a new archbishop of Canterbury was appointed, it was the custom for him to make the long journey to Rome to receive the pope's blessing and the **pallium**, a kind of scarf or band of white wool with six black crosses on it, which the pope bestowed on the archbishop as a sign of his authority. The archbishops would only wear the pallium on important solemn occasions, such as Christmas, Epiphany and Easter.

Language and style

Word order

The common pattern of word order in Old English is characterized by a sentence from the *Life of Guthlac* (see Unit 16):

sona swá he þa cartan **geseah,** þa **genam** he hig sona
as soon as he saw the parchment, he took it at once

This pattern can be summed up by the following rule:

subordinate clause – verb goes to the end (**geseah**)
main clause – verb comes as second element (**genam**)

In the above annal D 1022, there are two events recorded, Cnut's foray to the Isle of Wight and Æthelnoth's journey to Rome. These two events are recounted in separate sentences, each being given a main-clause word order:

connector + subject	verb	adverbials
(1) Her Cnut kyning	for	ut mid his scypum to Wihtlande
(2a) And Æþelnoð biscop	for	to Rome...

A clause then follows with the same subject, Æthelnoth, with the auxiliary verb in second place and the main verb (the past participle) towards the end, but with a long emphatic prepositional phrase in final position:

(subject) + auxiliary verb + adverb + past participle + final elements				
(2b) and	wæs	þær	underfangen	mid mycclan weorðscype ... papan

The remaining clauses in the annal each begin with the co-ordinating word **and**. Since they all have a main verb, some of them could be analysed as separate sentences, but the position of the verb in each case speaks against this. Although not, strictly speaking, subordinate, these clauses beginning with **and** behave like subordinate clauses in their word order because the verb tends to come towards the end:

subject	other elements	verb	final element
(2c) and he	mid his agenum handum him pallium on	asette,	
(2d) and	to arcebiscope swiðe arwurðlice	gehalgade & gebletsade	on Nonas Octobris

Here the verbs appear at the end or towards the end of the clause, with one emphatic phrase *on the nones of October* in final position. The pattern continues with the new subject *the archbishop* in (2e) and the effect of this is to make the series of clauses (2e)–(2h) effectively subordinate to the main clause (2a), with verbs postponed and the occasional emphatic element (always a prepositional phrase **on + noun**) in final position:

connector	other elements	verb	final element
(2e) and se arcebiscop	sona þærmid mæssan	sang	on þam sylfan dæge
(2f) and	syððan þæræfter mid þam sylfan papan arwurðlice	gereordade	
(2g) and	eac him seolf þone pallium	genam	on Sancte Petres weofode
(2h) and	þa seoððan bliðelice ham to his earde	ferde	

St Alphege

The story of the Translation of St Alphege appears in D 1023. It is a typical account of the veneration of a new saint, whose mortal remains must be honoured by being 'translated' to a more suitable and worthy resting place, which then becomes a place of pilgrimage. A late eleventh-century account in Latin by Osbern of Canterbury tells of trouble at the ceremony, with some Londoners wanting their favourite martyr to remain within the city and clashing with the housecarls or royal guards. Probably there were political reasons for this, at a time when England was ruled by the Danish king Cnut (see Lawson in **bibliography**). But the Old English version in D sets a wholly celebratory tone for the events of the day. With regard to sentence structure, the narrative is longer and more complex than D 1022, with several relative clauses at (1b), (4a) and (4c). Largely, however, it follows a similar style and word order, with *and* clauses usually taking verb-final order but allowing occasional prepositional phrases to follow the verb. Examples are clauses (1d), (2b), (2c), (3b) and (3c). It is, of course, likely that the two adjacent annals D 1022 and D 1023 about Æthelnoth's role as archbishop were written by the same Chronicle author. But on stylistic grounds, arguably, this supposition is supported by the sentence structure.

Her Cnut kyning binnan Lundene on Sancte Paules mynstre
Here king Cnut in London at Saint Paul's

(1a) Her Cnut kyning binnan Lundene on Sancte Paules mynstre sealde fulle leafe Æðelnoðe arcebiscope and Bryhtwine biscope and eallon þam Godes þeowum (1b) þe heom mid wæron (1c) þæt hi moston nyman up of þam byrgene þone arcebiscop Sancte Ælfheah, (1d) and hi þa swa dydon on .vi. Idus Iunii.

se þeow *servant*
nyman *take*
se byrgen *burying place, sepulchre*
dydon *did* (from **dōn**, see Unit 15)

(2a) And se brema cyng and se arcebiscop and leodbiscopas and eorlas and swiðe manege hadode and eac læwede feredon on scype his þone halgan lichaman ofer Temese to Suðgeweorke, (2b) and þær þone halgan martyr þan arcebiscope and his geferum betæhton, (2c) and hi þa mid weorðlican weorode and wynsaman dreame hine to Hrofesceastre feredan.

se brema cyng *the glorious king* (base form of the word is **breme**)
se lichaman *body*
ofer Temese to Suðgeweorce *over the Thames to Southwark*
se gefera *companion*
betæhton from **betæcan** *entrust* 'beTAIchan'
weorðlic *worthy*
se weorod *host, troop*
wynsam (also **wynsum**) *delightful*
se dream *joy*
to Hrofesceastre *to Rochester*
feredan *conveyed* from **ferian**

(3a) Ða on þam þryddan dæge com Imma seo hlæfdie mid hire cynelican bearne Hardacnute, (3b) and hi þa ealle mid mycclan þrymme and blisse and lofsange þone halgan arcebiscop into Cantwarebyri feredon, (3c) and swa wurðlice into Cristes cyrcan brohton on .iii. Idus Iunii.

Imma seo hlæfdie *Emma the Lady*, an honorific title for queen Emma
cynelic *royal*
þæt bearn *child*
se þrymm *glory*
seo bliss *happiness* (also spelt **bliþs**, from **bliþe** *happy*)
se lofsang *song of praise*

(4) Eft syððan on þam eahteoðan dæge, on .xvii. Kalendas
Iulii, Æðelnoð arcebiscop and Ælfsie biscop and Bryhtwine
biscop, and ealle (4a) þa þe mid heom wæron,

(4b) gelogodon Sancte Ælfeages halgan lichaman on
norðhealfe Cristes weofodes, Gode to lofe, and þam halgan
arcebiscope to wurðmynte, and eallon þam to ecere hælðe
(4c) þe his halgan lichoman þær mid estfulre heortan and mid
ealre eadmodnysse dæghwamlice seceað.

(5) God ælmihtig gemiltsie eallum Cristenum mannum þurh
Sancte Ælfeges halgan gegearnunga.

Eadsige

After a long period of service, Æthelnoth was succeeded in 1038
by Eadsige, formerly a chaplain at Cnut's court. It looks as if the
king was determined to have his own man in the archbishopric
eventually, and Eadsige was first of all appointed bishop at
St Martin's for the period 1035–38. During which time he appears
to have acted as Æthelnoth's deputy administrator; for example,

he helped to safeguard Canterbury from attempts by the king's reeve to levy excessive amounts of money on land owned by the cathedral (see text in **Test Yourself (2)** below). In the end, Cnut did make some concessions to the monastic establishment, in that Eadsige duly became a monk before he became archbishop. He held the see from 1038 to 1044, when he stood down for health reasons, but he served a second term as archbishop from 1048 to his death in 1050. It was Eadsige who crowned Edward as king at Easter in 1043 (see Unit 1).

TEST YOURSELF (1)

Reread the text of Anglo-Saxon Chronicle D 1022 and analyse
the use of adverbials (either single-word adverbs or multi-word
phrases); find the following types:

1 four adverbials of manner

2 four adverbials of place or direction

3 four adverbials of time

TEST YOURSELF (2)

Cnut protects the archbishop against the reeve AD 1035
(S 987; Harmer 29)

Translate the following text:

Cnut cyngc gret Eadsige biscop and Ælfstan abbot and Ægelric and
ealle mine þegnas on Cent freondlice. And ic cyþe eow þæt ic wylle
þæt Æþelnoð arcebiscop werige his landare into his bisceoprice nu eal
swa he dyde ær Ægelric wære gerefa and siððan he gerefa wæs forð
oð þis, and ic nelle na geþafian þæt man þam bisceope ænige unlage
beode beo gerefa se þe beo.

18

Archbishop Wulfstan greets king Cnut

This unit will cover:

texts
- *Wulfstan's letter to king Cnut and queen Emma*
- *agreements between archbishop Æthelnoth and Toki*
- *agreements between archbishop Eadsige and Toki*

grammar
- *personal pronouns: first and second person*
- *more on strong adjective endings*

vocabulary
- *the rich variety of the definite article*

◀⁾ **TR 51, 00:11**

Wulfstan arcebiscop gret Cnut cyning
Archbishop Wulfstan greets king Cnut

The MacDurnan Gospels

Now in the archbishop's library as London Lambeth Palace
1370, the MacDurnan gospel book is an attractive pocket-sized
copy of the four gospels in Latin. Written in Ireland, it belonged
to Mael Brigte mac Tornain (Maelbright MacDurnan), abbot of
Iona and 'head of the piety of all Ireland and of the greater part
of Europe' as an Irish chronicle puts it. The book later came into
the possession of Æthelstan, king of England from 924 to 939,
who presented it to Canterbury Cathedral. Here various texts
were added: a Latin poem commemorating the book's illustrious
owners, a letter from Wulfstan to king Cnut and queen Emma, and
two records of an agreement between successive archbishops of
Canterbury and a certain Toki (a name of Scandinavian origin).

The Latin inscription

The Latin poem appears on a blank page after the preface to
Matthew. It is written in a rhythmical style with alliteration
(a favourite English technique) and even contains an Old English
genitive plural ending on the word **Anglosæxna** *of the Anglo-Saxons*
in line three (in correct Latin this should be *Anglosaxonum*).
Try reading out loud, for the rhythmic and alliterative effects:

+ MÆIELBRIÞUS MAC DURNANI
ISTUM TEXTUM PER TRIQUADRUM
DEO DIGNE DOGMATIZAT
+ AST AETHELSTANUS ANGLOSÆXNA
REX ET RECTOR DORVERNENSI
METROPOLI DAT PER ÆVUM.

Mælbright MacDurnan
this text – through the wide world
to the honour of God – proclaims
but Æthelstan, the Anglo-Saxons'
king and ruler, to the Canterbury
metropolitan see, gives it for ever.

Wulfstan arcebiscop gret Cnut cyning
Archbishop Wulfstan greets king Cnut (S 1386)

This letter seems to have been sent to king Cnut and queen Emma shortly after Æthelnoth was appointed as archbishop (see Unit 17); the copy here appears on folio 69b (i.e. 69v) of the MacDurnan Gospels. As you read, study carefully the personal pronouns used in the text (*I, you, he* etc.) and refer to the first part of the **grammar** section below.

🔊 **TR 51, 00:11**

Wulfstan arcebiscop gret Cnut cyning his hlaford and Ælfgyfe þa hlæfdian eadmodlice. And ic cyþe inc leof þæt we habbað gedon swa swa us swutelung fram eow com æt þam biscope Æþelnoþe, þæt we habbað hine nu gebletsod. Nu bidde ic for Godes lufon, and for eallan Godes halgan þæt ge witan on Gode þa mæþe, and on þam halgan hade, þæt he mote beon þære þinga wyrþe þe oþre beforan wæron – Dunstan þe god wæs and mænig oþer – þæt þes mote beon eall swa rihta and gerysna wyrðe, þæt inc byð bam þearflic for Gode, and eac gerysenlic for worolde.

Archbishop Wulfstan greets king Cnut his lord and Ælfgyfu the lady humbly. And I declare to you dear ones [i.e. affectionately] that we have done as the declaration came to us from you concerning bishop Æthelnoth, that we have now blessed him. Now I pray for the love of God and for all God's saints that you may know reverence to God and to the holy office, that he might be worthy of the things which others were before (Dunstan who was good and many another) that this man might be also worthy of rights and honours. So that it will be – for both of you – profitable before God and also honourable before the world.

inc *you both* (see **grammar**)
leof *dear, beloved*
bletsian *to bless*
se halga *saint* (from **halig** *holy*; cf. *All Hallows* i.e. the feast of
   All Saints)
biddan *to pray*
seo mæþ *reverence*
mote *might* (subjunctive of **moste**)
se had *rank, order, status*
gerysna *what is fitting, dignity, honour*
gerysenlic *honourable*
bam, bæm *both* (dative of **begen**; see **grammar**)

Grammar

The personal pronouns *ic* and *ge*

In the accusative and dative cases the pronoun **ic** (pronounced to
rhyme with 'rich') changes to **me** 'may' meaning *me* and *to me*,
whereas **ge**, the plural *you* (pronounced 'yay' to rhyme with 'may'),
changes to **eow**:

> **me** þuhte þæt we bundon sceafas on æcere
> *it seemed **to me** that we were binding sheaves in the field*
> (Unit 6)

> ic cyðe **eow** þæt ic wylle beon hold hlaford (Unit 7)
> *I make known **to you** (i.e. I inform you) that I will be a
> gracious lord*

In the paradigm below, the forms of the first and second person
pronoun are arranged according to their grammatical case (the
usual four cases) and number (singular, dual, or plural); for

convenience, a length mark has been employed to indicate long vowels:

······································

personal pronouns

······································

first person

	singular	dual	plural
	I, me	*we-two, us-two*	*we, us*
nominative	ic	wit	wē
accusative	mē	unc	ūs
genitive	mīn	uncer	ūre
dative	mē	unc	ūs

second person

	you	you-two	you
nominative	þū	git	gē
accusative	þē	inc	ēow
genitive	þīn	incer	ēower
dative	þē	inc	ēow

It is worth reviewing the patterns of pronunciation in the commoner forms: **ic** 'itch', **me** 'may', **þe** 'thay', **we** 'way' and **ge** 'yay', and the long vowels in **us** 'oos', **min** 'meen', **þin** 'theen' and **ure** 'OOruh' and **eower** 'Éo-wer'. The last four pronouns also function as the possessive and survive in modern English as *mine*, *thine*, *our* and *your*.

For examples in use, look at Wulfstan's letter above. The second sentence is particularly rich in personal pronouns, including a switch from **ic** (the writer of the letter) to **we** (who carried out the blessing), and a change from the dual **inc** (you-two, pronounced 'ink') to the general plural **eow**:

·······································

And ic cyþe inc leof
þæt we habbað gedon
swa swa us swutelung fram eow com
æt þam biscope Æþelnoþe,
þæt we habbað hine nu gebletsod.

(Contd)

> *And I declare to you dear ones*
> *that we have done*
> *as the declaration came to us from you*
> *concerning bishop Athelnoth,*
> *that we have now blessed him.*

Wulfstan's choices of pronoun in this letter are open to interpretation. He may have used **ic cyðe inc** and later **inc byð bam** as opening and closing formulas of direct address to the king and lady. But in the middle of the letter he switched to **eow** and **ge** because it was a more natural way of speaking for the main part of his message. Alternatively, he may have switched to **ge** for the main message because the whole court was intended to hear it rather than only the royal couple. In this respect it should be remembered that letters, writs and declarations were almost certainly read out loud before the assembled gathering.

Archbishop Æthelnoth and Toki (S 1464) (from the MacDurnan Gospels, folio 115r)

Her swuteliað on ðisse Cristes bec Æþelnoðes arcebisceopes forword and Tokiges embe þæt land æt Healtune; þæt wæs þæt Tokig com to Hrisbeorgan to ðam arcebisceope syððan Æðelflæd his wif forðfaren wæs, and cydde him Wulfnoðes cwyde þæt he þæt land becweden hæfde into Cristes cyrcean æfter his dæge and his wifes, and bæd þone arcebisceop þæt he þæt land habban moste his dæg, and æfter his dæge þæt hit lage into Cristes cyrcean mid eallum þingum þe he þæron getilian mihte unbesacen, and cwæð þæt he wolde þam bisceop þances kepan and his mannum, and se arcebisceop him þæs tiðude, and sæde þæt he riht wið hine gedon hæfde þæt he sylf him for þam cwyde secgean wolde, þeh he hit ær ful georne wiste. And ðises wæs to gewitnysse Æþelstan æt Bleddehlæwe, and Leofwine his sunu, and Leofric æt Eaningadene, and feala oðra godra cnihta, þeh we hi ealle ne nemnon, and eall ðæs arcebiscopes hired, ge gehadude ge læwede.

bec 'baytch' dative singular of **seo boc** *book*
æt Healtune *at Halton* (Buckinghamshire)
to Hrisbeorgan *to Risborough* (Monks Risborough, Buckinghamshire)
cydde from **cyðan** *to proclaim*
se cwyde *will* (from **cweðan** *to speak*)
becweðan *to bequeath, leave in a will*
bæd *asked* from **biddan** *to ask, pray* **(bitt, bæd, bædon, gebeden)**
moste *be allowed*
lage past subjunctive from **licgan** *to lie* **(lið, læg, lægon, gelegen)**
getilian *to till, cultivate, produce*
þances kepan *to show gratitude*
kepan = cepan *to show, observe*
se arcebiscop him þæs tiðude *the archbishop granted him this*
tiðian *to permit, grant* (followed by dative of the person and genitive of the thing granted)
secgean = secgan *say*
þeh = þeah *although*
ær *previously*
ær… wiste *had known*
ful georne *perfectly well*
æt Bleddehlæwe *at Bledlow*
æt Eaningadene (location unidentified)
feala *many*

QUICK VOCAB

Archbishop Eadsige and Toki (S 1466) (from the MacDurnan Gospels, folio 114r)

+ Eadsige arcebiscop cyþ on ðisse Cristes bec þæt Tokig sende to me to Hrisbeorgan his twegen cnihtas oðor hatte Seaxa oðor hatte Leofwine, and bæd me þæt þa forword moston standan þe Æðelnoð arcebishop and he geworht hæfdon ymbe þæt land æt Healtune þæt he his bruce his dæg, and eode æfter his dæge into cristes cyricean and ic him ðæs tiðude on manegra godra manna gewitnysse and ealles mines hiredes ge gehadudra ge læwedra.

Language and style

The rich variety of the definite article

King Alfred's chronicler

Take two versions of the Chronicle and you will find that for any
common annal the two texts are not spelled exactly the same in
each case. During Alfred's war with the Danes in the ninth century,
for example, the Chronicle reports on the movements of the Danish
army as follows:

*A 892 Here in this year the great army which we spoke about
earlier travelled back from the East Kingdom (East Francia) to
Boulogne, and there they were provided with ships...*

The original text of the A Chronicle scribe can be compared with
that of the later scribe who copied the annal into the D Chronicle:

A 892 Her on þysum geare for se micla here þe we gefyrn ymbe
spræcon eft of þæm eastrice westweard to Bunnan, & þær wurdon
gescipode...

D 893 Her on þyssum geare for se mycla here þe we fyrn ær ymbe
spræcon eft of þam eastrice westweard to Bunan, & þær wurdon
gescipude...

As further perusal of the whole passage in the two versions would
show, the later writer consistently prefers to write þam where the
A scribe has þæm. This is one kind of scribal variation, probably
based on the house style of a particular scriptorium that was in
operation at the time of writing.

Byrhtferth

Another kind of variation occurs in a passage from Byrhtferth's
Handbook (I.i.92), where þæne and its variant þone (masculine

accusative) appear in close proximity even in the same sentence. Describing the creation of the heavens Byrhtferth writes:

God... gesceop sunnan and monan and tungla and steorran, and he gesette twegen sunnstedas, **þæne** ænne on .xii. kalendas Ianuarii and **þone** oþerne on .xii. kalendas Iulii.

God created sun and moon and planets and stars, and he established two solstices, the one on the twelfth of the kalends of January, the other on the twelfth of the kalends of July.

The relevant part of this sentence is structured as follows:

nominative	verb	accusative
God	gesceop	sunstedas: **þæne** ænne... **þone** oþerne
God	*created*	*solstices: the one... the other*

There may be several reasons for the contrast between the preferred form þæne and the (in this text) less frequent þone. But looking at the vowels in þæne ænne... þone oþerne (æ... æ, o... o) one might speculate that Byrhtferth – or the scribe who copied the text – enjoyed the way the sounds in each phrase echoed from one word to the next.

The Lady Emma

A further reason for spelling variation is the influence of the spoken language, particularly the way the inflected endings on Old English words could be pronounced less distinctly in the eleventh century. So a fairly common variant in some texts is þan instead of þam. This almost certainly reflects the pronunciation. The dative þan occurs in the following short document of king Edward's reign (S 1229), also written for safekeeping in a de-luxe gospel book. Here Ælfgyfu the Lady (Emma) makes a declaration about a property transaction that took place during the reign of her husband Cnut:

ælfgyfu seo hlæfdige, Eadweardes cyninges modor,
geærndede æt Cnute cyninge minum hlaforde þæt land æt
Niwantune and þæt þærto hyrð into Cristes cyrcean, þa
Ælfric se þegen hit hæfde forworht þan cyninge to handan.
And se cyning hit geaf þa into Cristes cyrcean þan hirede to
fosterlande for uncre beigra sawle.

*I Ælfgyfu the lady, king Edward's mother, acquired from king
Cnut my lord the land at Newington and what pertains to it
for Christ Church, when Ælfric the thegn had forfeited it to the
king. And the king gave it to Christ Church for the community
to use as fosterland, for the benefit of both our souls.*

To understand this passage it must be remembered that one legal
sanction for serious crime was to deprive a man of his property,
which then was taken over by the monarch. This had occurred in
the case of a certain Ælfric, for crimes unspecified, or in Emma's
words:

þa Ælfric se þegen hit hæfde forworht þan cyninge to handan
*when Ælfric the thegn had forfeited it to the king into (his)
hands*

Here the idiomatic use of the definite article **þan** (dative) has
possessive meaning **þan cyninge to handan** *into the king's
hands*.

The forfeiture was not the end of the story. Not one to leave the
matter entirely in the king's hands, Emma intervened with the
request that the property be donated to Christ Church, the cathedral
abbey in Canterbury, to be used as **fosterland** (**fostorland**), i.e. land
that is granted to the recipients to use for food.

From the point of view of structure, the final sentence could be broken down as follows:

subject	object	verb	adverbs: of time
se cyning	hit	geaf	þa

adverbs: of place	of purpose	of reason
into Cristes cyrcean	þan hirede to fosterlande	for uncre beigra sawle

The adverbial of purpose (which in classic Old English would have been þam hirede to fosterlande) could be explained as another 'possessive' use of the dative definite article þan, but meaning literally to *the community for fosterland*.

Grammar

More on strong adjective endings

In the table or paradigm below, the strong endings are presented for the adjective gōd *good* (pronounced 'goad' and sometimes written by the scribes as gód):

	masculine	neuter	feminine	
nominative singular	gōd	gōd	gōdu	good
accusative	gōdne	gōod	gōde	good
genitive	gōdes	gōdes	gōdre	of good
dative	gōdum	gōdum	gōdre	to good
nominative plural	gōde	gōdu	gōda	good
accusative	gōde	gōdu	gōda	good
genitive	gōdra	gōdra	gōdra	of good
dative	gōdum	gōdum	gōdum	to good

Variants include nominative and accusative plural in -e in all genders; in later Old English the -um ending is often replaced by the form -an. Possessive adjectives such as min and þin decline like god. The adjectives bisig and micel are uninflected in the nominative singular feminine, and nominative and accusative plural.

Reading

Cnut gives Æthelnoth his legal powers
(S 986; Harmer 28)

In the following text, from folio 114b of the MacDurnan Gospels, Cnut gives to Æthelnoth sacu and socn or *sake and soke*, the right to hold a court and exact fines, especially for such misdemeanours as griðbryce *breach of sanctuary*, hamsocn *attacking a man in his own home*, forsteall *ambush and assault*. He also grants him the right to *fine thieves* caught in his jurisdiction, i.e. infangene-þeof, and to exact penalties for flymena fyrmð the *harbouring of fugitives* (flymena: genitive plural of flyma *fugitive*).

> Cnut cyncg gret ealle mine biscopas and mine eorlas and mine gerefan on ælcere scire þe Æþelnoð arcebiscop and se hired æt Cristes cyrcean land inne habbað freondlice. And ic cyðe eow þæt ic hæbbe geunnen him þæt he beo his saca and socne wyrðe and griðbryces and hamsocne and forstealles and infangenes þeofes and flymena fyrmðe ofer his agene menn binnan byrig and butan and ofer Cristes cyrcean and ofer swa feala þegna swa ic him to lætan hæbbe. And ic nelle þæt ænig mann aht þær on teo buton he and his wicneras for þam ic hæbbe Criste þas gerihta forgyfen minre sawle to ecere alysednesse, and ic nelle þæt æfre ænig mann þis abrece be minum freondscipe.

se gerefa *reeve*

seo sacu *conflict, lawsuit, contention*

seo sōcn *seeking, visit, attack; right to take fines; district where this right holds sway*

þæt grið *truce, protection, sanctuary*

se forsteall, foresteall *hindrance, assault, ambush*

se þeof *thief*

infangene from **fon** *to seize* (**fēhð, fēng, fēngon, ge-fangen**)

seo fyrmð *harbouring*

lætan also spelled **læten** *granted* (**lætan, lætt, lēt, læten**)

ic nelle *I do not want*

aht *anything*

þær on teo *take from it* **tēon** *to take, pull* (**tȳhð, tēah, tugon, togen**)

se wicnere *bailiff, officer*

seo sāwol, sāwel *soul* (dative **sawle**)

seo ālȳ sednes *redemption* (**ālīesan** *release*)

abrece *break* present subjunctive of **ābrecan** (**-bricð, bræc, bræcon, brocen**)

se freondscipe *friendship*

TEST YOURSELF

1 In the above reading text, find and translate phrases containing strong adjectival endings, e.g. **on ælcere scire** *in every shire*.

2 Find phrases in the study texts meaning:
   a many other retainers
   b with the witnessing of many good men
   c after his lifetime
   d with all things
   e in this gospel book
   f I inform you both

19

How Wynflæd summoned her witnesses

This unit will cover:

texts
- *the lawsuit Wynflæd v. Leofwine*
- *extract from King Alfred's Boethius*
- *from Chronicle C 1006: the Vikings at Cwichelm's Barrow*

grammar
- *reported speech*
- *modal verbs* (can, could, would, should, etc.)

writing
- *the Tironian* nota

◀ TR 53

Hu Wynflæd gelædde hyre gewitnesse
How Wynflæd summoned her witnesses

Wynflæd

The document we will consider in this unit provides a series of snapshots from a significant episode in a woman's life (S 1454 in Sawyer's catalogue and no. 66 in Robertson's *Anglo-Saxon Charters*). Recorded as a **swutulung** or *declaration*, it tells how

Wynflæd defended herself before the law against the man Leofwine, who seized some disputed land from her in the years 990–92, during the reign of Æthelred. The dispute concerned two estates in Berkshire, which had belonged originally to a certain Ælfric (a common name at the time – see below). The Ælfric of the dispute apparently gave Hagbourne and Bradfield to Wynflæd in return for an estate in Buckinghamshire. But Leofwine (who must be Ælfric's son) questions this during the proceedings of the court, perhaps because he is worried about some gold and silver belonging to his father which was now allegedly in Wynflæd's possession. How she may have acquired it is not stated. Did Leofwine also pay her some money? Or was the gold and silver somehow left on the property itself? Apart from the royal treasury, there were few places where money could be deposited safely, and it was customary to provide for the future by concealing stores of silver coin as treasure hoard. Perhaps this money had been hidden away and so had remained on the two estates after the transaction.

The Tironian *nota*

In the text, note the use of the symbol 7. This is known as the Tironian *nota* after the Roman writer M. Tullius Tiro (assistant to the famous orator Cicero), who developed the form of shorthand from which it was taken. The sign 7 represents the word **and** (sometimes also **ond**), which quite simply means *and*; most introductory textbooks of Old English expand this abbreviation for clarity's sake, but the *nota* is very common in the manuscripts and standard editions, and it is worth familiarizing yourself with its use, for it makes a difference to the appearance of the page, and perhaps to the way it was read. The Tironian *nota* certainly prevents the superfluous writing out of the word **and**; arguably also, it served as a kind of supplementary punctuation mark to distinguish items in lists.

◀) TR 53

Hu Wynflæd gelædde hyre gewitnesse
How Wynflæd summoned her witnesses (S 1454)

Her cyþ on þysum gewrite hu Wynflæd gelædde hyre
gewitnesse æt Wulfamere beforan Æþelrede cyninge: þæt
wæs þonne Sigeric arcebiscop 7 Ordbyrht biscop 7 Ælfric
ealderman 7 Ælfþryþ þæs cyninges modor, þæt hi wæron
ealle to gewitnesse þæt Ælfric sealde Wynflæde þæt land æt
Hacceburnan 7 æt Bradanfelda ongean þæt land æt Deccet.
Þa sende se cyning þær rihte be þam arcebiscope 7 be þam þe
þær mid him to gewitnesse wæron to Leofwine 7 cyþdon
him þis. Þa nolde he butan hit man sceote to scirgemote. Þa
dyde man swa.

◀ TR 54

Þa sende se cyning be Æluere abbude his insegel
Then the king sent his seal by abbot Ælfhere

Þa sende se cyning be Æluere abbude his insegel to þam
gemote æt Cwicelmeshlæwe 7 grette ealle þa witan þe þær
gesomnode wæron: þæt wæs Æþelsige biscop 7 Æscwig
biscop 7 Ælfric abbud 7 eal sio scir 7 bæd 7 het þæt hi
scioldon Wynflæde 7 Leofwine swa rihtlice geseman swa
him æfre rihtlicost þuhte. And Sigeric arcebiscop sende his

(Contd)

swutelunga þærto 7 Ordbyrht biscop his. Þa getæhte man
Wynflæde þæt hio moste hit hyre geahnian; þa gelædde hio
þa ahnunga mid Ælfþryþe fultume þæs cyninges modor: þæt
is þonne ærest Wulfgar abbud 7 Wulfstan priost 7 Æfic þara
æþelinga discsten 7 Eadwine 7 Eadelm 7 Ælfelm 7 Ælfwine 7
Ælfweard 7 Eadwold 7 Eadric 7 Ælfgar 7 Eadgyfu abbudisse
7 Liofrun abbudisse 7 Æþelhild 7 Eadgyfu æt Leofecanoran
7 hyre swustor 7 hyre dohtor, 7 Ælfgyfu 7 hyre dohtor 7
Wulfwyn 7 Æþelgyfu 7 Ælfwaru 7 Ælfgyfu 7 Æþelflæd 7
menig god þegen 7 god wif þe we ealle atellan ne magon þæt
[þær] forþcom eal se fulla ge on werum ge on wifum.

Cultural contexts

Names in the document

Apart from king Æthelred and his mother Ælfthryth, the most
important figure in the list of witnesses is Sigeric, archbishop of
Canterbury from 990 to 995. Sigeric is known to have been a
patron of religious literature and actively involved in politics,

particularly (as Chronicle accounts reveal) in devising peaceful ways of dealing with the Viking threat by buying off the invaders with tribute.

The name Ælfric ('Alfritch') was common in this period. Another man of the same name witnesses the first stage of the dispute; this Ælfric – the ealdorman of Hampshire – features, chiefly for his notorious treachery, in the dramatic Anglo-Saxon Chronicle accounts of the 990s and early 1000s. Two important churchmen of the time also shared the name Ælfric; one was to be consecrated as archbishop of Canterbury in 996 as archbishop Sigeric's successor. The other Ælfric, a monk and priest who lived at Cerne Abbas in Dorset, was the most prolific writer of the period. He composed the first volume of his renowned *Catholic Homilies* in the period 990–92 and sent a copy with a dedicatory preface to archbishop Sigeric.

Document S 1454 is remarkable for the number of women's names it contains.

Insight

Wynflæd was able to count on the assistance of **Ælfþryþ þæs cyninges modor**, 'Ælf-thryth thes kininges mo-dor', i.e. the king's mother, a powerful force in the early years of Æthelred's reign; this probably helped her to muster a strong contingent of female witnesses in support of her case.

The names are the typical dithematic ones consisting of two parts (as discussed in Unit 1), with the common naming elements **Wyn-** *joy*, **Ælf-** *elf*, **Ead-** *blessed*, **Liof-** *dear*, **Æþel-** *noble* and **Wulf-** *wolf* for the first part of the name and **-flæd** *beauty*, **-þryþ** *power*, **-gyfu** *gift* and **-run** *counsel* for the second part of the name, as well as the perhaps more surprising **-hild** *battle* and **-waru** *protection*. Many of these elements were still productive and meaningful words in their own right and reflect something of the values of the parents who so named their children.

The use of particular names can also reveal family connections. As we saw in Unit 1, there were many kingly names beginning

Ead- in the tenth century, and children sometimes shared one of their name elements with a parent. St Wulfstan, godson of archbishop Wulfstan, was born about this time (1008) but was not necessarily named after his baptismal sponsor, since his father was called Æthelstan and his mother Wulfgifu; as the Latin *Life of St Wulfstan* puts it, in the translation by M. Winterbottom and R. Thomson:

He was given the name Wulfstan, made up of the first part of his mother's and the second of his father's. The child had fair hopes, and fair too the omen which gave him a name taken from both parents, considering that he was destined to pour into himself the sanctity of both, and perhaps to surpass it beyond all comparison.

Oath helping

The so-called **oath helping** was a common legal practice in many early medieval societies. It required that a plaintiff in a dispute should gather together a number of supporters who then swore to his or her good character. This is what seems to be happening in the case of Wynflæd's lawsuit; there is a distinction between witnessing, i.e. to establish her **ontalu** *claim*, and oath helping, i.e. to act as **ahnung** *proof of ownership*. First, Wynflæd gathers her witnesses (archbishop Sigeric, bishop Ordbryht, ealdorman Ælfric and the dowager Ælfthryth), who all witness to the fact of the earlier land transaction. Next, Wynflæd summons her character witnesses (the longer list of names in the second paragraph), **eal se fulla ge on werum ge on wifum** *all the plenitude*, as the text states, *of both men and women*, who are all prepared to undertake the oath helping.

....

◀) TR 55

Þa cwædon þa witan þe þær wæron
Then the counsellors who were there said

Þa cwædon þa witan þe þær wæron þæt betere wære þæt man
þene aþ aweg lete þonne hine man sealde, forþan þær syþþan
nan freondscype nære 7 man wolde biddan þæs reaflaces þæt

he hit sciolde agyfan 7 forgyldan 7 þam cyninge his wer. Þa
let he þone aþ aweg 7 sealde Æþelsige biscope unbesacen land
on hand þæt he þanon forð syþþan þæron ne spræce.

[This part of the text is translated in the section on **reported
speech**, below.]

wære *was, would be* (subjunctive form of **wæs** *was*)
þene = þæne, þone
se āþ *oath, judicial swearing* 'ahth'
lete subjunctive of **lǣtan** *let, leave* (**lǣtt, lēt, lēton, lǣten**)
aþ aweg lǣtan *dispense with the oath*
aþ sellan *give (i.e. swear) an oath*
forþan *because*
nære *would not be* from **ne** + **wære** (subjunctive of **wæs**)
þær syþþan nan freondscype nære *there would not be any
  friendship afterwards*
biddan *ask, demand* (with genitive)
þæt rēaflāc *robbery*
agyfan *to give up*
forgyldan *to compensate* (e.g. for loss of income from rents)
wer = wergild *legal compensation* (see Unit 7)
unbesacen *undisputed*
þæt *so that*
þanon forð *thenceforth, from then on*
spræce *lay claim* to (legal term) subjunctive of **sprecan** *speak*

QUICK VOCAB

◀》 **TR 56**

Þa tæhte man hyre þæt hio sciolde bringan his fæder gold 7
siolfor
*Then they told her that she should bring his father's gold and
silver*

Þa tæhte man hyre þæt hio sciolde bringan his fæder gold 7
siolfor eal Þæt hio hæfde, þa dyde hio swa hio dorste hyre
aþe gebiorgan. Þa næs he þagyt on þam gehealden butan hio
(Contd)

sceolde swerian þæt his æhta Þær ealle wæron. Þa cwæþ hio
þæt hio ne mihte hyre dæles ne he his.

And þyses wæs Ælfgar þæs cyninges gerefa to gewitnesse
7 Byrhtric, 7 Leofric æt Hwitecyrcan, 7 menig god man
toeacan him.

Grammar

Reported speech in the subjunctive

The 'conjectural subjunctive'

Reported speech, otherwise known as indirect speech or indirect
discourse, is a grammatical term for dialogue which is reported
indirectly by verbs of saying and speaking. In modern English, the
direct utterance 'I am well' can be reported indirectly by a sentence
such as 'he said that he was well'. Here the present tense verb *is*
becomes past tense *was*. In similar contexts in Old English, instead
of a change of tense, the verb goes into the subjunctive mood. In
the Wynflæd dispute for example the counsellors' spoken decision
is reported in the subjunctive:

þa <u>cwædon</u> þa witan þe þær <u>wæron</u> þæt betere **wære** þæt
man þene aþ **aweg lete** þonne hine man **sealde**, forþan

þær syþþan nan freondscype **nære**, 7 man **wolde** biddan
þæs reaflaces þæt he hit **sciolde** agyfan 7 forgyldan, 7 þam
cyninge his wer.

Then the counsellors who were there said that it was better that
one should dispense with the oath than give it because there
would not be any friendship afterwards (between them) and
people would ask of the stolen property that he should return it
and pay compensation for it, and pay the king his wergild.

The verbs in the subjunctive in this passage are marked in bold and
those in the indicative are underlined. It will be seen that the basic
principle of the 'subjunctive as conjecture' (see Unit 13) applies
also to reported speech. The facts of the narrative – that is, what
was done – are given in the indicative, while the ephemeral words –
what was said – are reported in the subjunctive. Particularly
distinctive are the past subjunctive forms **nære**, which corresponds
to the past indicative næs, and **lete**, which corresponds to the
normal past let, as seen in the subsequent sentence:

Þa let he þone aþ aweg, 7 sealde Æþelsige biscope unbesacen land
on hand þæt he þanon forð syþþan þæron ne **spræce**.

Then he dispensed with the oath, and gave the land undisputed
into the hands of bishop Æthelsige (promising) that thenceforth
thereafter he would make no other claim to it.

The subjunctive **spræce** (equivalent to indicative spræc) in the
phrase **þæron ne spræce** is here translated as *would make no other*
claim to it; it expresses conjecture and anticipation, and as reported
speech it implies that this is the substance of the words Leofwine
used when he promised not to lay claim to the land thereafter.

Shortcomings of the subjunctive

It will be seen in the two sentences just quoted that **sealde** *gave*
has the same form in both subjunctive and indicative. To see how
this happens it is worth reviewing verb conjugation, taking the 3rd
person singular and plural of **sellan** *to give* and **sprecan** *to speak*:

	weak	strong
present indicative	he selð, hi sellað	he spricð, hi sprecað
present subjunctive	he selle, hi sellen	he sprece, hi sprecen

	weak	strong
past indicative	he sealde, hi sealdon	he spræc, hi spræcon
past subjunctive	he sealde, hi sealden	he spræce, hi spræcen

Comparing tenses, it can be said that the subjunctive is most
distinctive in the present tense because of its -e or -en ending, which
contrasts with the indicative 'th' sound in its endings -ð or -að. In the
past, it is the strong verb which has the most distinctive subjunctive
(**spræce**) while the weak verb cannot easily distinguish the two moods.

Modal verbs

Modal verbs express the idea of volition, obligation, necessity. The
main group includes **cann** *know*, **dearr** *dare*, **mæg** *can*, **mót** *must*,
sceal *must*, **þearf** *need*. They are known in Old English grammar
as preterite present verbs, preterite being the alternative name for
the past tense. The distinguishing feature is that in the present tense
these verbs resemble past tenses of strong verbs in their form.

modal verb	strong verb (class III)
present tense	**past tense (preterite)**
ic cann *I know*	**ic sang** *I sang*
þu cannst *you know*	**þu sunge** *you sang*
he cann *he knows*	**he sang** *he sang*
hi cunnon *they know*	**hi sungon** *they sang*

The historical development of these verbs is an interesting case of
adaptation. Because of the past tense form but present tense meaning,
these verbs had to create new past tenses, and the solution was to use

a weak (consonantal) verb form, so that the past tense of **ic cann** is **ic cuðe** *I knew* and the plural form is **we cuðon** *we knew*.

The two verbs *sceal* **and** *mæg* **contrasted with** *wille* **want**
The modal verbs **sceal** and **mæg** are preterite present verbs. An exception to this pattern is **willan** *to want*; its forms are closer to those of an ordinary weak verb. For example:

cyning **sceal** rice healdan (Unit 2)

a king must rule a country

Ymbe þa feower timan we **wyllað** cyðan iungum preostum ma þinga, þæt **hig magon** þe ranclicor þas þing heora clericum geswutelian (Unit 5) *About the four seasons we wish to proclaim to young priests more things, so that they can explain the more boldly these things to their clerics.*

present indicative

ic sceal *I must*	**ic mæg** *I can*	**ic wille** *I want*
þu scealt *you must*	**þu meaht** *you can*	**þu wilt** *you want*
heo sceal *she must*	**heo mæg** *she can*	**heo wile** *she wants*
we sculon *we must*	**we magon** *we can*	**we willað** *we want*

past indicative

ic sciolde *I had to*	**ic mihte** *I could*	**ic wolde** *I wanted*
þu scioldest	**þu mihtest**	**þu woldest**
we scioldon	**we mihton**	**we woldon**

Other irregular verbs you should recognize are:

ic cann, we cunnon *know*	**ic cuðe** *I knew*
ic ann, we unnon *grant*	**ic uðe** *I granted*
ic þearf, we þurfon *need*	**ic þorfte** *I needed*
ic dearr, we durron *dare*	**ic dorste** *I dared*
ic mot, we moton *am-are allowed*	**ic mōste** *I was allowed*

Cultural contexts

Ancient barrows and mounds

Taplow

One of the ancient features of the landscape recorded in Old English place names is the barrows and burial mounds of the period. Taplow in Buckinghamshire, for instance, was the site of an Anglo-Saxon burial, probably of the very man, Tappa, after whom the mound was named. Like the spectacular burial goods of the nowadays better known Sutton Hoo, Tappa's mound was richly furnished with weapons and metalwork. But as well as the early Saxon burials, there were older mounds and prehistoric features and these also tended to become associated with figures of Old English legend and history.

Sites along the Ridgeway

In Berkshire, for instance, there is the old green road known as the Ridgeway. As its name suggests this is a long high ridge; the bedrock is chalk, well drained and hence a good surface underfoot. It has been a highway since prehistoric times, with numerous archaeological sites along its route, as the 1:50 000 map for Newbury and Wantage testifies (Ordnance Survey sheet 174). Beginning south of Swindon at the earthwork of Liddington Castle, travellers on foot follow the high ground eastwards along Æscesdune or Ashdown, site of Alfred's pitched battle against the Danes in 871. As the Chronicle put it: **ond þæs ymb .iiii. niht gefeaht Æþered cyning 7 Ælfred his broþur wiþ alne þone here on Æcesdune,** *and after four nights king Æthelred and his brother Ælfred fought with all the Viking army at Ashdown.*

Passing further eastwards along the ridge you come first to Wayland's Smithy, a chambered long cairn looking northwards to present-day Ashbury and Compton Beauchamp, then to the earthwork of Uffington Castle and the famous White Horse, a leaping figure of chalk cut out of the turf on the north-facing slope.

From here the route continues eastwards to a large earthwork ring at Segsbury Down just south of Wantage, birthplace of king Alfred. The Ridgeway then passes various mounds and other sites such as Scutchamer Knob and Grim's Ditch before dividing near the site of an old Roman temple and making for the Thames at Streatley by the southerly route and the Thames at Cholsey by the northerly path.

Cwichelm's Low

Several of these sites must have been known in Anglo-Saxon times. Wayland's Smithy is a prehistoric monument to which the Old English name Welund was attached – named after the legendary Germanic blacksmith who features briefly in the Old English version of the *Consolation of Philosophy* and in the poem *Deor* of the Exeter Book. To the east is the mound now called Scutchamer Knob near the village of East Hendred. At a high point on the ridge, and now surrounded by trees, this barrow still commands a wide view of the surrounding countryside. In Old English texts this landmark was known as **Cwichelmeshlæw** or Cwichelm's Barrow after an early West Saxon king; in the tenth century it served as a meeting place for the shire assembly, presumably because of its ancient associations.

Reading

The Old English Boethius on Wayland Smith

Hwæt synt nu þæs foremeran þæs wisan goldsmiðes ban Welondes? Forði ic cwæð 'þæs wisan' forþy þam cræftegan ne mæg næfre his cræft losigan, ne hine mon ne mæg þonne eð on him geniman ðe mon mæg þa sunnan awendan of hire stede. Hwær synt nu þæs Welondes ban, oððe hwa wat nu hwær hi wæron?

(*Alfred's Boethius,* ed. Sedgefield, p. 46)
(*Contd*)

*What became of the bones of Welund the famous wise
goldsmith? The reason I say 'the wise' is that you cannot ever
deprive the artist of his art; nor could you deprive him of it
any more easily than you could turn the sun from its track.
Where now are the bones of Wayland, or who knows now
where they were?*

Cwichelm's Barrow and the Vikings

Þa hit winterlæhte, þa ferde seo fyrd ham. 7 se here com þa
ofer þa Sancte Martines mæssan to his friðstole Wihtlande
7 tylode him þær æghwær þæs ðe hi behofedon, 7 þa to
ðam middan wintran eodan him to heora gearwan feorme
ut þuruh Hamtunscire into Bearrucscire to Readingon, 7 hi
a dydon heora ealdan gewunan, atendon hiora herebeacen
swa hi ferdon. Wendon þa to Wealingaforda and þæt eall
forswældon, 7 wæron him þa ane niht æt Ceolesige, 7
wendon him þa andlang Æscesdune to Cwicelmeshlæwe, 7
þær onbidedon beotra gylpa, forðon oft man cwæþ, gif hi
Cwicelmeshlæw gesohton, þæt hi næfre to sæ gan ne scoldon,
wendon him þa oðres weges hamwerd. Þa wæs ðær fyrd
gesomnod æt Cynetan, 7 hi þær togædere fengon, 7 sona þæt
wered on fleame gebrohton 7 syþþan hiora herehyþe to sæ
feredan, ac þær mihton geseon Wincester leode rancne here 7
unearhne ða hi be hiora gate to sæ eodon, 7 mete 7 madmas
ofer .l. mila him fram sæ fetton.

(from annal C 1006 of the Anglo-Saxon Chronicle)

*When winter came the national levy went home. And the
Viking army came then at St Martin's Mass to its refuge
on the Isle of Wight, and acquired there what it needed,
and then at Midwinter they went to their ready feast out
through Hampshire into Berkshire to Reading. And they
practised their old custom and lighted their alarm beacons
as they travelled. They came to Wallingford and burned it
all, and were then one night at Cholsey, and so moved along*

Ashdown to Cwichelm's Barrow. There they awaited the [fulfilment of the] boasts (because it was often said that if they reached Cwichelm's Barrow, they would never get back to the sea) and returned home by a different route. By this time the national levy was assembled at Kennet, and they came together, and at once they put the levy to flight and afterwards transported their plunder to the sea. So there the people of Winchester could see the proud bold army as they passed their gates towards the sea, and they had taken food and money from fifty miles distance from the sea.

Wordhoard

Wynflæd's wardrobe

In a tenth-century will drawn up by a certain Wynflæd, although perhaps not by the same lady as the winner of the legal dispute, her best items of clothing and jewellery are carefully described. Such documents are a rich source for the vocabulary of women's lives, which would not otherwise be well documented in the period. The mention of dark (undyed woollen) garments suggests the kind of clothing worn for religious occasions (see G. Owen-Crocker in the **bibliography**):

hyra bestan dunnan tunecan *her best brownish tunic*
hyre blacena tunecena *(one) of her black tunics*
hyre ealdan gewiredan preon *her antique filigree brooch*

TEST YOURSELF (1)

Questions on the study text

1 What happened at Woolmer?

2 How did Leofwine react to the message from the king?

3 Did the king attend the meeting at Cwichelm's Barrow?

4 Why did Leofwine dispense with the oath?

5 What was Wynflæd required to do at the settlement of the dispute?

TEST YOURSELF (2)

1 Read through the Wynflæd v. Leofwine narrative again and identify one more verb (other than those verbs discussed in the grammar section) which is unambiguously in the subjunctive both in its form and function in the sentence. Translate the sentence.

2 Are there any verbs in the passage which could be either indicative or subjunctive according to their form and their use in the sentence? In each case translate the clause or sentence in question. What helps the reader to decide which mood is intended?

20

Act like thegns, and deliver my message to the assembly

This unit will cover:

texts
- **the Herefordshire Dispute**
- **Wulfstan's Promotion Law**
- **extract from** The Battle of Maldon

manuscripts
- **the Old English Illustrated Hexateuch**
- **reading Old English script**
- **word and image**

vocabulary
- **traditional poetic words**
- **innovations in eleventh-century English**
- **Old Norse words in the language**
- **French influence**

◀️ **TR 57**

> Doð þegnlice, and wel abeodað mine ærende to þam gemote
> *Act like thegns, and deliver my message to the assembly*

Be Cnutes dæge cinges *In the time of king Cnut*

In the latter half of the reign of king Cnut, a shire assembly (**scirgemot**) gathered at Ailnothstan (now Aylton) in Herefordshire, presided over by the local bishop Athelstan, and attended by **ealle þa þegnas on Herefordscire**. Its purpose was to hear the pleading of a lawsuit by one Eadwine son of Enneawn. The following is the text (S 1462).

🔊 **TR 57, 00:13**

Be Cnutes dæge cinges *In the time of king Cnut*

Her swutelað on þissum gewrite þæt an scirgemot sæt æt Ægelnoðesstane be Cnutes dæge cinges. Þær sæton Æðelstan biscop, and Ranig ealdorman, and Edwine þæs ealdormannes sunu, and Leofwine Wulsiges sunu, and Ðurcil Hwita. And Tofig Pruda com þær on þæs cinges ærende. And þær wæs Bryning scirgerefa, and Ægelgeard æt Frome, and Leofwine æt Frome and Godric æt Stoce and ealle þa þegnas on Herefordscire. Ða com þær farende to þam gemote Edwine Enneawnes sunu, and spæc þær on his agene modor æfter sumon dæle landes, þæt wæs Weolintun and Cyrdesleah. Ða acsode þe bisceop hwa sceolde andswerian for his moder. Ða andsweorode Ðurcil Hwita and sæde þæt he sceolde, gif he þa talu cuðe. Þa he ða talu na ne cuðe, ða sceawode man þreo þegnas of þam gemote ðær þær heo wæs – and þæt wæs æt Fæliglæh – þæt wæs Leofwine æt Frome, and Ægelsig þe Reada, and Winsig scægðman.

sceawian *to look at, appoint*
Fæliglæh *Fawley* nine miles south west of Aylton (perhaps means *hay pasture*)

Insight

In the sentence **Ða acsode þe bisceop hwa sceolde andswerian for his moder** *Then the bishop asked who would reply for his mother*, note the pronoun **hwa,** which declines nominative **hwa,** accusative **hwæne** (or **hwone**), genitive **hwæs** (cf. modern English *whose*) and dative **hwæm** (cf.*whom*); the neuter form was **hwæt** (cf. *what*).

◀ **TR 58**

Þa acsoðon heo hwylce talu heo hæfde
Then they asked what claim she had

And þa þa heo to hire comon þa acsoðon heo hwylce talu heo hæfde ymbe þa land þe hire sunu æfter spæc. Ða sæde heo þæt heo nan land hæfde þe him aht to gebyrede, and gebealh heo swiðe eorlice wið hire sunu, and gecleopade ða Leoflæde hire magan to hire Ðurcilles wif and beforan heom to hire þus cwæð, 'Her sit Leoflæde min mage þe ic geann ægðer ge mines landes, ge mines goldes, ge rægles, ge reafes, ge ealles þe ic ah æfter minon dæge.' And heo syððan to þam þegnon cwæþ, 'Doð þegnlice, and wel abeodað mine ærende to þam gemote beforan eallum þam godan mannum. And cyðaþ heom hwæm ic mines landes geunnen hæbbe, and ealre minre æhte – and minan agenan suna næfre nan þing! And biddað heom beon þisses to gewitnesse.'

---

gebyrian *to belong*
gebelgan *to become angry* **(gebelgan, belhð, bealh, bulgon, gebolgen)**
eorlice *angrily* (cf. **ierlic** *angry*)
gecleopade past tense of **cleopian** *to call*
þæt rægl = þæt hrægl *clothing*
ic ah *I own*

þegnlice *in a thegnly manner* (adverb in **-lice**)
abeodan *announce* 'ah-BAIo-dan'
þæt ærende *message* 'AIR-en-deh'
hwæm *to whom* (dative)

◀ TR 59

Ða astod Ðurcil hwita up on þam gemote
Then Thorkell the White stood up at the assembly

And heo ða swæ dydon; ridon to þam gemote and cyðdon
eallon þam godan mannum hwæt heo on heom geled
hæfde. Ða astod Ðurcil hwita up on þam gemote, and bæd
ealle þa þægnas syllan his wife þa land clæne þe hire mage
hire geuðe. And heo swa dydon. And Ðurcill rad ða to
sancte Æþelberhtes mynstre, be ealles þæs folces leafe and
gewitnesse, and let settan on ane Cristes boc.

QUICK VOCAB

ridon *they rode* 'riddon' (**rídan, rítt, rád, ridon, geriden**)
geled, geléd, gelegd 'yuh-laid' from **lecgan** *to lay* (**legð, legde, legdon, gelegd**)
lecgan on *to charge with*
astod *stood up* 'a-STOHD' (**ā + standan, stent, stód, stódon, gestanden**)
clæne *cleanly, completely*
seo mage *kinswoman* 'mah-yuh'

Cultural contexts

'Thegnly' behaviour

The status of thegns in late Anglo-Saxon society was discussed
briefly in Unit 7, particularly the terms **twelfhynde** and **twihynde**
referring to the amount of wergild for different ranks of society.

In the Herefordshire Lawsuit, there is a rare occurrence of the adverb þegnlice, which connotes not only social status but also behaviour appropriate to that rank:

> **Doð þegnlice, and wel abeodað mine ærende to þam gemote beforan eallum þam godan mannum.**
> *Act thegnly, and present my statement well at the Assembly, before all the good men.*

What does 'thegnly' behaviour entail? Two Old English texts throw some light on the connotations of this word: the *Promotion Law* by Wulfstan archbishop of York yields information on the status of *þegenriht*, the rights and privileges of a thegn, while a line in the poem *The Battle of Maldon* gives information on the kind of actions or attitudes that 'thegnly' might imply.

Wulfstan's Geþyncðo *Promotion Law*

The text by Wulfstan known as **Geþyncðo** or the *Promotion Law* is recorded in two manuscripts: the Corpus Wulfstan Anthology (Corpus Christi College, Cambridge manuscript 201), already mentioned earlier since it contains the *Joseph* story (see Unit 14), and the *Textus Roffensis*, an anthology of legal texts compiled at Rochester in the twelfth century. Compared with the Corpus Christi text, the Rochester version contains a few extra details on the legal requirements for thegnly status; this is the text given here. The translation below poses a number of problems, since it is difficult to represent the rhyme of *cheorl* and *eorl* and the alliteration of *thegn* and *theoden* (a traditional poetic word for *prince*). Especially difficult is the question of how to translate **ceorl** ('cheorl'). Normally the word refers to a low-ranking landowner or freeman, but the modern English *churl* and *peasant* have the wrong connotations.

Hit wæs hwilum on Engla lagum þæt leod and lagu for be geþincðum; and þa wæron leodwitan weorðscipes wyrðe ælc be his mæðe, eorl and ceorl, þegen and þeoden. And gif ceorl geþeah þæt he hæfde fullice fif hida agenes landes, cirican and kycenan, bellhus and burhgeat, setl and sundernote on cynges healle, þonne wæs he þanon forð þegenrihtes weorðe.

(Contd)

> *Once it was in the laws of the English that nation and law*
> *proceeded by rank; and at that time counsellors were worthy*
> *of honour each according to his degree: earl and cheorl,*
> *thegn and theoden (prince). And if a freeman flourished so*
> *that he had five hides of his own land, a church and kitchen,*
> *a bell-house and a castle-gate, a seat and special office in the*
> *king's hall, then he was thenceforth worthy of thegnly legal*
> *status.*

Here the key term is **þegenriht** *thegnly legal status*; this is something that can be acquired: a freeman can rise through the ranks. Recent archaeological research has confirmed the thegnly status of the various objects named: it seems that by the eleventh century high-ranking nobility were living in fortified settlements equipped with a stone castle-gate, a stone tower such as the one at Earls Barton in Northamptonshire, a kitchen, and – in contrast to the previous pattern of communal minsters – with their own private chapel or church. It is not strictly correct to call this kind of **burh** a *castle*, since the word **castel** came into Old English from French in the eleventh century to denote the particular motte and bailey as built by some of Edward the Confessor's continental supporters and by the Normans after 1066. Nevertheless such accoutrements make the thegn seem very similar in status to the knight who was shortly to appear on the medieval English social scene (for further details see **bibliography**).

From *The Battle of Maldon*
This passage (lines 286–94) comes from the end of the poem as the warriors each in turn declare their intentions to fight on despite the certainty of imminent defeat. In keeping with the warrior theme there are a number of traditional poetic words and martial images, including three words for *battle*: **hild**, **here** and **wælstow**; three words for *lord*: **frea**, **beahgifa** and **þeoden**; and one word for the traditional lord–retainer relationship: **beotian** *to make a formal vow of service*. Such passages are often cited to show the Anglo-Saxon adherence to an ancient Germanic type of heroic code, as celebrated in poems in an older style such as *Beowulf*, *The Wanderer* and (with a religious application) *The Dream of the Rood*. But *The Battle of Maldon*

mixes the old and the new. In the light of the previous passage from Wulfstan's *Promotion Law* it is interesting to see here an evocation of riding **hale to hame,** *safely home* to the thegnly **burh,** a day-dream that is contrasted with the reality of the battle from which Offa will not return. Instead the *thegn* will lie next to his fallen *theoden* (note the same alliterative pattern as in Wulfstan); he will not desert his lord. Here the word **þegnlice** connotes courage and absolute loyalty, *thegnly* qualities.

Raðe wearð æt hilde Offa forheawen;
he hæfde ðeah geforþod þæt he his frean gehet,
swa he beotode ær wið his beahgifan
þæt hi sceoldon begen on burh ridan,
hale to hame, oððe on here crincgan,
on wælstowe wundum sweltan:
he læg ðegenlice ðeodne gehende.

Quickly Offa was cut down at the battle;
he had nevertheless accomplished what he promised his lord
as he had vowed to his ring-giver
that they would both ride into the castle,
safely home, or else fall in the fighting,
on the battlefield die of their wounds:
he lay in a thegnly manner close to his theoden.

Wordhoard

The changing English vocabulary

In the Herefordshire Lawsuit, three thegns are appointed to learn the details of the lady's claim to the land: **Leofwine æt Frome, Ægelsig þe Reada,** and **Winsig scægðman.** Their names throw light on the state of the Old English language as society moved from the time of king Cnut to the age of Edward the Confessor. Apart from the names of these thegns, some interesting insights can be also gained from two other names, both of mixed origin: **Tofi Pruda** and **Eadwine Enneawnes sunu**.

Leofwine æt Frome: traditional names and new bynames

The first of the three thegns is **Leofwine æt Frome**. Leofwine is a traditional Old English dithematic name; of its two elements **leof** *dear* was still in current use, whereas **wine** *friend* was otherwise confined to verse contexts, e.g. **goldwine** *gold-friend* i.e. *lord or patron*, a poetic compound akin to **beahgifa** *ring-giver* in line 288 of *The Battle of Maldon* (see extract above). In everyday prose, by contrast, the word for *friend* was **freond**. Leofwine's by-name **æt Frome** indicates the location of his residence, perhaps a fortified place of the kind described in Wulfstan's *Promotion Law*. Under later Norman and French influence, the preposition **æt** in such names was replaced by **de**.

Ægelsig þe Reada *Æthelsige the Red*: the first uses of the word *the*

With hindsight, we can see that the name **Ægelsig þe Reada** (in traditional Old English **Æþelsige Reada** or perhaps **Æþelsige se Reada**) points to various ways in which the English language was changing at this time. Firstly, instead of using the definite article **se** – or indeed missing it out as with **Þurcil Hwita** *Thorkell the White* – the name **Ægelsig þe Reada** demonstrates one of the first occurrences in the language of the definite article **þe**. This was to become *the* in Middle English and modern English. Another change is phonetic rather than grammatical: the name **Æþelsige** is simplified, dropping its 'th' sound and final syllable -e to become **Ægelsig**. A similar loss of 'th' occurred in the name **Æðelræd**, which became **Ailred**; in the twelfth century a famous Latin religious writer signed his name **Ailred de Rivaulx**, his domicile being one of the great Yorkshire monasteries of the French-based Cistercian order. Such changes are more likely to occur first in personal names, which are on people's lips all the time, rather than in the phrases of formal writing. In the eleventh century the Old English written standard was taught alongside Latin in the monastic and cathedral schools; this was less common in the twelfth century, thus allowing such linguistic changes to continue more freely.

Winsig scægðman *Winsig the Viking*: **Old Norse in English**

Of the three thegns delegated to hear the lady's claim at Fawley in the Herefordshire Dispute, the third – **Winsig** – has an interesting Old Norse byname **scægðman**, to be translated *shipman* or even *viking*. Old Norse was the language spoken by the Vikings, although with dialectal variants, throughout Scandinavia and in parts of England – especially the region known as the Danelaw. Cognate with Old English, Old Norse had many similar sounding words but significantly different grammatical structures. In king Cnut's day, **be Cnutes dæge cinges**, Old Norse was heard at the royal court in Winchester and the skalds performed their poems not far from the church where archbishop Wulfstan declaimed his Old English sermons and lawcodes. It is no surprise that in this context a number of words connected with Anglo-Danish rule were borrowed from Old Norse into Old English; the following are some common examples:

Maritime: **lib** *fleet*, **æsc** *warship*, **barda** *beaked ship*, **cnear** *small warship*, **ha** *rowlock*, **hamele** *oarlock*, **hæfene** *haven*, **lænding** *landing-site*, **butsecarl** *sailor*, **steormann** *pilot*, **scegðmann** *Viking, shipman*.

Legal: **feolaga** *fellow*, **formal** *treaty*, **grið** *truce* or *sanctuary*, **husting** *tribunal*, **lagu** *law*, **lahbryce** *breach of the law*, **lahmenn** *lawmen*, **mal** *law suit*, **niðing** *outlaw*, **sac** *guilty*, **sacleas** *innocent*, **utlaga** *outlaw*, **utlagian** *to outlaw* (see Unit 4).

Military: **brynige** *mailshirt*, **genge** *troop*, **targa** s*mall round shield*.

Politics: **eorl** *earl*, **huscarl** *housecarl or member of king's guard*.

Monetary: **gersum** *treasure*.

By the time Edward the Confessor came to the throne in 1042, most of these words were firmly entrenched in the language; they occur with increasing frequency in the later annals of the Anglo-Saxon Chronicle (especially E, which continues up to 1154).

Tofi Pruda *Tofi the Proud*

Tofi (a Danish name) was a prominent figure in Cnut's England, known elsewhere as a witness to charters and as one of the main protagonists in a Latin history composed in the twelfth century known as the Waltham Chronicle. Tofi is also connected with a dramatic incident that took place shortly before the accession of Edward the Confessor: Cnut's son Harthacnut was taken seriously ill at the wedding feast of Tofi with Gytha, daughter of Osgod Clapa, a Danish landholder from the Eastern shires. Interestingly, Tofi's name has cosmopolitan implications, for this important Anglo-Danish aristocrat Tofig Pruda has a French byname. Like **sott** *fool* (see Unit 4), **prud** *proud* appears to derive from French, as do **tur** *tower*, **capun** *capon* and **castell** *castle* – signs of the wide cultural connections of late Old English society. This tendency to borrow from French increased enormously with the prestige of French in the later medieval period (see **bibliography**).

Edwine Enneawnes sunu

Little is known of this name other than these lines in the document. Since the dispute takes place in Herefordshire, in the border country, it is possible that Enneawn was a Welshman. It is a reminder that another language culture existed near at hand in Wales; its literature was to flourish under the Welsh princes in the 12th century.

Reading

Further study of Old English

For those interested in taking their Old English further, there are many directions to choose from here and many periods of Old English history and literature to explore in greater depth, from the earliest Northumbrian poems of the eighth century to the annals of the Peterborough Chronicle in the twelfth century. For now your attention is drawn briefly to one area of further study: the reading

of a manuscript. Recommendations for your future learning of
Old English are given in the final **bibliography**.

Reading a manuscript in facsimile

Compared with later periods up to and including the Renaissance,
the handwriting of Old English scribes is relatively easy to read.
For practice, it is recommended that you begin with a text you
already know. For our purposes here we will use the Old English
Hexateuch. This has already been the focus of several units in
this book and its text is written in a clear late Old English scribal
hand. For those who wish to read the text in its original script the
facsimile of the manuscript is available in good research libraries
(see **bibliography**). Folio 63v, Joseph's second meeting and feast
with his brothers, is reproduced in this unit in black and white and
on the inside front cover of this book. Some guidance on text and
script will be given shortly; but to start, try reading the first line:

Soþlice hiledon forð heoralac ongean þæt iosep ineode . 7 feollon

Practising transcription

Use the old method of look and listen: in order to familiarize
yourself with the scribal conventions, turn to the facsimile and
listen to the recording through once, following the text with your
finger. Next, try to transcribe the text. Then compare your text
with the transcription here. Letters that are difficult to make out
at first are **d**, which curls back on itself (see **ledon** in line 1), **f** and
r, which extend below the line (e.g. **forð**). Note the shape of **g**
in **ongean** and the alternative form of the letter **s** (a little like the
modern letter 'r') as it appears in **iosep** (Joseph). The Tironian *nota*
represents **and** and the main punctuation mark is a point. Capital
letters are used sparingly: the initial **S** marks a new section, but
Iosep is written with lower case **i** in line 1 and upper case
I in line 2. One interesting feature is word division by phrase:
smaller words tend to be written together with the larger stressed
word that follows (e.g. **ineode**). Watch out in particular for the

round 'w' rune known as **wynn** *joy*, e.g. **wiþ hine** in the middle of line 2.

Soðlice hi ledon forð heora lac
So they brought out their gifts

Soðlice hi ledon forð heora lac
So they brought out their gifts (facsimile)

Soðlice hiledon forð heoralac ongean þæt iosep ineode.
7 feollon onþa eorðan. 7 geeaðmeddon wiþhine. Iosep
hioncneowða arful lice. 7 axode hi hwæðer heora fæder
wære hal. Þehihim fore sædon oþþehwæðer heleofode.
þacwædon hi gesund isþin þeow urefæder
5 gyt he leofaþ. Ðaiosep geseah hisge meddredan broþor
beniamin. Þacwæþ he. isþis secnapa þegeme foresædon. 7 eft
he cwæþ godgemilt sige þe sunu min. 7 he wearð swaswiðe
astyrod þæthim feollon tearas for his broþor þingon. 7 he
eode into his bed cleofan 7 weop. 7 Þahe þæs geswac. þa
eode he ut tohim 7 hiæton. Onsundron. þaegyptiscean.
10 hit næs na alifed þæthiætgædere æton. 7 himan oferdrencte.

282

Soðlice his ledon forð heora lac
So they brought out their gifts [lightly edited transcription]

Soðlice hi ledon forð heora lac ongean þæt Iosep in eode,
7 feollon on þa eorðan, 7 geeaðmeddon wiþ hine. Iosep hi
oncneow þa arfullice, 7 axode hi hwæðer heora fæder
wære hal, þe hi him foresædon oþþe hwæðer he leofode. þa
cwædon hi gesund is þin þeow ure fæder gyt he leofaþ. ða
Iosep geseah his gemeddredan broþor Beniamin, þa cwæþ
he, is þis se cnapa þe ge me foresædon. 7 eft he cwæþ God
gemiltsige þe sunu min. 7 he wearð swa swiðe astyrod þæt
him feollon tearas for his broþor þingon. 7 he eode into his
bedcleofan 7 weop. 7 þa he þæs geswac, þa eode he ut to him
7 hi æton. Onsundron þa egyptiscean: hit næs na alifed þæt
hi ætgædere æton. 7 hi man oferdrencte.

*So they brought out their gifts as Joseph came in, and fell
on the ground and prostrated themselves before him. Joseph
acknowledged them graciously, and asked them whether
their father was well, whom they had mentioned before, or
whether he lived. Then they said, 'Your servant our father is
well, he is still living.' When Joseph saw his maternal brother
Benjamin, then he said, 'Is this the boy you mentioned to
me?' And again he said, 'God protect you, my son.' And
he was so deeply moved that his tears fell for the sake of
his brother, and he went to his bedchamber and wept. And
when he had stopped, he went out to them and they ate. The
Egyptians separately. It was not allowed that they should eat
together. And they gave them too much to drink.*

Manuscript illustrations

It is possible with some caution to use manuscript illustrations as a
source of information on the material culture of the period. In the
illustration accompanying the text of Joseph and his brothers, the

figures of the men wear tunics of varying colours and 'flat, black ankle shoes, with a white strip down the front' (G. Owen-Crocker, *Dress in Anglo-Saxon England*, p. 259; see **bibliography**). Many of the men wear cloaks fastened with a round brooch at the shoulder. They eat with large prominent knives (the Saxon type known as a *seax*) and take their wine in drinking horns and beaker cups – the Egyptians with forked beards form a group in the chamber in the lower left of the picture, while on the right are the Hebrews, who appear to be drinking more prominently.

In the upper picture, the brothers bring gifts to the man they call **se landhlaford** *lord of the land* (their unrecognized brother Joseph); the picture shows an assemblage of goods: a money bag, a tall jar with a lid, a cup, a golden goblet, a drinking horn and a bowl. Such assemblages appear in other manuscripts, where they clearly represent the idea of treasure. In contrast to the brothers, Joseph carries a sword with a trilobed pommel, a symbol of his authority. On the far right of the picture he departs with cloak held to his eyes to weep unseen in his chamber. The location of the meeting is a hall with tiled roof and carved columns. Like the assemblage of rich goods, this is, of course, an icon rather than a realistic depiction; it represents the idea of the **heall** *hall* or, as the text calls it (Genesis 44: 13), the **burh** *stronghold* where the **landhlaford** resides.

Test yourself

Translate the text of the Herefordshire Lawsuit into natural idiomatic English.

21

....

The tide went out

This unit will cover:

text and vocabulary
- *extract from* The Battle of Maldon, **lines 55b–83**

manuscripts
- *capitalization and punctuation in manuscripts*
- *text layout and questions of interpretation*

There follows an extract from the classic poem *The Battle of Maldon* (for the full text along with supporting notes and commentary, see the website). It raises the issue of the modern-day presentation of Old English poems, and how closely this should follow the authentic layout and punctuation of the original manuscript (for a facsimile of the unique surviving transcript, see D.G. Scragg 1991 in the **bibliography** for Unit 21, under *The Battle of Maldon*).

In August of the year 991, the same year in which Wynflæd won her lawsuit at Cwichelm's Barrow (see Unit 19), a battle was fought against Viking invaders at the estuary near Maldon in Essex, the East Saxon region of England. The **ealdorman** or governor of the region, called Byrhtnoth, raised the **fyrd** or army of levies to deal with the threat. Some time after 991, the events of the day were revisited, and an anonymous poet composed an Old English poem on the battle in a traditional style, which we call *The Battle of Maldon*. In the passage quoted here, the two armies face each other across the river Pante. (This is usually identified with the the river Blackwater that separates Northey

Island from the mainland). Byrhtnoth is addressing the **wicinga ar**, the anonymous Viking messenger, perhaps the interpreter for the Norse-speaking Viking leader, whom the poem does not name. The Vikings have demanded the payment of *tribute* (spelt **gafol** or **gofol**) in return for **grið** *truce* or *protection*, but Byrhtnoth rejects their offer.

The Battle of Maldon, lines 55b–83

Lines 55b–61: 'the grim game of battle – before we give tribute!'

'To heanlic me þinceð   55b
þæt ge mid urum sceattum   to scype gangon
unbefohtene,   nu ge þus feor hider
on urne eard   in becomon.
Ne sceole ge swa softe   sinc gegangan;
us sceal ord and ecg   ær geseman   60
grim guðplega,   ær we gofol syllon.'

to heanlic *too shameful*;
ge *you* (plural); **mid urum sceattum** *with our payments*;
unbefohtene *unfought*; **nu** *now*; **hider** *here, hither*;
ur-ne *our*; **in becomon** *have come in*;
ne sceole ge *nor should you*; **swa softe** *so agreeably*; **sinc** *treasure*;
ord and ecg *point and edge*; **ær** *first*; **geseman** *reconcile*;
guðplega *battle-play*; **ær** *before*; **gofol** *tribute*

Lines 62–67: the waters joined

Het þa bord beran,   beornas gangan
þæt hi on þam easteðe   ealle stodon
ne mihte þær for wætere,   werod to þam oðrum.
þær com flowende   flod æfter ebban;   65
lucon lagustreamas.   To lang hit him þuhte
hwænne hi togædere   garas beron.

þa *then*; **bord** *shields*; **beornas** *men*;
hi *they*; **on þam easteðe** *on the river bank*;
for wætere *because of the water*; **werod to þam oðrum**
  one troop (reach) to the other;
flowende *flowing*; **æfter ebban** *after the ebb-tide*;
lucon *joined*; **lagustreamas** *streams of water*; **to lang** *too long*;
hwænne *until the time when*; **beron** *they would bear*

QUICK VOCAB

Lines 68–71: they stood along the river Pante in great array

Hi þær Pantan stream   mid prasse bestodon
Eastseaxena ord   and se æschere
ne mihte hyra ænig   oþrum derian   70
buton hwa þurh flanes   flyht fyl gename.

mid prasse *in great array*;
se æschere: *æsc* *ash-wood* i.e. *ship* + **here** *army*;
hyra ænig *any of them*; **derian** *cause harm*; **oþrum** *to the others*;
þurh flanes flyht *through the flight of an arrow*; **fyl** *fall*; **gename**
  might take

QV

Lines 72–73: the tide went out

Se flod ut gewat   þa flotan stodon gearowe
wicinga fela,   wiges georne.

Se flod *the flood-tide*; **ut** *out*; **gewat** *went*; **þa flotan**
  the seamen; **gearowe** *ready*;
wicinga *Vikings*; **fela** *many*; **wiges georne** *eager for battle*

QV

Lines 73–83: hold the bridge

Het þa hæleða hleo   healdan þa bricge
wigan wigheardne   se wæs haten Wulfstan   75
cafne mid his cynne   þæt wæs Ceolan sunu
þe ðone forman man   mid his francan ofsceat
þe þær baldlicost   on þa bricge stop.
þær stodon mid Wulfstane   wigan unforhte,

Ælfere and Maccus   modige twegen,   80
þa noldon æt þam forda   fleam gewyrcan,
ac hi fæstlice   wið ða fynd weredon
þa hwile þe hi wæpna   wealdan moston.

Capitalization and punctuation in manuscripts

As we saw in Unit 20, Old English scribes copied texts using conventions of capitalization, punctuation, spacing and word-division that are very different from those of the present. Even more striking is the way in which Old English verse was recorded in writing; a short example from the Exeter Book is given in Unit 22 below. The scribes copied the poems as though they were paragraphs of continuous prose writing: it is not possible to see or count the number of lines simply by looking at a poem laid out on the page – this despite the fact that Latin poetry of the period was laid out in lines of verse. Though the conventions are flexible, the beginning of the Old English verse paragraph was often marked by a capital letter and ended with a point or **punctus**, or a **punctus versus**, which looks like a kind of semi-colon. Spacing of words and syllables and the arrangement of words on the page contributed, it seems, to the rhetoric: to the sound and fury of the performance before an audience, probably in the hall of a **burh**, or in the reading room of a minster.

The only extant copy of the poem *The Battle of Maldon* is an 18th-century transcript in the Bodleian Library in Oxford, the closest we can now come to what the scribe originally wrote; a facsimile is available for comparison in Scragg 1991 (see **bibliography** for Unit 21). On the next page you will see a representation of folio 8v of the Bodleian manuscript. The study of its layout and punctuation is illuminating. Unlike many modern editions, the capitalization and punctuation of the transcript appear to follow the manuscript, so that a letter in bold marks a new section, and the **punctus** or point marks a pause, while the **punctus versus** (here a semi-colon or colon) marks the end of a section.

Insight

Notice the two examples of a large bold letter **h**, which marks a new section clearly in the transcript and perhaps follows the practice of the original scribe. There is a colon after **fyl gename** suggesting an original **punctus versus** followed by a capital **S**. Another new section appears to start shortly afterwards: a point follows **wiges georne**, and a new section arguably begins with the slightly larger **h** of **het þa hæleða hleo**. These divisions arrest the narrative and may have served to mark the ebb and flow of the tide, which obviously occupied a duration of several hours. In this way the poet and/or the scribe marked the long passage of time at this stage in the narrative.

On the practice of adding commas and semi-colons to the text in order to clarify the sentence structure, Edward B. Irving has written of how modern editors bear 'the burden of furnishing sometimes misleading modern punctuation to the text, simply because convention seems to demand it'. By departing from the editorial convention, going back as far as possible to the punctuation of the original Old English text and comparing it with that of modern editions, you will be able to explore different readings and interpretations of the language of the poem (see website for more discussion).

A page of the transcript (*Battle of Maldon* lines 56b–81)

Oxford, Bodleian Library, manuscript Rawlinson B 203, folio 8r is set
out as follows (for a facsimile reproduction, see Scragg 1991, p. 5):

gangon unbe fohtene nuge þus feor hider on urne eard inbecomon ne sceole
ge swa softe sinc ge gangan us sceal ord
7 ecg ærge seman grī guð plega ærþe
gofol syllon.

het þa bord beran beornas gangan þ
hi on þā ea steðe ealle stodon ne mihte
þærfor wætere. werod to þā oðrum þær
com flowende flod æfter ebban lucon
lagu streamas to lang hit him þuhte
hwænne hi to gædere garas beron

hi þær pantan stream mid prasse
be stodon eastseaxena ord 7 se æsc here
ne mihte hyra ænigoþrū derian buton
hwa þurh flanes flyht fylgename : Se
flod ut ge wat þa flotan stodon gearowe
wicinga fela wiges georne. het þa hæleða hleo healdan þa bricge wigan wigheardne se wæs haten wulfstan cafne mid his cynne þ wæs ceolan sunu
þe ðone forman man mid his francā
of sceat þe þær baldlicost on þā
bricge stop. þær stodon mid wulfstāe
wigan unforhte. ælfere 7 maccus modige twegen. þa noldon æt þā forda
  fleāge

For further reading on the battle and the poem, see **bibliography**;
for the full text of *The Battle of Maldon*, with a language
commentary and other related documents, see the website
(teachyourself.com).

22

I was by the shore

This unit presents – for further reading and interpretation – three short texts from books owned by Leofric of Exeter, the continental cleric of English origins who rose to prominence in England during the reign of Edward the Confessor (see Unit 3):

Two riddles

▶ Riddle 30b **Ic eom ligbysig** *I am beset with flames* (for title, see Treharne in **bibliography**)
▶ Riddle 60 **Ic wæs be sonde** *I was by the shore*

The Old English coronation oath

▶ **Ic þreo þing behate** *I promise three things* – as perhaps used by Edward when he was consecrated at Winchester in 1043 (see Unit 1).

For the manuscript contexts and related historical texts, and for further discussion, see the **bibliography** and website.

Two riddles

Riddle 30b (manuscript layout)

Ic eom lig bysig lace mid winde [...fire damage in the manuscript] dre ge somnad fus forð weges fyre gemylted [...]

blowende byrnende gled ful oft mec gesiþas sendað
æfter hondū þærmec weras 7wif wlonce gecyssað þōn
ic mec onhæbbe hion hnigað tome modge miltsum
swa ic mohgum sceal ycan up cyme eadignesse :7

Riddle 60 (manuscript layout)

Ic wæs besonde sæ wealle neah æt mere
faroþe minum gewunade frum staþole fæst. fea
ænig wæs. monna cynnes þæt minne þær on an æde
eard be heolde. ac mec uhtna gehwam yð sio brune
lagu fæðme beleolc lyt icwende þ ic ær oþþe sið.
æfre scolde ofer meodu muð leas sprecan wordum wrix
lan þ is wundres dæl onsefan searolic þā þe swylc ne
conn. humec seaxeð ord 7seo swiþre hond eorles inge
þonc 7ord somod þingum geþydan þæt ic wiþþe sceolde
for unc anum twan ærend spræce abeodan bealdlice
swa hit beorna ma uncre word cwidas widdor ne
mænden :7

Riddle 30 (text edited with readings from riddle 30a)

Ic eom ligbysig   lace mid winde
wuldre bewunden   wedre gesomnad
fus forðweges   fyre gemylted
bearu blowende   byrnende gled
ful oft mec gesiþas   sendað æfter hondum   5
þær mec weras ond   wif wlonce gecyssað
þonne ic mec onhæbbe   hi onhnigað to me
modge miltsum   swa ic mongum sceal
ycan upcyme   eadignesse :7

Riddle 60 (lightly edited text)

Ic wæs be sonde   sæwealle neah
æt merefaroþe   minum gewunade
frumstaþole fæst.   fea ænig wæs.

monna cynnes   þæt minne þær
on anæde   eard beheolde.   5
ac mec uhtna gehwam   yð sio brune
lagufæðme beleolc   lyt ic wende
þæt ic ær oþþe sið.   æfre scolde
ofer meodu   muðleas sprecan
wordum wrixlan   þæt is wundres dæl   10
on sefan searolic   þam þe swylc ne conn.
hu mec seaxes ord   ond seo swiþre hond
eorles ingeþonc   ond ord somod
þingum geþydan   þæt ic wiþ þe sceolde
for unc anum twan   ærendspræce   15
abeodan bealdlice   swa hit beorna ma
uncre wordcwidas   widdor ne mænden :7

The Old English coronation oath

The Old English coronation oath, entitled in Latin PROMISSIO
REGIS, *The king's promise*, was copied into a manuscript belonging
to Leofric bishop of Exeter in the reign of Edward the Confessor
(see Unit 1). The text gives us the English words of the oath sworn
by Edward's father Æthelred the Unready when he was consecrated
king by St Dunstan at Kingston in 978. In the intervening reigns,
it is likely that king Cnut and his sons had used another crowning
ceremony, but we may speculate that Edward spoke the same words
as his father Æthelred had done before him for his consecration at
Winchester in 1043.

••

◀)) TR 61

Ic þreo þing behate *I promise three things*

Þis gewrit is gewriten be stæfe be þam gewrite þe Dunstan
arcebisceop sealde urum hlaforde æt Cingestune, þa on dæg
þa hine man halgode to cinge, and forbead him ælc wedd to
                                                    (Contd)

syllanne butan þysan wedde þe he up on Cristes weofod léde,
swa se bisceop him dihte:

On þære halgan þrinnesse naman ic þreo þing behate
Cristenum folce and me underðeoddum: án ærest, þæt Godes
cyrice and eall Cristen folc minra gewealda soðe sibbe healde;
oðer is, þæt ic reaflac and ealle unrihte þing eallum hádum
forbeode; þridde, þæt ic beháte and bebeode on eallum
dómum riht and mildheortnisse, þæt us eallum arfæst and
mildheort God þurh his ecean miltse forgife, se lifað and rixað.

I promise three things

*This document is written according to the letter from the
document that archbishop Dunstan gave to our lord at
Kingston on the day when he consecrated him as king and
forbade him from giving any oath except the oath which he
laid on Christ's altar, as the bishop dictated to him:*

*In the name of the Holy Trinity, I promise three things to my
Christian people and subjects: first, that God's church and
all Christian people of my domains should keep true peace;
the second is that I forbid robbery and all unjust acts to all
orders of society; third, that I promise and command in all
the laws justice and mercy, which gracious and merciful God
may grant us all through his eternal favour, who liveth and
reigneth.*

Bibliography

General bibliography

John Blair, *Anglo-Saxon England: A Very Short Introduction* (Oxford: Oxford University Press, 2000)

Kenneth Cameron, *English Place Names*, new edition (London: Batsford, 1996)

David Crystal, *The Stories of English* (London: Penguin, 2004)

Malcolm Godden and Michael Lapidge, *The Cambridge Companion to Old English Literature* (Cambridge: Cambridge University Press, 1991)

Barbara Raw, *The Art and Background of Old English Poetry* (London: Edward Arnold, 1978)

Andrew Reynolds, *Later Anglo-Saxon England: Life and Landscape* (Stroud: Tempus, 1999)

Michael Wood, *In Search of England: Journeys into the English Past* (London: Penguin, 2000)

Barbara Yorke, *The Anglo-Saxons* (Stroud: Sutton, 1999)

Translations

S.A.J. Bradley (trans.), *Anglo-Saxon Poetry* (London: Dent, 1982; reprinted London: Everyman, 1995)

Kevin Crossley Holland, *The Anglo-Saxon World*, new edition (Woodbridge: Boydell Press, 2002)

Richard Hamer (ed. and trans.), *A Choice of Anglo-Saxon Verse* (London: Faber & Faber, 1970)

Seamus Heaney (trans.), *Beowulf* (London: Faber & Faber, 1999)

Michael J. Swanton (trans.), *Anglo-Saxon Prose* (London: Dent, 1975)

Essential reference works and collections of texts

Florence E. Harmer (ed.), *Anglo-Saxon Writs*, 2nd edition (Stamford: Paul Watkins, 1989)

David Hill, *An Atlas of Anglo-Saxon England* (Oxford: Basil Blackwell, 1981)

Michael Lapidge, John Blair, Simon Keynes and Donald Scragg (eds), *The Blackwell Encyclopedia of Anglo-Saxon England* (Oxford: Blackwell, 1999)

A.J. Robertson (ed. and trans.), *Anglo-Saxon Charters* (Cambridge: Cambridge University Press, 1939)

Peter H. Sawyer, *Anglo-Saxon Charters: An Annotated List and Bibliography* (London: Royal Historical Society, 1968)

Frank M. Stenton, *Anglo-Saxon England*, 3rd edition (Oxford: Oxford University Press, 1998)

Approaches to language learning

Two good guides are Stella Hurd and Linda Murphy (eds), *Success with Languages* (London: Routledge, 2005) and Vivian Cook, *Second Language Learning and Language Teaching*, 4th edition (London: Hodder Education, 2008). The challenge to purely grammar-based methods is taken up by Michael Lewis, *The Lexical Approach. The State of ELT and a Way Forward*

(Andover: Heinle, 2008). On different types of language learner see
the specialist study by P. Skehan, *Individual Differences in Second-
Language Learning* (London: Edward Arnold, 1989). Still worth
reading are the surveys by H.H. Stern, *Fundamental Concepts of
Language Teaching* (Oxford: OUP, 1983), and by W.F. Mackey,
Language Teaching Analysis (London: Longman, 1965).

Language learning and Old English

The now classic work on the subject, *The Practical Study of
Languages* (London: Dent, 1899), was written by the phonetician
and Old English specialist Henry Sweet, author of *An Anglo-Saxon
Reader*, 1st edition (Oxford: Clarendon Press, 1876), 15th edition
(Oxford: Clarendon Press, 1967). Sweet's insightful, context-based
approach to language learning was lost sight of by twentieth-
century Anglo-Saxon studies. For discussion, see two articles by
M. Atherton, 'Henry Sweet's psychology of language learning',
in Klaus D. Dutz and Hans-J. Niederehe (eds), *Theorie und
Rekonstruktion* (Münster: Nodus, 1996), pp. 149–168; and 'Priming
the poets: the making of Henry Sweet's *Anglo-Saxon Reader*' in
David Clark and Nicholas Perkins (eds), *Anglo-Saxon Culture and
the Modern Imagination* (Woodbridge: Boydell & Brewer, 2010).

Follow-up reading for units

Introduction

The poem 'Bone Dreams' is found in Seamus Heaney, *North*
(London: Faber & Faber, 1975) and Seamus Heaney, *Opened
Ground: Poems 1966–1996* (London: Faber & Faber, 1998).
Another approach to Old English poetry is outlined in J.R.R.
Tolkien, *The Monsters and the Critics and Other Essays* (London:
George Allen & Unwin, 1983). For the development of the
language see David Crystal, *The Stories of English* and Melvyn
Bragg, *The Adventure of English 500 AD–2000: the Biography of
a Language* (London: Hodder & Stoughton, 2003).

1 Here Edward was consecrated as king

Frank Barlow, *Edward the Confessor*, new edition (London: Yale University Press, 1997)

2 A king must hold a kingdom

Paul Cavill, *Maxims in Old English* (Cambridge: D.S. Brewer, 1999); Victor Watts (ed.), *The Cambridge Dictionary of English Place-Names* (Cambridge: Cambridge University Press, 2004).

3 Say what I am called

Frank Barlow, *Leofric of Exeter: Essays in Commemoration of the Foundation of Exeter Cathedral Library in* AD 1072 (Exeter: Exeter University Press, 1972); John Porter, *Anglo-Saxon Riddles* (Hockwold-cum-Wilton: Anglo-Saxon Books, 2003)

4 Here in this year

M.K. Lawson, *Cnut: England's Viking King* (Stroud: Tempus, 2004); Katherine O'Brien O'Keeffe (ed.), *The Anglo-Saxon Chronicle: A Collaborative Edition Vol. 5: Manuscript C* (Cambridge: D.S. Brewer, 2001); A.R. Rumble, *The Reign of Cnut: King of England, Denmark and Norway* (London: Leicester University Press, 1994); Michael J. Swanton (trans.), *The Anglo-Saxon Chronicles* (London: Phoenix, 2000).

5 About the four seasons

P.S. Baker and M. Lapidge (eds), *Byrhtferth's Enchiridion*, Early English Text Society, supplementary series vol. 15 (Oxford: Oxford University Press, 1995). The original Old English semantic system is reviewed in an article by Earl R. Anderson, 'The Seasons of the Year in Old English', in the journal *Anglo-Saxon England* 26 (1997), pp. 231–63.

6 I saw in a dream

The text of the Joseph story is in Genesis, chapters 37–50. The standard edition of the Old English is Samuel J. Crawford (ed.), *The Old English Version of the Heptateuch*, Early English Text Society vol. 160 (London: OUP, 1969). *The Dream of the Rood* is edited with parallel translation in Richard Hamer, *A Choice of Anglo-Saxon Verse*.

7 King Cnut greets his archbishops

Richard Sharpe, 'The Use of Writs in the Eleventh Century', *Anglo-Saxon England* 32 (2003), pp. 247–91. N.P. Brooks, *The Early History of the Church of Canterbury. Christ Church from 597 to 1066* (Leicester: Leicester University Press, 1984), pp. 288–90, discusses archbishop Lyfing. For the seal of Godwine, see John Blair, *Anglo-Saxon Oxfordshire* (Thrupp: Sutton Publishing, 1994). For a photograph of a friþstol and some background to the reigns of Cnut and Edward the Confessor, read Richard A. Fletcher, *Bloodfeud: Murder and Revenge in Anglo-Saxon England* (London: Penguin, 2003).

8 He promised her the land at Orleton

Christine Fell, *Women in Anglo-Saxon England* (London: British Museum Publications, 1984); A. Fischer, *Engagement, Wedding and Marriage in Old English* (Heidelberg: C. Winter Universitätsverlag, 1986). Carole Hough, 'The Early Kentish "Divorce Laws": a Reconsideration of Æthelberht, chs. 79 and 80', *Anglo-Saxon England* 23 (1994), 19–34; A.J. Robertson, *Anglo-Saxon Charters*, no. 76.

9 I seek my brothers, where they are keeping their herds

The economic and cultural life of the period is presented in Robert Lacy and Danny Danziger, *The Year 1000. What Life was Like at the Turn of the First Millennium* (London: Abacus, 2000). For a facsimile of the manuscript illustration see **bibliography** to Unit 14.

The relevance of the past to the present is a theme in N. Howe, *Migration and Mythmaking in Anglo-Saxon England* (London and New Haven: Yale University Press, 1989) and S. Nichols, *Romanesque Signs: Early Medieval Literature and Iconography* (New Haven: Yale University Press, 1983).

10 These are the bounds of the pasture at Hazelhurst

On charter bounds and literature: Nicholas Howe, 'Writing the boundaries', ch.1 of his book *Writing the Map of Anglo-Saxon England. Essays In Cultural Geography* (New Haven and London: Yale University Press, 2008). On topography: John Blair, *Anglo-Saxon Oxfordshire* (Thrupp: Sutton Publishing, 1994), p. xxv; on boundaries and meeting places: Margaet Gelling, *Signposts to the Past: Place-Names and the History of England* (London: J.M. Dent, 1978), pp. 191–214. T.G. Allen describes the excavation of a Roman villa at Fawler in the journal *Oxoniensia* liii (1988), pp. 293–315. For discussion of the name **denn**, see Kenneth Cameron, *English Place Names*, p. 204 and for **leah**, pp. 201–3. The scribe Eadwig Basan is discussed by N.P. Brooks, *The Early History of the Church of Canterbury*, pp. 257–60, 267–70, 289–90. His work as an artist is surveyed by Michelle P. Brown, *Manuscripts from the Anglo-Saxon Age* (London: British Library, 2007), p. 132; this book prints a colour facsimile of Eadwig's calligraphic script and signature at p. 155 and examples of his splendid manuscript illumination on pp. 154–9, including his own self-portrait as a monk kneeling at the feet of St Benedict. The poem *The Ruin* is printed with parallel translation in Richard Hamer, *A Choice of Anglo-Saxon Verse*. For a map of the charter bounds of a typical estate, Stanton St Bernard in Wiltshire, see Andrew Reynolds, *Later Anglo-Saxon England: Life and Landscape* (Stroud: Tempus, 1999), pp. 82–83, figure 28 with photographs of the area in colour plates 2, 3, 4 and 5.

11 Here is declared in this document

Ann Williams, *Kingship and Government in Pre-Conquest England, c. 500–1066* (London: Macmillan, 1999), especially pp. 109–15. On the formulaic phrase **her swutelað,** see Benjamin C. Withers, *The Illustrated Old English Hexateuch, Cotton Claudius B.iv. The Frontier of Seeing and Reading In Anglo-Saxon England* (London: British Library and Toronto: Toronto University Press, 2007), pp. 191–5.

12 I saw a creature travel on the wave

D.R. Howlett, 'The Iconography of the Alfred Jewel,' in the journal *Oxoniensia* 39 (1974), pp. 44–52. For further vocabulary work consult Stephen Pollington, *Wordcraft: Concise Dictionary and Thesaurus. Modern English–Old English* (Pinner: Anglo-Saxon Books, 1993).

13 *And dydon hyne on þone wæterleasan pytt* (And they put him into the waterless well)

Text in S.J. Crawford, *The Old English Version of the Heptateuch.* Randolph Quirk and C. L. Wrenn, *An Old English Grammar,* 2nd edition (London: Methuen, 1957) has a very useful section on prefixes. For approaches to metaphorical language, try George Lakoff and Mark Johnson, *Metaphors we Live by* (London: University of Chicago Press, 2003); Peter Stockwell, *Cognitive Poetics* (London: Routledge, 2002). On the plot and characters of the original Joseph story, see Robert Alter, *The Art of Biblical Narrative* (London: George Allen & Unwin, 1981) and Laurence A. Turner, *Genesis* (Sheffield: Sheffield Academic Press, 2000).

14 *Nys se cnapa her* (The boy is not here)

Double negation in English is described by James Milroy and Lesley Milroy, *Authority in Language. Investigating Standard English*, 3rd edition (London: Routledge, 1999), pp. 53–4. For the text of Joseph, see the edition cited in the bibliography for Unit 6. For black-and-white reproductions of the manuscript text and illustrations of the Joseph story, consult C.R. Dodwell and P.A.M. Clemoes (eds), *The Old English Illustrated Hexateuch, Early*

English Manuscripts in Facsimile, vol. 18 (Copenhagen, 1974).
For a colour facsimile see the CD attached to the book by Benjamin
C. Withers, *The Illustrated Old English Hexateuch, Cotton
Claudius B.iv. The Frontier of Seeing and Reading In Anglo-Saxon
England* (London: British Library and Toronto: Toronto University
Press, 2007). Literary approaches to the Old English Joseph story
are found in Mary Richards, 'Fragmentary Versions of Genesis in
Old English Prose: Context and Function', in Rebecca Barnhouse
and Benjamin C. Withers, *The Old English Hexateuch. Aspects
and Approaches* (Kalamazoo: Medieval Institute Publications,
2000), pp. 145–64; Benjamin C. Withers, 'Unfulfilled Promise: the
Rubrics of the Old English Prose Genesis', *Anglo-Saxon England*
28 (1999), pp. 111–39; and Daniel Anlezark, 'Reading "The story
of Joseph" in MS Cambridge, Corpus Christi College 201', in
Hugh Magennis and Jonathan Wilcox (eds), *The Power of Words:
Anglo-Saxon Studies Presented to Donald G. Scragg on his
Seventieth Birthday* (Morgantown: West Virginia University Press,
2006), pp. 61–94.

15 I always wanted to convert to the monastic life

Debby Banham, *Monasteriales Indicia; The Anglo-Saxon
Monastic Sign Language* (Pinner: Anglo-Saxon Books, 1991).
Two monks appear to be communicating in sign language in an
illustration drawn in a Latin book of the Psalms (London, British
Library, Arundel 155, folio 10r); for a photograph see Francis
Wormald, *English Drawings of the Tenth and Eleventh Centuries*
(London: Faber & Faber, 1952), plate 24(b) (I owe this reference
to Barbara Raw). The anonymous *Life of Euphrosyne,* which
appears in a manuscript of *Ælfric's Lives of the Saints*, is edited
by W.W. Skeat, *Ælfric's Lives of Saints,* Early English Text Society
original series 76, 82, 94, 114 (Oxford: Oxford University Press,
1881–1900). Fred C. Robinson, 'European Clothing Names and
the Etymology of Girl', in his *The Tomb of Beowulf and other
Essays on Old English* (Oxford: Blackwell, 1993), pp. 175–81.
Richard Gameson, 'The Origin of the Exeter Book of Old English
Poetry', *Anglo-Saxon England* 25 (1996), pp. 135–85.

16 *Ðæt gelamp on sumere nihte* (It happened one night)

The Prose Life of Guthlac is edited by P. Gonser, *Das angelsächsische Prosa-Leben des heiligen Guthlac* (Heidelberg: C. Winter, 1909) and discussed by Jane Roberts, 'The Old English Prose Translation of Felix's *Vita Sancti Guthlaci*', in Paul E. Szarmach, *Studies in Earlier Old English Prose* (Albany: State University of New York Press, 1986). See also Mary Clayton, 'Hermits and the Contemplative Life in Anglo-Saxon England' in Paul E. Szarmach (ed.), *Holy Men and Holy Women: Old English Prose Saints' Lives and their Contexts* (Albany: State University of New York Press, 1996). For the Old English story of Fursey see the edition with parallel translation by Thomas Miller (ed.), *The Old English Version of Bede's Ecclesiastical History of the English People*, Early English Text Society original series 95 and 96 (Millwood: Kraus Reprint, 1990). *Guthlac A*, the Exeter Book poem on the life of the hermit in his fenland retreat, is discussed by Catherine A.M. Clarke, *Literary Landscapes and the Idea of England, 700–1400* (Cambridge: D.S. Brewer, 2006), pp. 36–66.

17 And bishop Æthelnoth travelled to Rome

Æthelnoth's predecessors also travelled to Rome; in one case the itinerary has been preserved; it is discussed by Veronica Ortenberg, 'Archbishop Sigeric's Journey to Rome in 990', *Anglo-Saxon England* 19 (1990), pp. 197–246; see also her *The English Church and the Continent in the Tenth and Eleventh Centuries: Cultural, Spiritual, and Artistic Exchanges* (Oxford: Clarendon Press, 1992). For Æthelnoth's career see N.P. Brooks, *The Early History of the Church of Canterbury. Christ Church from 597 to 1066* (Leicester: Leicester University Press, 1984), pp. 257–60, 273, 291–2; M.K. Lawson, *Cnut: England's Viking King* (Stroud: Tempus, 2004). For the election of an abbot, read H.E. Butler (ed. and trans.), *The Chronicle of Joscelin of Brakelond* (London: Thomas Nelson, 1949).

18 *Wulfstan arcebiscop gret Cnut cyning* **(Archbishop Wulfstan greets king Cnut)**

J. Armitage Robinson, *The Times of St Dunstan* (Oxford: Clarendon Press, 1923); Simon Keynes, 'King Athelstan's Books', in Michael Lapidge and Helmut Gneuss, *Learning and Literature in Anglo-Saxon England* (Cambridge: Cambridge University Press, 1985), pp. 143–201.

19 How Wynflæd summoned her witnesses

The text of the dispute is printed in A.J. Robertson, *Anglo-Saxon Charters*, no. 66. For a general explanation of the judicial process and oath-swearing, see Andrew Reynolds, *Later Anglo-Saxon England: Life and Landscape* (Stroud: Tempus, 1999), pp. 99–100. The Wynflæd–Leofwine case is discussed by Ann Williams, *Kingship and Government in Pre-Conquest England c. 500–1066* (London: Macmillan, 1999), pp. 11–12. 'The Life of St Wulfstan' is the principal piece in M. Winterbottom and R.M. Thomson (eds and trans.), *William of Malmesbury: Saints' Lives* (Oxford: Oxford University Press, 2002). Walter J. Sedgefield (ed.), *King Alfred's Old English Version of Boethius De Consolatione Philosophiae* (Oxford: Clarendon Press, 1899). For women's clothing, see Gale R. Owen-Crocker, *Dress in Anglo-Saxon England* (Woodbridge: The Boydell Press, 2004).

20 Act like thegns, and deliver my message to the assembly

The Herefordshire Lawsuit
The Herefordshire Lawsuit occurs on folio 134r and 134v of a Latin gospel book (shelfmark P. I. 2) at Hereford Cathedral Library; the original text is edited by Robinson, *Anglo-Saxon Charters*, no. 78 and by Dorothy Whitelock in *Sweet's Anglo-Saxon Reader* (Oxford: Clarendon Press, 1966); for a literary–critical approach, see Daniel Donoghue, *Old English Literature: A Short Introduction* (Oxford: Blackwell, 2004), pp. 1–5 and a photograph of the actual document at p. 3. The case is discussed

at length by Clare A. Lees and Gillian R. Overing, *Double Agents: Women and Clerical Culture in Anglo-Saxon England* (Philadelphia: University of Pennsylvania Press, 2001), pp. 72–89.

Anglo-Saxon thegns

On the lifestyle of later Old English thegns, see *Later Anglo-Saxon England: Life and Landscape* (Stroud: Tempus, 1999) in which Andrew Reynolds discusses the Promotion Law at p. 60, the place name Yatesbury corresponding to **burhgeat** at p. 93, and the tower at Earl's Barton Northamptonshire at p. 96 and colour plate 8. See also Ann Williams, 'A Bell-House and a Burh-Geat: the Lordly Residences in England before the Norman Conquest', in C. Harper-Bill and R. Harvey (eds), *Medieval Knighthood IV* (Woodbridge: Boydell, 1992), pp. 221–40.

Old Norse and Old French

Old Norse developed into various modern languages in mainland Scandinavia, but modern Icelandic is essentially the same language. A starting point for learning Old Norse, therefore, is basic Icelandic; see Hildur Jónsdóttir, *Teach Yourself Complete Icelandic* (London: Hodder & Stoughton, 2004). For Old French, consult E. Einhorn, *Old French: A Concise Handbook* (Cambridge: Cambridge University Press, 1974). For an example of Old Norse–Old English communication see Robert McCrum, Robert MacNeil and William Cran, *The Story of English*, 3rd edition (London: Faber & Faber, 2002), p. 69. Borrowings from Old Norse and Old French are discussed in David Crystal, *The Stories of English*; Dennis Freeborn, *From Old English to Standard English*, 2nd edition (Basingstoke: Palgrave, 1998). Melvyn Bragg's television series *The Adventure of English* showed some interesting survivals of Norse in the English dialects of Cumbria and Yorkshire; see his *The Adventure of English 500 AD–2000: the Biography of a Language* (London: Hodder & Stoughton, 2003).

Old Norse Poetry in England

Roberta Frank, 'Cnut and his Skalds', in Alexander Rumble (ed.), *The Reign of Cnut,* pp. 106–24; also Matthew Townend,

'Contextualizing the Knútsdrápur: Skaldic Praise-Poetry at the Court of Cnut', *Anglo-Saxon England* 30 (2001), pp. 145–79.

Manuscripts

A good introduction is Michelle Brown, *Anglo-Saxon Manuscripts* (London: British Library, 1991). Basic reference works are: Helmut Gneuss, *Handlist of Anglo-Saxon Manuscripts: A List of Manuscripts and Manuscript Fragments Written or Owned in England up to 1100* (Tempe: Arizona Centre for Medieval and Renaissance Studies, 2001); N.R. Ker, *Catalogue of Manuscripts Containing Anglo-Saxon* (Oxford: Clarendon Press, 1990); Elzbieta Temple, *Anglo-Saxon Manuscripts 900–1066* (London: Harvey Miller, 1976).

Art and manuscript illumination

Janet Backhouse, D.H. Turner and Leslie Webster, *The Golden Age of Anglo-Saxon Art 966–1066* (London: British Museum, 1984); Richard Gameson, *The Role of Art in the Late Anglo-Saxon Church* (Oxford: Clarendon Press, 1995); D.M. Wilson, *Anglo-Saxon Art from the Seventh Century to the Norman Conquest* (London: Thames & Hudson, 1984).

21 The tide went out

Editing issues and punctuation

Many of the problems are discussed in Bruce Mitchell's article 'The dangers of disguise: Old English Texts in modern punctuation', published in the journal *Review of English Studies* new series 31 (1980), pp. 385–413. See also Sarah Larratt Keefer and Katherine O'Brien O'Keeffe (eds), *New Approaches to Editing Old English Verse* (Cambridge: D.S. Brewer, 1998). For the 18th-century copying of this text, see H.L. Rogers, '*The Battle of Maldon*: David Casley's transcript', in the journal *Notes & Queries*, new series, vol. 32 (1985), pp. 147–55.

The Battle of Maldon

D.G. Scragg (ed.), *The Battle of Maldon* (Manchester: Manchester University Press, 1981); D.G. Scragg (ed.), *The Battle of Maldon*

AD 991 (Oxford: Blackwell, 1991); Janet Cooper (ed.), *The Battle of Maldon: Fiction and Fact* (London: Hambledon, 1993). For the documents of the period see Ann Williams, *Æthelred the Unready: The Ill-Counselled King* (London: Hambledon, 2003).

Other editions of *The Battle of Maldon*

E.V.K. Dobbie, *The Anglo-Saxon Minor Poems* (New York, 1942),
E.V. Gordon, *The Battle of Maldon* (London, 1937), Richard
Marsden, *The Cambridge Anglo-Saxon Reader* (Cambridge, 2004),
B.J. Muir, *Leoð: Six Old English Poems* (New York, 1990),
J.C. Pope, *Seven Old English Poems* (Indianapolis, 1966),
D. Whitelock, *Sweet's Anglo-Saxon Reader* (London, 1970).

Related material

For translations, vocabulary, notes and further documents related
to the battle at Maldon see teachyourself.com

22 I was by the shore

The texts of the Exeter Book

At some stage in the course of his career, Leofric acquired the
tenth-century anthology of traditional poetry now known as the
Exeter Book, which he left in his will to Exeter cathedral in 1072
(Exeter, Cathedral Library, 3501). The two poems are to be found
on folio 122v and 123r of the manuscript. For translations, see
Bradley and Hamer. For a full edition see Bernard J. Muir (ed.),
The Exeter Anthology of Old English Poetry, 2 vols (Exeter:
University of Exeter Press, 1994). For a discussion of riddles 30a
and 30b see the article by A.N. Doane, 'Spacing, placing and
effacing: scribal textuality and Exeter Riddle 30a/b', in Keefer and
O'Keeffe, *New Approaches to Editing Old English Verse*, pp. 45–65;
and Roy M. Liuzza, 'The texts of Old English Riddle 30', in
Journal of English and Germanic Philology 87 (1988), pp. 1–15.
For facsimile plates of riddle 30b, riddle 60 and *The Husband's
Message*, see Anne L. Klinck, *The Old English Elegies: A Critical
Edition and Genre Study* (Montreal: McGill-Queen's University

Press, 1992). For a more general study see Carol Braun Pasternack, *The Textuality of Old English* (Cambridge: Cambridge University Press, 1995).

The coronation oath
The text occurs in the 11th-century manuscript London, British Library, Cotton Cleopatra B.xiii, and in Oxford, Bodleian Library Junius 60, a copy of the lost manuscript Cotton Vitellius A.vii. There is an edition and translation in A.J. Robertson, *The Laws of the Kings of England: From Edmund to Henry I* (Cambridge, 1925). For more dicussion of Leofric, see Elaine M. Treharne, 'The bishop's book: Leofric's Homiliary and 11th-century Exeter', in Stephen Baxter, Catherine Karkov, Janet Nelson and David Pelteret (eds), *Early Medieval Studies in Memory of Patrick Wormald* (London: Ashgate, 2009), pp. 521–37.

Interpreting Old English literature
John Hines, *Voices in the Past: English Literature and Archaeology* (Cambridge: D.S. Brewer, 2004); David F. Johnson and Elaine Treharne, *Readings in Medieval Texts: Interpreting Old and Middle English Literature* (Oxford: Oxford University Press, 2005); Clare A. Lees, *Tradition and Belief: Religious Writing in Late Anglo-Saxon England* (London: University of Minnesota Press, 1999); Katherine O'Brien O'Keeffe, *Reading Old English Texts* (Cambridge: Cambridge University Press, 1997); Andy Orchard, *A Critical Companion to Beowulf* (Cambridge: D.S. Brewer, 2003); Phillip Pulsiano and Elaine Treharne, *A Companion to Anglo-Saxon Literature* (Oxford: Blackwell, 2001); T.A. Shippey, *Old English Verse* (London: Hutchinson, 1972).

Further study of Old English language
Apart from books on Old English already mentioned, the following two textbooks are recommended: the first, Chris McCully and Sharon Hilles, *The Earliest English: An Introduction to Old English* (Harlow: Pearson Education, 2005), presents pronunciation, phonology, metre and grammar in interesting and accessible ways. The second, Peter S. Baker, *Introduction to*

Old English (Oxford: Blackwell, 2003), contains a grammar followed by a good selection of poems and prose.

For a selection of texts and parallel translations see Elaine Treharne, *Old and Middle English c.890–c.1400. An Anthology*, 2nd edition (Oxford: Blackwell, 2004). There are two useful beginners' editions of *Beowulf* (with vocabulary on facing page or in margins): Michael Alexander (ed.), *Beowulf* (London: Penguin, 2003) and George Jack (ed.), *Beowulf. A Student Edition* (Oxford: Clarendon Press, 1994). A portable paperback dictionary is J.R. Clark Hall, *A Concise Anglo-Saxon Dictionary* (Toronto and London: University of Toronto Press reprint, 2000). A standard survey and reference work for Old English, with full bibliography, is Richard M. Hogg, *The Cambridge History of the English Language. Volume I. The Beginnings to 1066* (Cambridge: Cambridge University Press, 1992).

For more material and resources on Old English, visit the website teachyourself.com

Test Yourself answers

Unit 1

(1) 1(a) (literal translation) Eadsige archbishop him hallowed and before all the people him well taught, and to his own need and of-all people well admonished. 1(b) Archbishop Eadsige consecrated him and instructed him before all the people and admonished him well for his own need and that of all the people. 1(c) þam 'tham', lærde 'LAIRdeh', arcebiscop 'AR-chuh-bi-shop', agenre 'AH-yun-reh'. 1(d) (suggested answer): the preposition 'to his own need', the -de ending on the past tenses; note also that hine, the word for *him*, precedes the three verbs '… consecrated, … taught, … admonished'. 1(e) (modernized, with some endings omitted) Eadsie archebishop him halwade, and tofor all tha folk him wel lærde, and to his awen neod and all folks wel manude.

2(a) And Stigant priest was blessed to bishop to East Angles. 2(b) And the priest Stigant was consecrated as bishop of East Anglia. 2(c) biscop 'BIshop'. 2(d) Note the preposition *to* after *blessed* and, on word order, the way the word for a rank or profession *priest* comes after the name to which it refers, e.g. Eadsige arcebiscop, Stigant preost. 2(e) (suggested modernization) And Stigant preost was i-bletsad to bishop to East-englum.

(2) 1 (some famous men) Ælfræd, Æþelstan, Eadgar, Æþelræd, Eadweard, Wulfstan, Godwine [explanations: 1 Ælfræd (Alfred the Great), Æþelstan (Athelstan the tenth-century king), Eadgar (Edgar the Peaceable, king of England 959–75), Æþelræd (Ethelred the Unready), Eadweard (Edward the Confessor), Wulfstan (archbishop of York), Godwine (father of Harold II)]

2 (some famous women) Æþelþryþ, Eadgifu, Eadgyð, Ælfþryþ, Ælfgifu, Godgifu, Eadgyð [explanations: Æþelþryþ (St Æthelthryth, also St Etheldreda in Bede's *History*, later form of name was Audrey), Queen Eadgifu (tenth century, king Edgar's grandmother), Eadgyð

(St Edith daughter of king Edgar), Queen Ælfþryþ (Ælfthryth, mother of Æthelred), Queen Ælfgifu (also called Emma, married first to Æthelred and then to Cnut), Godgifu (Lady Godiva, wife of the earl of Mercia), Eadgyð (Edith wife of Edward the Confessor and sister of Harold Godwineson, i.e. king Harold II)]

Unit 2

1 beagas bera; eald egesfull ea; flodgræg feran fyrd; tirfæstra getrum treow; wisdom were wudu; blædum blowan beorh; grene God; dæda demend 2 (a) Bera sceal on hæðe, eald and egesfull. (b) Ea of dune sceal flodgræg feran. (c) Wudu sceal on foldan blædum blowan. (d) Beorh sceal on eorþan grene standan. 3 (a) **cinges tun or cynges tun** *king's estate* (b) **sumor** *summer* (c) **norð** *north* (d) **suð** *south* (e) **ac** *oak* (f) **mere** *lake* (g) **scip** *ship* or **sceap** *sheep* (h) **oxena ford** *ford of the oxen* (i) **here** *army* (j) **heort** *hart* i.e. *stag* (cf. the common English pub name The White Hart) (k) **niw** *new* and **brycg** *bridge*

Unit 3

1 (suggested solutions only) (a) ice (b) dog (c) hen

Unit 4

(1) 1 Thorkell was outlawed by king Cnut. 2 Cnut must have ordered a naval sortie to the Isle of Wight, while Athelnoth's visit to Rome involved a papal ceremony of inauguration as archbishop of Canterbury. 3 Cnut had Thorkell's son at his court to ensure Thorkell's loyalty. 4 Cnut had the relics taken from London to Canterbury.

(2) 1 (a) gewunode, gewunade (b) nam (c) forðferde (d) let (e) gehalgode (f) betæhte 2 (a) for (b) geseah (c) geutlagode (d) gehalgodon 3 D 1026 Here bishop Ælfric went to Rome, and received the pallium from Pope John on the second of the ides of November (12th November). D 1031 Here king Cnut went to Rome. And as soon as he returned home, he then went to Scotland, and the king of the Scots submitted to him and became his man,

but he kept it only for a little while. 4 The C version emphasizes Olaf's sanctity after his death, while D sounds more secular in its insistence that Olaf died in battle. D explicitly explains Cnut's active involvement in Norway and his driving out of Olaf, while C omits or assumes this information. C mentions the loss at sea of earl Hakon.

Unit 5

1 (a) wyllað (b) gæð (c) hæfð (d) springað (e) weaxað (f) ripiað (g) byð 2 Concerning the sun we speak thus. When it rises it makes (the) day. When it is gone down then it brings the night. 3 (a) is called, it, can, it (b) touch, burns (c) it, wanes (d) is

Unit 6

(1) (a) cwæð (b) ðuhte (c) bundon (d) stodon (e) abugon (f) cwædon (g) hatedon (h) hæfdon

(2) 1 (a) When Joseph was 16, he kept his father's herd with his brothers. (b) When his brothers saw this, they shunned him. (c) Then his brothers said, 'Are you our king, or are we your courtiers?' 2 In Joseph's dream the sun and moon and eleven stars represent Joseph's family, who take exception to the idea that their upstart brother has dreamt of lording it over them. 3 Etymologies: 'dream' from Old English **dream** *joy;* 'walk' from **wealcan** *to roll;* 'tell' from **tellan** *to count* (cf. modern English 'teller' *bank clerk, counter of votes in Parliament*); 'tumble' from **tumbian** *to leap, dance;* 'main' from **mægen** *power;* 'fear' from **fær** *danger;* 'wedge' from **wecg** *piece of money*

Unit 7

(1) (a) (plurals) arcebiscopas, leodbiscopas, eorlas, gewritu, word 2 prominent alliteration falls on C̲nut c̲yning, e̲alle his e̲orlas, t̲welfh̲ynde and t̲wyh̲ynde, h̲old h̲laford, Godes ge-r̲ihtum and to r̲ihtre woroldlage, ic nam m̲e to ge-m̲ynde þa ge-w̲ritu and þa

<u>w</u>ord, <u>f</u>ull <u>f</u>rið 3 Antonyms include **twelfhynde and twyhynde** *rich and poor*, **gehadode** and **læwede** *clergy and laity*, **aræran** *raise up* **alecgan** *put down*; the opposite of *hold loyal* is implied in the **swicende** *deceitful* of **unswicende**; divine and secular spheres of law are suggested by the phrase to **Godes gerihtum** and to **woroldlage.**

(2) 1 (suggested hierarchy) casere, cyning, hlaford, hlæfdige, aþeling, eorl, ealdorman, scirgerefa, wita, þegn, burhmann, cypa, ceorl, þeowa 2 The list first needs dividing according to monastic and secular clergy. Secular clergy, who take mass and perform other services for the laity, are **arcebiscop, biscop,** and **preost** or **mæssepreost.** The monastic list could divide according to gender: **abbod, munuc, mynstermann;** and **abbodesse, mynecen.** There is some overlap between these lists, as a monk could be a priest and an abbot could later become a bishop. The anomaly is **ancor** *anchorite* or *hermit*, who was unregulated, and perhaps also the **capellan,** who might be a priest or chaplain at the royal court. 3 se biscop, þone biscop *the bishop*, þæs biscopes *of the bishop*, þam biscope *to the bishop*, þa biscopas, þa biscopas *the bishops*, þara biscopa *of the bishops*, þam biscopum *to the bishops* 4 (a) Lyfing's grievance was that Christ Church did not seem to enjoy as much freedom (e.g. exemption from rent payments) as it had once had. (b) Cnut offered Lyfing a new royal charter of freedom. (c) Realizing that the old charters needed to be renewed and made effective, Cnut placed them with his own hands on the altar of the cathedral.

Unit 8

1 (a) hyne (b) hi (c) hyne (d) hym or hyne (e) hi 2 (a) Euphrosyne was famed for her wisdom and learning and virtuous living. (b) The father's words *God's will be done* are a polite form of refusal to the young suitors, at the same time they suggest that he believes St Euphrosyne must follow the divine vocation ordained for her. (c) The father only changed his mind when approached by a man of the thegnly class who was wealthier than the other suitors and could pledge a larger sum of money.

Unit 9

(1) 1 Their father was worried about why his brothers were delayed and sent Joseph to see whether it was well with them and then to report back to him. 2 When he meets the man Joseph appears to be wandering aimlessly on Shechem. 3 The man has overheard his brothers talking about going to Dothaim.

(2) 1 ic blissie, þu blissast, heo blissaþ, we, ge, hi blissiaþ; blissiende; ic blissode, þu blissodest, heo blissode, we, ge, hi blissodon; geblissod 2 (a) hit gelamp (b) we swuncon (c) hi gewunnon (d) ic swamm (e) heo arn (f) we druncon (g) þu hit funde

Unit 10

1 (a) þone (b) þære (c) þære (d) þære (e) þære (f) þam (g) þa

2 From the ditch end into the stream. From the stream into the sandy road; after the road northwards onto the bishop's measure of land, over the bishop's land to the innermost flax field way. From the flax field into the hedge; after the hedge on badger hole way. From badger hole way into the croft. From the croft by the enclosure into Leofsunu's croft. 3 (a) ðæs (b) fearnleges burnan (c) Holan beames (d) Holan beames (e) þære (f) þam (g) þam (h) þæne (i) þæne (j) þæs

Unit 11

1 (a) gret (b) mine (c) freondlice (d) cyðe (e) birig, byrig (f) wuda (g) forð 2 I Thored grant the land at Horsley to the community at Christ Church for the sake of my soul as fully and completely as I myself owned it. 3 These are the lands which Thorketel grants to God and St Mary and St Edmund: that is, the land at Culford that was his own, as it stands, with food and labour provision, and with jurisdiction, and all the land at Wordwell, and the land at Ixworth as it stands with food and labour provision. 4 (a) þes ceorl (b) he hatað þisne cyning (c) he lufað þas cwen (d) þyses cynges land (e) he hit geaf þyssum ceorle (f) þas eorlas (g) he hit geaf þyssum eorlum

Unit 12

(1) (a) numbers: four feet below the stomach, eight feet on its back, two wings, twelve eyes, six heads; proposed solution: a ship with four oars, four rowers and two sails; the six heads are the four seamen and the two figureheads of the ship (see Porter, Anglo-Saxon Riddles, p. 135) (b) one eye, two ears, two feet, twelve hundred heads, one neck, two sides; proposed solution: a one-eyed seller of garlic

(2) 1 The **annus solaris** (solar year) has 365 days and 52 weeks, and in fact the year has 8,066 hours. 2 (a) feower and twentig (b) eahta and feowertig (c) twa and hundseofontig (d) an hund tida and twentig tida

(3) 1 woodland pasture for cows; **seo cu** 2 dairy farm for sheep; **se sceap** 3 ford for goats; **se gat** 4 eagle clearing; **se earn** 5 crane ford; **se cran** 6 horse ford; **þæt hors** 7 woodland pasture for sheep; **þæt scip sheep** 8 stream for stags; **se heort** 9 wolf clearing; **se wulf** 10 dairy farm for herds; **seo heord** 11 island of the calves; **þæt cealf** 12 estate with dogs; **se hund** 13 boar wood; **se eofor** 14 sheep stream; **se scip**

Unit 13

1 The brothers deprived Joseph of his coat. 2 They were about to eat when they saw the traders. 3 Ruben presents his motivation to his brothers as one of propriety: it is better to keep their hands clean of bloodshed. In fact he wants to rescue Joseph from the well and return him to his father. Judah, contrariwise, has no wish to return Joseph to their father. He agrees with Ruben about the impropriety of murdering their own brother, a member of their own kin, but instead proposes selling Joseph as a slave. 4 The thirty pieces of silver would recall the Gospel narrative of how Judas betrayed Jesus for thirty pieces of silver.

Unit 14

(1) 1 The brothers killed a goat kid and dipped the tunic in its blood. 2 Ruben and Jacob both tear their clothes as an expression

of grief; in both illustrations this action is clearly indicated to the right of the picture. 3 The Midianites sold Joseph to Potiphar, captain of the guard.

(2) 1 (a) Alliteration on the stressed syllables of witan, ge-wearð, wurðe (b) full rhyme in gesealde, sealde, gewealde (c) understande se ðe wille 2 (a) mare and mænigfealdre … manige, forsworene and swiðe (b) forsworene, forlogone, tobrocene (c) oft and gelome 3 MAnige sind forSWOrene, and swiðe forLOgene, and WED synd toBROcene, OFT and geLOme. 4 strong adjective endings on oþerne, fremdum, micele, egeslice, forsworene, forlogone, tobrocene

Unit 15

(1) 1 Her father will look for her in the women's convent and then take her away to marry her bridegroom. 2 Euphrosyne disguises herself in men's clothing and waits until evening. 3 The visitor falls at the abbot's feet to receive a blessing. 4 The visitor has heard of the reputation of the monastery and claims to have been at the king's court, but there is no possibility of leading a monk's life in the city.

(2) 1 (a) magisters (b) teacher's 2 (a) syxes (b) knif 3 (a) briwes (b) briw (c) soup (d) soup 4 (a) sealt (b) seltan (c) salt (d) to salt

Unit 16

1 Æthelbald asked the man Wilfrid to lead him to the hermitage. 2 Wilfrid had left his gloves in the ship; Guthlac knew by divine inspiration: God made known to him all secret things. 3 They realized that the gloves had been stolen by ravens. 4 The raven obeyed Guthlac's command. 5 The three men struck the signal – presumably a bell – to announce their arrival at the landing place. 6 They also wanted a period of conversation with the hermit. 7 **mid bliðum andwlite and gode mode** *with happy countenance and good disposition*; **smerciende** *smiling* 8 first episode: **on sumere nihte** (feminine), **þæt gewrit** (neuter), **þa cartan** (feminine accusative), **on þæne fenn** (masculine accusative), **se foresæda cuma** (masculine),

þone hrefen (masculine accusative), **se halga wer** (masculine), þone
broðor (masculine accusative), **se hrefn** (masculine), **þa fennas**
(masculine plural), **þa fenland** (neutral plural), **seo carte** (feminine),
to þære cartan (feminine), second episode: **wið þone halgan wer**
(masculine accusative), **ealle þa diglan þingc** (neuter plural),
se fugel (masculine), **þæt westen** (neuter), **þa glofe** (feminine
accusative), **to þære hyðe** (feminine dative), **ane glofe** (feminine
accusative), **his bletsunge** (feminine accusative)

Unit 17

(1) 1 four adverbials of manner: mid mycclan weorðscype, mid his
agenum handum, arwurðlice, bliðelice 2 four adverbials of place or
direction: ut, to Rome, on Sancte Petres weofode, ham to his earde
3 four adverbials of time: on Nonas Octobris, sona þærmid, on
þam sylfan dæge, syððan þæræfter

(2) King Cnut sends friendly greetings to bishop Eadsige and abbot
Ælfstan and Æthelric and all my thegns in Kent. And I inform
you that I wish that Æthelnoth shall keep his landed property in
his episcopal see now just as he did before Æthelric was reeve and
after he was reeve until the present time, and I will not allow any
wrong to be done to the bishop, whoever the reeve may be

Unit 18

1 swa feala þegna so many thegns, minre sawle to ecere alysednesse
to the eternal salvation of my soul, be minum freondscipe *by my
friendship* 2 (a) feala oðra godra cnihta (b) on manegra godra
manna gewitnysse (c) æfter his dæge (d) mid eallum þingum (e) on
ðisse Cristes bec (f) ic cyþe inc

Unit 19

(1) 1 Wynflæd presented her witnesses at Woolmer before the
king, and they confirmed that Ælfric had given Wynflæd the
land at Hagbourne and at Bradfield in return for the estate at
Datchet. 2 He refused to accept the decision and insisted that the

case should be referred to the shire court. 3 The king sent abbot Ælfhere (Æluere) to the assembly with his message of greetings and an instruction to work out a just agreement between the two parties. 4 When he saw that Wynflæd's claim was supported by a formidable array of oath helpers, Leofwine must have realized that his counterclaim would fail. The counsellors at the meeting advised him not to take an oath as this would spoil the chance of an amicable agreement. If the verdict had then been against him, Leofwine would have had to pay not only compensation to Wynflæd, for holding her estates illegally, but also his wergild to the king, as punishment for his theft of the property. 5 Wynflæd was instructed to give back any of Leofwine's father's gold and silver that she still had; in fact she gave back as much as she could.

(2) 1 þa nolde he butan hit man **sceote** to scirgemote. *He would not do this except that it was referred to the shire court.* 2 þa getæhte man Wynflæde þæt hio **moste** hit hyre geahnian *then they instructed Wynflæd that she should prove her ownership*; þa tæhte man hyre þæt hio **sciolde** bringan his fæder gold and siolfor eal þæt hio hæfde *then they instructed her that she should bring his father's gold and silver, all that she had* (or *all that she might have* – if subjunctive); þa næs he þagyt on þam gehealden butan hio **sceolde** swerian þæt his æhta þær ealle wæron *then he was still not satisfied until she would swear that all his possessions were there* (**butan** governs the subjunctive earlier in the text); þa cwæþ hio þæt hio ne **mihte** *then she said that she could not...*

Unit 20

Here is declared in this document that a shire assembly sat at Æthelnoth's Stone in the time of king Cnut. Bishop Æthelstan and ealdorman Ranig sat there, and Edwine the ealdorman's son and Leofwine Wulfsige's son, and Thorkell the White. And Tofi the Proud came there on the king's business. Bryning the shire-reeve was there, and Æthelgeard of Frome, Godric of Stoke, and the thegns of Herefordshire. Then Edwine Enneawn's son travelled to the assembly and sued his own mother there for a certain portion of land, which was Wellington and Crawley. Then the bishop asked who would answer for the mother, and Thorkell the White answered that he would if he knew the claim. Since he did not know the claim, they appointed three thegns from the assembly (to go) where she was, which was at Fawley, and these were Leofwine of Frome, and Æthelsige the Red, and Wynsige the Shipman. When they came to her, they asked what claim she had to the land for which her son was suing. But she said that she did not have any land that belonged to him in any way. And she became extremely angry with her son; and she called her kinswoman Leofflæd to her – Thorkell's wife – and in their presence spoke to her as follows: 'Here sits Leofflæd my kinswoman to whom I grant both my land and also my gold, clothing and garments and all I possess, after my lifetime.' And after that she spoke to the thegns: 'Act thegnly and present my statement well at the assembly, before all the good men. And have them know who I have granted my land to, and all my possessions, and to my own son never a thing! And let them be witness to this.' And they did so. They rode to the assembly and made known to all the good men what she had charged them with. Then Thorkell the White stood up at the assembly and petitioned all the thegns to give cleanly to his wife the lands which her kinswoman had granted to her. And they did so. And Thorkell then rode to Saint Æthelberht's Minster, with the consent and witness of all the people, and had it recorded in a Gospel Book.

Old English–English word index

The index covers words and phrases occurring in the **study texts**
and **Test Yourself** exercises.

The number indicates the unit in which the word or phrase occurs
prominently. You should refer back to that unit to study the
word in context; in that unit you will find further information on
grammar, usage, pronunciation, etymology and word formation.

Each word is translated briefly, according to its meaning in
context.

Occasionally where necessary, a grammatical explanation is given,
e.g. 'agen *own* (adj.) 1' (abbreviations used are: acc. accusative,
adj. adjective, conj. conjunction, dat. dative, fem. feminine, masc.
masculine, past part. past participle, subj. subjunctive).

Any words which occur only in the parallel-text reading sections
are not normally listed. This is to encourage the use of these texts
for wider reading, as a complement to the more intensive word-by-
word analysis of the study texts.

When learning a language it is important that you acquire words,
phrases and patterns as they appear in context. Use this index also
as a review or revision tool, to recall the original context in which
your learning took place.

æfentid *evening time* 15
æfre *ever* 19
æfter *after* 10
Ægelnoðesstan *Aylton* 20
ægðer ge... ge *both... and* 8
æhta *possessions* 19
ælc *each, every* 18
ælf *elf* 1
ælfere *Ælfhere* 21
ænig *any* 11, 21
ær *earlier, before* 4
ærende *message, errand* 20
ærendspræc *message* 22
ærest *first* 10
ge-ærndede æt Cnute *acquired from Cnut* 18
ærnemerigen *early morning* 5
ær ðam *before that* 4
ær ðam þe *before* (conj.) 13
ær wiste *had known* 18
æt *at* 4
æt: onfeng æt *received from* 4
æt: Godric æt Stoce *Godric of Stoke* 20
ætgædere *together* 20
æton *they ate* 20
ætsomne *together* 2
ætwitan *reproach* 21
æþeling *prince* 19
æþelred *king Æthelred the Unready* 21
afleogan *fly away* 16
afligeð *flies away* 16
afysan *drive away* 6, 14
agan *have, own* 11
agen *own* (adj.) 1
agenre *see* agen
ageotan *spill, pour out* 13, 14
agyfan *deliver, give over to* 13, 19
ageaf *gave back* 16
ah: ic ah *I own* 20
ahengce *hung* (subj.) 16

(ge)ahnian *possess* 4, 19
ahnunga *proofs of ownership* 19
ahrinest *you touch* 5
aht *anything* 18
ahte *owned* 11, 16
alecgan *put down, lay down* 7
alifed *permitted* 20
alysednes *release* 18
amber *pitcher, measure, amber* 11
an *one* 3, 4
anæd *solitude* 22
anda *enmity* 6
andland = andlang
andlang *along* 10
andswarode *answered* 9
andwlita *face* 16
ane *alone* (fem.) 3
Angelcynn *the English nation* 4
ann: ic geann *I grant* 11
annus solaris (Latin) *the solar year* 12
anræd *of single counsel, of one mind* 4
ar *messenger* 21
aræran *raise* 7
arcebiscop *archbishop* 1, 4
arfæst *gracious* 22
arfullice *graciously* 20
arwurð *venerable* 17
arwurðlice *honourably* 17
asette *put, placed* 17
asprang *sprang forth* 8
Assandun *Ashingdon* 4
astigen *descended* 5
astod *stood up* 20
astyrod *moved* 20
atellan *recount* 19
atiht: manige wurdon atihte *many were attracted* 8
aþ *oath* 19
aþreatode *rebuked* 6

Augustin: æt sancte Augustine *at St Augustine's* **10**

aþel *noble* **1**

aðreatode *rebuked* **6**

aweg *away* **19**

aweg lætan *dispense with* **19**

awrat *wrote down* **16**

awriten *written* **7, 16**

axode *asked* **9**

ge-axode ic *I have heard of* **15**

bæd *asked, requested* **18**

bædde *encouraged* **8**

baldlicost *most boldly* **21**

bam *both* (dative) **18**

bar *boar* **12**

be *about, by, concerning* **5, 10**

bead *commanded* **7**

beagas *rings* **2**

beah = beag *arm-ring* **8**

beahwriða *arm-ring* **8**

bealdlice *boldly* **22**

beam *tree* **10**

bearm *lap* **3**

bearn *sons* **14**

bearn *child, son* **17**

bearu *grove, wood* **22**

bebeodan *command* **20**

bec *book* (dat.) **18**

becomon *came* **21**

becweden *bequeathed* (past part.) **18**

becweðan *bequeath* **18**

befer *beaver* **9**

beforan *before* **18, 19**

begeat *received* **8**

begytan *acquire, receive* **8**

behatan *promise* **8**

beheolde *saw, beheld* **22**

behet *promised* **8**

beleolc *enclosed* **22**

(ge)belgan *become angry* **20**

belle *bell* **15**

beo *be* (imperative) **16**

beodan *command* **11**

beon *to be* **3**

beorh *hill* **2**

beorht *bright* **1**

beornas *men* **21**

beotian *to vow* **20**

beoð *are* **3**

bera *bear* (the animal) **2**

beran *carry, bear* **16**

bereafian *deprive* **13**

beron *they would bear* (subj.) **21**

bestodon *stood along* **21**

betæcan *entrust* **4, 17**

betæhte *entrusted* **4**

betere *better* **19**

betwux *among* **5**

betwux þysum *meanwhile* **15**

betwynan *between, among* **13**

beþencan *ponder* **13, 15**

bewunden *wound round* **6, 22**

biddan *to ask* **19**

bidde ic *I pray* **18**

binnan *within* **11**

(ge)biorgan *protect* **19**

bisceop *bishop* **1**

blæd-um *with fruits* **2**

Bleddehlæw *Bledlow* **18**

(ge)bletsad *blessed* **1**

bletsian *to bless* **18**

(ge)bletsod *blessed* (past part.) **18**

bletsung *blessing* **16**

bliss *happiness* **17**

blissian *to rejoice* **9**

bliðe *happy* **16**

bliðelice *happily* **17**

blowan *to flourish* **2**

blowende *flourishing* **22**

boc *book, charter* **10**

bocere *scholar* **5**

bord *shield* **21**

brad *broad* 10, 21
æt Bradanfelda *at Bradfield* 19
breme *famous* 17
bricg *bridge* 21
bringan *bring* 19
brocc *badger* 10
brohte *brought* 16
broðor *brother* 6
broðru *brothers* 6
broðrum *(with his) brothers* 6
bruce *enjoy* 8, 18
brun *dark, shining* 22
brycg *bridge* 2, 10
brydguma *bridegroom* 15
bufan *above* 10
bugan *to bend* 8
burg = burh
burh *city, stronghold* 2
burna *burn, stream* 10
butan *without* 11
butan *except that* 19
buton *unless* 21
byre *youth(s)* 8
byrgen *grave* 17
byrht *bright* 1, 5
(ge)byrian *belong* 20
byrig *city, stronghold* 11
byrnende *burning* 16, 22
bysig *busy* 22
byst ðu? *are you?* 6

caf *brave* 21
carta *parchment* 16
ceald *cold* 5
cealf *calf* 12
ceap *price, transaction* 13
ceaster *city* 2
cempena: cempena ealdor *captain of soldiers* 14
Cent *Kent* 7
ceorl *free peasant* 4, 20
(ge)ciged *called* 5

cild *child, young nobleman* 11
cing *king* 1
cirice *church* 20
clæne *cleanly, completely* 20
claðas *clothes* 14
(ge)cleopian *call* 20
cleric *clerk, cleric* 5
cnapa *boy* 14
cniht *retainer* 11
com *came* 4
conn: ne conn *does not know* 22
cran *crane, heron* 12
crawa *crow* 12
cristen *Christian* 7
Cristes boc *gospel book* 20
Cristes cyrice *Christ Church* 7
croft *croft* 10
cu *cow* 12
Culeforde *Culford* 11
cum *come* (imperative) 9
cuma *guest* 16
cuman *come* 13
cuð *known* 7
cuðe *knew* 19, 20
cwædon *(they) said* 6
cwæð *(he) said* 6
(ge)cweden *called* (past part.) 5
cwen *queen, consort* 8
cweðað *(they) say* 5
cweðende *saying* (present part.) 15
cweðe we *we say* 5
æt Cwichelmeshlæwe *at Cwichelm's Barrow* 19
cwyde *will, testament* 18
cydde *proclaimed* 18
cynelic *royal* 17
cyng *king* 4
cyning *king* 2
cynn *kin, kindred* 2, 3, 16, 21
(ge)cynd *nature* 16
cypa *merchant* 13
cyrcean: cyrice *church* 7

Cyrdesleah *Cradley* 20
cyrice, cirice *church* 7
(ge)cyrran *turn, convert* 15
(ge)cyssað *kiss* 22
cyð *tell* (imperative) 9
(ge)cyðan *proclaim, make known* 5
cyta *kite* (the bird) 12

dæd *deed* 2
dæg *day* 5
dæl *part* 5
dæl: hyre dæles *for her part* 19
dælan *share out* 2
daga *of days* 5
decanus *dean, prior* 17
Deccet *Datchet*
  (Buckinghamshire) 19
demend *judge* 2
dene: denu *valley* 9
Dene-mearc *Denmark* 4
denn *woodland pasture* 10
deor *animal* 12
derian *harm, damage* 14, 21
deþ *(he, it) does* 15
dic *ditch* 10
digel *secret* 15
dihtan *dictate* 22
discten = discþegn
discþegn *steward, seneschal* 19
dohtig *excellent* 4
dohtor *daughter* 19
dom: on eallum domum *in all the*
  laws 22
don *to put* 13
don *to do* 15
dorste *dared* 19
dream *joy* 17
drigge *dry* 5
Drihten *Lord, God* 1, 7
drohtnung *way of life* 15
dun *mountain* 2
dyde *did* 15

dydon *they put* 13
dydon *they did* 4, 17

ea *river* 2
eac *also* 16
ead, eadig *blessed* 1, 16
eadignesse *blessedness* 22
eadmodnys *humility* 17
eagan *eyes* 12
eage *eye* 12
eahta *eight* 12
eahteoð *eighth* 17
eald *old* 2
ealdor *captain, chief* 14
ealdorman *nobleman, prince* 4
eall *all* 4
eall-es *of all* 1
eall-um *all* 1
eal-ne *all* 2
earan *ears* 12
eard *region, land* 3
eardian *to live* 15
earn *eagle* 12
eart *you are* (singular) 3
east *east* 2
Eastenglas *East Angles,*
  East Anglia 1
to Eastenglum *to the*
  East Angles 1
Easterdæig *Easter Day* 1
ea-steð *river-bank* 21
Eastseaxe *East Saxons, Essex* 4, 21
eaxl *shoulder* 12
ebba *ebb-tide* 21
ece *eternal* 11
ecg *edge, sword* 21
eft *again, back again* 4, 10
eg *island* 12
ege *fear* 2
egesfull *terrible* 2
egeslic *terrible* 14
egland *island* 16

Egypta land *Egypt, land of the Egyptians* **13**
ehtuwe *eight* **12**
elles *else* **7**
embe *about* **18**
emniht *equinox* **5**
endleofan *eleven* **6**
engla *of angels* **3**
Engla *of the English* **4, 20**
Englaland *England* **4**
englisc *English*
eode *went* **4**
eofor *wild boar* **12**
eoh *horse* **12**
eom *(I) am* **3**
eorl *nobleman, earl* **2, 4**
eorlice *angrily* **20**
eorþe *earth* **2**
eow *to you* **7**
eower *your* **15**
engel *angel* **3**
ersc *stubble field* **10**
estful *devout* **17**
eþel *homeland* **3**
eunuchus *eunuch* **15**

fæder *father* **6**
Fæliglæh *Fawley* **20**
fæmne *maid, woman* **15**
fæmnena *of women* **15**
fæst *firm* **22**
fæstlice *firmly* **15, 21**
fæðm *embrace* **3**
far *go* (imperative) **9**
faran *to go, travel* **4**
farende *travelling* **20**
fea *few* **22**
(ge)feaht *fought* **19**
feala *many* **18**
fearn *fern* **10**
fela *many* **21**
feld *field* **11**

feng *to took* **16**
fenn *fenland* **16**
feoh *fee, cattle* **12**
feohtan *to fight* **2**
feoll *fell* **15**
feorran *from afar* **13, 17**
feower *four* **5, 12**
feowertig *forty* **11**
(ge)fera *companion* **4, 17**
feran *to depart, travel* **2, 12**
ferian *convey* **4, 17**
fet *feet* **12**
fif *five* **11**
fiftig *fifty* **3**
fingras *fingers* **15**
fisc *fish* **15**
fiþru *wings* **7**
flæsc *flesh* **13**
flan: flanes *of an arrow* **21**
fleah *flew* **16**
fleam *flight* **21**
flet *hall* **8**
flod *tide* **21**
flodas *floods* **3**
flod-græg *flood-grey* **2**
flot *sea* **21**
flotan *seamen, Vikings* **21**
flowende *flowing* **21**
flyht *flight* **21**
folc *people* **1**
folca *of nations* **8**
folces: ealles folces *of all the people* **1**
foldan: on foldan *on the earth* **2**
folde *earth* **2**
for *went, from* **faran** *go* **4**
for: for wætere *because of the water* **21**
forbead *forbade* **20**
forbeodan *forbid* **20**
ford *ford, river-crossing* **2, 21**
foresæd *aforesaid* (past part.) **16**

foresædon *they mentioned* **20**
forferde = forðferde *departed* **4**
forgenga, foregenga *predecessor* **11**
forgife *grant* **22**
forgyfen *granted* (past part.) **18**
forgyldan *compensate* **19**
forgyldon *(you) might buy off* (subj.) **21**
forleton *they left behind* **16**
forma *first* **1, 21**
forsteall *ambush* **18**
forstodan *were worth, stood for* **7**
for þam ðe *because* **6**
forþan = forðam *because* **19**
forðcom *came forth* **19**
forðferde *passed away* **4**
forðweg *onward journey* **22**
forun *they went* **13**
for ut set *out to sea* **4**
forwerda *terms of agreement* **8**
forword *agreement* **18**
forworht *forfeited* (past part.) **18**
fostorland *land given to recipients to use for food* **18**
fot *foot* **12**
fræton *devoured, ate* **13**
(ge)frætwod *adorned* (past part.) **8**
franca *spear* **21**
Frankland *France* **4**
frea *lord* **20**
frefrode *consoled* **16**
(ge)frefrodon *(they) consoled* **14**
frefrung *consolation* **14**
fremd *foreign* **11**
fremdan *to strangers* **11**
fremdum *to strangers* **14**
fremian *to benefit* **13**
freols *immunity, privilege* **7**
freond *friend* **6, 20**
freondlice *in a friendly manner* **7**
freondræden *friendship* **6**
freondscipe *friendship* **18**

frið *peace* **7**
friðusibb *peace-pledge* **8**
frumstaðol *foundation, first state* **22**
fugel *bird* **16**
fuhton *fought* (plural) **4**
ful georne *very well* **18**
fulla *fullness* **19**
full *full* **7**
full *fully* **11**
fultum *help* **19**
funde: ne funde *could not find* **14**
fundon *(they) found* **14**
fus *eager* **22**
fyl *fall* **21**
(ge)fylle *I fill* **3**
fynd *enemies* **6, 21**
fyr *fire* **22**
fyrd *army, militia* **2**

ga *(I) go* **14**
gaderung *the gathering in, harvest* **5**
gæð *goes* **5**
gafol *tribute* **21**
gan *go* **5**
gangan, gongan *walk* **12, 21**
gangon *they went* **21**
gegangan *obtain* **21**
gar *spear* **1**
garas *spears* **21**
gastlic *spiritual* **7**
gat *goat* **12**
ge *you* (plural) **3, 18**
ge... ge... *both... and...* **19**
ge-ærndede æt Cnute *acquired from Cnut* **18**
geaf *gave* from **gifan 18**
ge-ahnian *take possession* **4**
ge-ahnian *prove possession* **19**
ge-ahnade him eall þæt land *claimed all the land as his* **4**
ge-ann *(I) grant* **11**

geard *enclosure* **10**
gear *year* **4**
geare: on þissum geare *in this year* **4**
gearowe *ready* (plural) **21**
geat *gate* **10**
geatweard *gatekeeper* **15**
ge-axode *he heard of* **15**
ge-bealh *she became angry* **20**
ge-biorgan *protect* **19**
ge-bletsad *blessed* (past part.) **1**
ge-bletsade *he blessed* **17**
ge-bletsod *blessed* (past part.) **18**
ge-bohte *bought* **11**
ge-broðru *(group of) brothers* **4, 6**
ge-byrede *belonged* **20**
ge-ciged *called* (past part.) **5**
ge-cleopade *called, summoned* **20**
ge-cneow *he recognized* **14**
ge-cweden *called* (past part.) **5**
ge-cynd *nature* **16**
ge-cyrran *turn, convert* **15**
ge-cyssað *kiss* **22**
ge-don *done* (past part.) **18**
ge-dwola *error, wandering* **9**
ge-earnunga *favours* **21**
ge-eaðmeddon *they humbled themselves* **20**
ge-feaht *fought* **19**
ge-fera *companion* **4**
ge-frætwod *adorned* (past part.) **8**
ge-frefrodon *(they) comforted* **14**
ge-fylle *I fill* **3**
ge-ga *go* **11**
ge-gaderian *gather* **5**
gegangan *to obtain* **21**
ge-gearnunga *merits* **17**
ge-gierwed *equipped, clothed* (past part.) **12**
ge-gyrla *garment, dress* **15**
ge-hadod *ordained* (past part.) **7**
ge-hadud *ordained* (past part.) **18**

ge-halgian *consecrate* **4**
ge-halgod *consecrated* (past part.) **1**
ge-healden *satisfied* **19**
ge-hwæde *little* **15**
ge-hydde *hid* **15**
ge-hyrde *heard* **9**
ge-lamp *happened* **6**
ge-lædde *led* **19**
ge-lærednys *learning, skill* **8**
geldan *pay* **11**
ge-led *charged with* **20**
ge-lede *laid* **7**
ge-lede *lead* **16**
ge-limpan *to happen* **9**
ge-logodon *(they) placed* **17**
ge-lome *frequently* **14**
ge-meddred *maternal* **20**
ge-met *way, means, manner* **15**
ge-metfæst *moderate* **16**
ge-metgung *moderation* **5**
ge-miltsige *have mercy* (subj.) **20**
ge-mittan *meet, find* **9**
ge-mot *assembly, meeting* **4**
ge-mylted *consumed* **22**
ge-mynd *mind, memory* **7**
ge-nam *took* **16**
ge-name *might take* (subj.) **21**
ge-nemned *named* (past part.) **5**
ge-nerian *save, rescue* **13**
generienne *in order to rescue* **13**
ge-nog, genuh *enough* **4, 7**
geofan *give* **11**
geondhwearf *processed* **8**
geong *young* **8**
geong *went* **8**
georn *eager* **21**
georne *eagerly* **14**
ger *year* **4**
ger: þæs geres ær ðam *earlier in the year* **4**
ge-ræhte *reached* **16**
ge-refa *reeve* **17**

ge-reordade *feasted* **17**

ge-riht *right, justice, obligation* **4**

ge-riht: on geriht *straight on* **10**

ge-rysna *what is fitting, dignity, honour* **18**

ge-rysenlic *honourable* **18**

ge-sæde *said* **13, 18, 20**

ge-sæton *(they) sat* **15**

ge-samnodan *(they) gathered* **14**

ge-sawon *(they) saw* **3, 6, 13**

ge-scrydde *(she) clothed* **15**

ge-seah *(he) saw* **6**

ge-sealde *gave* **14**

ge-seman *reconcile* **19, 21**

ge-siðas *companions* **22**

gesohton *they sought out* **13, 19**

ge-somnod *gathered* (past part.) **19**

ge-specen *spoken* **11**

ge-swac *ceased* **20**

ge-swutelian *clarify* **5**

ge-syne *seen* **13**

ge-synscipe *marriage* **8**

ge-tæhte *instructed* **19**

ge-tæle *counting* **12**

ge-tilian *produce* **18**

ge-trahtniað *(they) explain, expound* **5**

ge-þafian *allow* **17**

ge-þeah *flourished* **20**

ge-þyncðo, geþincðo *rank, degree* **20**

ge-unnan *grant* **11**

ge-utlagian *to outlaw* **4**

ge-wat *departed, went* **15, 21**

ge-weald *power, dominion* **14, 22**

ge-wearð *occurred* **14**

ge-wendan *to turn, return* **4**

ge-winnan *strive* **9**

ge-witnes *witness, cognisance* **7, 11**

ge-worht *made* **8**

ge-wregan *to accuse* **6**

ge-writ *letter, writ, document* **7**

ge-writen *written* (past part.) **20**

ge-wunelic *usual* **15**

ge-wunian *remain* **2, 4**

ge-wurþe Godes willa *God's will be done* **8**

gif *if* : **gif eower willa þæt bið** *if it is your wish* **15**

gifu *gift* **1**

gim, gimm *jewel* **2**

gled *ember, flame* **22**

glof *glove* **2, 16**

God *God* **5, 8, 11, 13, 15**

god *good* **1, 11, 20**

godes *well-being* (genitive) **21**

goddra manna *of good men* **7**

gofol = gafol *tribute* **21**

gold *gold* **11**

gongan *walk, walking* **12**

græg *grey* **2**

graf *grove* **10**

grene *green* **2**

greniað *become green* **5**

gret *greets* **7**

gretan *greet* **7**

grette *greeted* **19**

grim *fierce* **21**

grið *truce, protection* **18, 20, 21**

griðbryce *breach of protection* **18**

grund *depth, ground* **3**

guð *battle* **21**

guðplega *battle-play* **21**

gyf *if* **7**

gyfan, to gyfene *to give* **8**

gyrd *staff* **16**

gyrnan *seek, yearn for* **8**

gyt *still, yet* **20**

Gyxeweorðe *Ixworth* (Surrey) **11**

habban *to have* **6**

habbað *(we) have* **18**

æt Hacceburnan *at Hagbourne* (Berkshire) **19**

(ge)hadode *ordained clergy* **7**
(ge)hadude *ordained clergy* **18**
hæbbe *I have* **11**
hæfde *had* **4, 7, 11**
hæfð *has* **5**
hælð *health, salvation* **17**
hæleða *of warriors* **21**
hære sack *cloth, hair-shirt* **14**
hæsel *hazel* **10**
hæð *heath* **2**
hafuc *hawk* **2, 12**
hal *safe, healthy* **20**
halga *saint* **18**
halgade *consecrated* **1**
(ge)halgod *consecrated*
  (past part.) **1**
halig *holy* **4**
ham home: ham com *came home* **4**
hamsocn *attack at home* **18**
hand *hand* **4, 12, 13**
hand: on hand *into his hands* **19**
hangiende *hanging* **15**
hangode *hung, was hanging* **16**
haten *called* (past part.) **5, 21**
hatian *to hate* **6**
ic hatte *I am called* **3, 12**
he *he or it* (masc.) **5**
heafda *of heads* **12**
heafdu: siex heafdu *six heads* **12**
heafod *head* **12**
healdan *hold, rule* **2**
to healdenne *to rule* **4**
healf *half, side* **4, 21**
heall *hall*: **on healle** *in the hall* **2**
Healtun *Halton*
  (Buckinghamshire) **18**
heanlic *shameful* **21**
hege *hedge* **10**
heo, hio *she or it* (fem.) **5, 16**
heofenas *heavens* **2**
on heofenum *in the heavens* **2**
heold *held, kept* from **healdan 4**

heom *them* **4**
heora *their* **9**
heorde *herds* **6**
heort *hart, stag* **2**
heorte *heart* **17**
her *here* **4**
her on ðissum geare *here in*
  this year **4**
here *army* **2**
het *commanded* **6**
hi, hig *they* **3**
hid *hide* (of land) **10**
hider *here, hither* **15**
hie *her*
him *to him* (dat.) or *to them* (dat.) **8**
hine *him* (acc.) **1, 8**
hio, heo *she or it* (fem.) **5, 16**
hira *their* **8**
hire *her* **8**
hired *community* **8**
hired *household, court* **15**
hit *it* **5**
hlæfdie *lady* **17**
hlæfdige *lady* **10**
hlaford *lord* **7**
hleo *protector* **21**
hlisa *fame* **8**
hnigan *drop, incline* **3**
hol *hollow* **10**
hol *hole, cave* **10**
hold *gracious, loyal* **7**
holt *wood* **12**
hond: æfter hondum *from hand to*
  hand **22**
hors *horse* **3, 12**
Horslege *Horsley* **11**
hrefn *raven* **16**
hreod *reed* **16**
hreodbedd *reed-bed* **16**
hrine: ic hrine *I touch* **3**
hring *ring* **6, 8**
Hrisbeorga *Risborough* **18**

Hrofesceaster *Rochester* **17**
hrycg *back* **12**
hu *how* **9**
hund *hundred* **12**
hund *dog* **12**
hundseofontig *seventy* **5**
hundnigontig *ninety* **5**
hunig *honey* **15**
hwa *who* **20**
hwæm *to whom* **20**
hwæne *each* **6**
hwænne *until* **21**
hwæt *what* **3**
hwæðer *whether* **9**
hwar *where* **14**
hwil *while, period of time* **4**
hwilum *at times* **8**
hwita: Þurkil hwita *Thorkell the White* **20**
æt Hwitecyrcan *at Whitchurch* **19**
hwyder *where to* **14**
hy *them* **7**
hyne *him* **6, 8**
(ge)hyran *hear* **9**
(ge)hyrað *hear* **6**
hyre *her* **19**
hyrmen *servants* **6**
hyrsumode *obeyed* **16**
hyrð *belongs to* **18**
hys *his* **6**
hyt *it* **6**

ic *I* **3**
ides *lady* **3**
idus (Latin) *ides* (in Roman calendar) **4, 5**
ieg *island* **12**
ilca *the same* **17**
inc *you both* (dual) **18**
infangene-þeof *the right to take and fine a thief caught in one's area of jurisdiction* **18**

ingeþonc *thought* **22**
innan *into* **10**
inne *inside, within* **18**
innmæst, innemest *inmost, deep* **10**
insegel *wax seal on documents* **19**
insegl = insegel *wax seal* **7**
Ismahelitisc *Ismaelite* **6**
iung *young* **5**

kepan: þances kepan *to show gratitude* **18**
kyning = cyning *king* **17**

lac *present, gift* **15**
lædan *to lead, carry* **13**
(ge)lædde *presented, led* **19**
læddon *carried* **13**
læg *lay* **18**
lærde *taught* **1**
(ge)lærednys *learning, skill* **8**
læs *pasture* **9**
læssa *smaller* **3**
læswum: on læswum *in the pastures* **9**
lætan = læten *granted* (past part.) **18**
lætan *order, command* **4**
lætan *leave, let* **19**
læwede *lay people* **7**
lace *leap, fly, play* **22**
lage *would lie* (subj.) **18**
lagon *(they) lay* **18**
lagu *law* **7**
lagu-fæðm *sea-embrace* **22**
lagu-stream *sea-current, water* **21**
land *land* **10**
land-ar *landed property* **11**
landgemæru *charter bounds* **10**
lange *long:* **to lange** *too long* **9**
lange tide *for a long time* **14**
leafe: leaf *leave, permission* **17**

leah *ley, clearing* **9**
leawede *lay people* **8, 11**
geled *laid, charged* (past part.) **20**
(ge)lede *laid* **7, 22**
lengten-tima *spring season* **5**
leod *nation* **20**
leodbiscop *suffragan bishop* **7**
leodwita *counsellor* **20**
leof *dear, beloved* **1, 7, 18**
leofaþ *lives, liveth* **22**
æt Leofecanoran *of Lewknor* **19**
leofest *dearest* **8**
leoht *light* **3**
let *ordered* **4**
lete *should leave* (subj.) **19**
lichoman *body* **17**
lif *life* **4, 15**
lifað *lives, liveth* **22**
lig *fire, flame* **22**
lin *flax, lint* **10**
lið *lies, is lying* **18**
loca *look, see* **9**
lof *praise* **17**
lof-sang *hymn* **17**
lucon *joined, enclosed* **21**
lufian *love* **6**
lufode *loved* **6**
Lunden *London* **17**
lyfde *granted* **7**
lyt *little* **22**
lytle hwile *for a short while* **4**

ma *more* (comp. adv.) **4**
maccus *Maccus* **21**
mæg *can* **2, 4, 5, 19**
mænden *declared* **22**
mænig *many* **11, 18**
mænigfeald *manifold, numerous* **12**
(ge)mære *boundary* **10**
mære *famous, great* **15**
mæru *famous, great* (fem.) **8**

mæssan: to Martins mæssan *on the feast of St Martin* **4**
mæssan = mæsse *holy mass* **4, 17**
mætte: me mætte *I dreamed* **6**
mæð *measure, degree* **20**
mæþ *reverence* **18**
mæðel *speech*: on mæðlu *in council* **7**
mage *kinswoman* **20**
magon *they can* **5**
man *they, one* **4**
mancus *one eighth of a pound* **8**
mancsas *plural of mancus* **16**
manega *many* **4**
manig *many a* **11**
mannum *men, people* (dat.) **5**
manude *admonished* **1**
mara *greater* **3**
martyr *martyr* **17**
mearc *border* **10**
menig *many a* **19**
meodu *mead* **22**
mere *sea, lake* **3**
mere-faroþ *surging of the waves* **22**
mere-stream *sea water* **3**
mergen *morning* **15**
mete *food provision* **11**
metest *you'll find* **16**
ge-metfæst *moderate* **16**
mette: me mette *I dreamed* **6**
micel *great, big* **3, 4**
mid *with* **4**
middan: on middan *in the midst* **6**
middangeard *world* **3**
mid heom *with them* **4**
mid him *with him* **4**
mid mannum *with provision of labour* **11**
mid mete *with food provision* **11**
mid þan þe *when* **16**
Mierce *Mercia* **4**
miht *power* **7**

mihte *it could* **13**
mihton *they could* **6**
mildheort *merciful* **20**
(ge)miltsie *have mercy* **17**
miltse *mercy, favour* **20**
miltsum *with favour, with humility* **22**
min *my, mine* **6,9, 15, 18**
mod mind: mode snottre *with a wise mind* **12**
modige *brave* (plural) **21**
modge *proud* (plural) **22**
modor *mother* **6**
mona *moon* **3**
monað *month* **5**
monðas *months* **5**
mongum *for many* **22**
monige *many* **3**
(ge)mot *assembly, meeting* **4**
moste *be allowed* **7** *should* **19**
moston *they should* **17**
mote *might* **18**
mund *security, protection* **7**
munuc *monk* **17**
munucas *monks* **17**
munuclic *monastic* **15**
muðleas *mouthless* **22**
myccel, mycel *great* **1**
ge-mylted *consumed* **22**
(ge)mynd *mind, memory* **7**
mynster *church, minster* **4**

na *not at all* **17, 20**
nænig *none* **16**
næfre *never* **20**
nære *would not be* **19**
næs *was not* **20**
nam *took* **4**
(ge)nam *took* **16**
nama *name* **5, 17**
(ge)name *might take* (subj.) **21**
namon *they took* **14**
nan *none* **14, 19**

ne *not* **14**
neadunga *forcibly* **15**
neah *near* **16**
nebb *face* **16**
nelle *(I) do not want* **18**
nemnan *to name* **18**
(ge)nemned *named* (past part.) **5**
neod *need* **1**
nerian *save* **12**
niðer *down* **10**
niman *take* **15, 16, 21**
niw *new* **7**
Niwantun *Newington* **18**
nolde *did not want* **19**
nonas *the nones* (calendar) **5, 17**
norð *north* **2**
nosu *nose* **12**
nyðer *down* **5**
nyxstan: æt nyhstan *at last* **8**
nu *now* **10**
nyman *to take* **17**
nys *is not* **14**

of *from, off* **2**
ofdyde *took off* **15**
ofer *over* **3**
oferstigan *climb over* **3**
ofsceat *shot down* **21**
ofslagen, ofslægen *slain, killed* **4**
ofslægen: he wearð ... ofslægen *he was slain* **4**
ofslean: to ofsleane *to slay, kill* **13**
oft *often* **14**
oftalu *counter-claim* **7**
olfenda *camel* **13**
onbyrnende *burning* **5**
oncneow *acknowledged, recognised* **20**
ond = and *and* **12**
onfeng *received* **4**
ongean *in exchange for* **19**
ongean *against* **13, 21**

ongean *back* **16, 21**
ongean þæt *as* **20**
onginnan *begin* **7**
onhæbbe: mec onhæbbe *raise myself* **22**
onhnigað *(they) bow* **22**
onriht *justly* **7**
onscunian *shun* **6**
ontalu *claim* **7**
ord *point, spear* **21**
ord *vanguard* **21**
os- (in names) *a god* **1**
oð *until* **10**
oððæt *until* **7**
oðer *second* **5**
oðer *other, another* **6, 21**
oðer... oðer *the one... the other* **8**
oððæt *until* **7, 21**
oððe, oþþe *or* (conjunction) **4, 22**
oðrum *to the other* **21**
oxa *ox* **2**
oxena *of oxen* (gen. plural) **2**

pallium *pallium, ceremonial scarf* **4, 17**
pantan *stream river Pante* **21**
papa *pope* **17**
peneg *penny* **11, 13**
prass *military array* **21**
preost *priest* **1**
priost *priest* **19**
prud *proud* **20**
pund *pound* **11**
pytt *well-pit* **13**

rad *rode* **20**
ræce *reach, extend* **3**
ræd *advice* **1**
rægl = hrægl *clothing* **20**
(ge)ræhte *reached* **16**
ranclicor *more boldly* **5**
raðe *quickly* **20, 21**

read, reod *red* **11**
reaf *clothing* **14, 20**
reaflac *robbery* **19, 22**
rehte *told* **6**
reliquias *relics* **4**
reordian *to feast* **17**
reow *rowed* **16**
reþnys *cruelty* **16**
ric *powerful* **1**
rice *kingdom, authority* **2**
ridon *they rode* **20**
(ge)riht *right, privilege, obligation* **7**
rihte *right away* **19,**
rihte *properly, correctly* **21**
rihtlice *justly* **19**
rihtlicost *most just* **19**
rihtwisnys *righteousness* **12**
ripiað *ripen* **5**
ripung *ripening* **5**
rixað *reigns, reigneth* **20**
ruh *rough* **10**

sæ *sea* **3**
(ge)sæde *said from* **secgan 18**
sæton *sat* (plural) from **sittan 4**
sacu and socn *jurisdiction* **18**
saga *say* (imperative) **3**
(ge)samnodon *they gathered* **14**
sanct *saint* **11**
sandiht *sandy* **10**
sarig *sad* **16**
sawle: sawol *soul* **11**
(ge)sawon *they saw* **6**
scægðman *shipman* **20**
sceaf *sheaf* **6**
sceal *must* **2**
sceap *sheep* **2**
sceatt *coin, price* **11**
sceawa *look* (imperative) **14**
sceawian *to look at, appoint* **20**
sceolde *should, would* **19**
sceoldon *had to* **20**

sceole: ne sceole ge *you should not* **21**

sceolon *must* **6**

sceotan *to shoot, appeal to* **19**

scep *sheep* **9, 12**

scinan *shine* **4**

scioldon = sceoldon *they should* **19**

scip = scep *sheep* **12**

scip *ship* **7**

scipon: mid his scipon *with his ships* **4**

scipum: mid fiftig scipum *with fifty ships* **4**

scir *shire* **18**

scirgemot *shire-court* **19**

scirman *shire-governor* **7**

scirgerefa *shire-reeve, sheriff* **20**

scolde, sceolde *must, should, had to* **7**

Scotta: Scotta cyng *king of the Scots* **4**

Scottas *the Scots* **3**

scrydde hyne *clothed himself* **14**

(ge)scrydde *clothed* **15**

scyp *ship* **21**

se *the* (masculine) **5**

(ge)seah *saw* **2**

sealde *gave* **8**

sealde wið *sold for* **13**

searolic *ingenious* **22**

seax, syx *knife* **15, 20, 22**

secan *look for, seek* **9**

sece *I'm looking for* **9**

secgan *say* **13**

secgean = secgan *say* **18**

secð *is looking for* **15**

sefa *mind* **22**

sellan *to give, sell* **11**

selre *better* **13**

(ge)seman *to reconcile* **19, 21**

sendan *are* **11**

sende *sent* **8**

seo *the* (fem.) **5**

seofon *seven* **5**

seolf *self* **17**

seolfor *silver* **11**

seoððan *afterwards* **17**

setl *seat* **8**

settan *compose, place* **11, 15**

se þe *who* **7, 17**

sibb *peace* **22**

sibban *to relatives* (dat.) **11**

sida twa *two sides* **7**

side *widely* **3**

siex *six* **12**

sige *victory* **1**

sihter *drain, ditch* **10**

sinc *treasure* **21**

siolfor *silver* **19**

sið: ær oþþe sið *before or after* **22**

ge-siðas *companions* **22**

siðon *times, multiplied* by **5**

slogon *struck* **16**

smerciende *smiling* **16**

smiþðe *forge, smithy* **10**

snoter, snotor *prudent* **12**

snoternys *wisdom* **5**

socn *see* sacu

softe *softly, easily* **21**

sohte *sought* **9, 13**

(ge)sohton *(they) sought* **13, 19**

(ge)somnad *gathered, united* **22**

(ge)somnode *gathered* **19**

somod *together* **22**

sona *immediately* **5**

sona swa *as soon as* **4, 13, 16**

sond *shore, sand* **22**

soð *true* **22**

soðlice *truly* **5, 6**

spæc *spoke* **7**

(ge)specen *spoken* **11**

spræc *claim* **7**

spræce *should lay claim to* **19**

sprecan *speak* **7, 19**

springað *spring up* **5**
stæf *letter* **22**
stænt *stands* **11**
stan *stone* **1**
stancynn *a kind of stone* **5, 16**
standan *to stand* **2**
stent *stands* **5**
steorra *star* **6**
stode (subj.) *stood* **6**
stodon *they stood* **21**
stop *advanced* **21**
stow *place* **10**
stræt *road, highway* **10**
stream *river* **21**
strengð *strength* **5**
strynan *to gain, beget* **6**
sum *a certain* **16**
sumor *summer* **5**
sunne *sun* **5**
sunstede *solstice* **5**
sunu *son* **4**
suð *south* **2**
swa *so, as* **16**
swaþu: on swaþe *on the track* **3**
sweart *black* **16**
swefn *dream* **6**
swefniend *dreamer* **13**
sweora *neck* **12**
swerian *swear* **19**
swift *swift* **3**
swincan *toil, labour* **9**
swiðe *greatly, very* **6**
swiðor *more* **6**
swiþre *stronger* **22**
swustor *sister* **19**
(ge)swutelian *clarify, declare* **5**
swutelað *declares, is declared* **11**
swutelung *declaration* **11**
swylc *such* **22**
swylce *as it were* **6**
swymð *swims* **15**
swyðe *very* **16**

sy *is* (subj.) **8, 9, 11, 13**
sylf *self* **3**
sylf *the same* **17**
syllan, sellan *give* **13**
syllan to ceape *sell* **13**
syllene, to syllene *to give* **8**
symle *always* **15**
syndan *are* **10**
syððan *afterwards* **4**
syx *six* **12**
syxtig *sixty* **12**

tacen *sign* **15**
(ge)tacnian *to signify* **5**
(ge)tæhte *instructed* **19**
(ge)tæle *counting* **12**
tær *tore* **14**
talu *claim* **7, 20**
teo *take* (subj. from **teon***)* **18**
tid *hour* **5**
tida *of hours* (genitive) **12**
(ge)tilian *till, cultivate, produce* **18**
tima *time, season* **5**
tir *glory* **2**
tirfæst *glorious* **2**
tiðude *granted* **18**
to *to* **1**
toeacan *in addition* **to 8**
toforan *before* **1**
togædere gesæton *they sat together* **15**
togeanes: him togeanes *against him* **4**
totær: totær his reaf *tore his clothing* **14**
(ge)trahtniað *(they) explain, expound* **5**
treow on eorle *loyalty in a man* **2**
treow *tree* (neuter) **6**
tu *two* (fem. and neuter) **7**
tugon *pulled* from **teon 13**
tun *estate, farm* **2**

tunece *coat* 6, 13
tunge *tongue* 12
tungol *star* 3
twa *two* (fem. and neuter) 3, 12
twan *two* 22
twegen *two* (masc.) 3, 12, 21
twelf *twelve* 12
twelfhynde *high-ranking* 7
twentig *twenty* 5
twihynde *low-ranking* 7
tyrwa *resin* 13

þa *then, at that time* 1, 4
þa... þa *when... then* 6
þa *the* (fem. acc.) 6, 10
þa *the* (plural) 7
geþafian *allow* 17
þæc *thatch, roof* 16
þæne *the* (masc. acc.) 10
þær *there* (adverb) 4
þær *where* (conj.) 15
þære *of the* (fem.) 7, 10
þære *to the* (fem.) 10
þæron: þæron getilian *produce on it, cultivate from it* 18
þær rihte *straightaway* 19
þærto: þærto hyrð *belongs to it* 11
þærto *to it, to that place* 19
þæs *of the* (masc. or neuter) 7, 10
þæt *the* (neuter) 5, 10
þæt *that, so that* 5
þagyt *still, yet* 19
þam *to the* (masc.) 10
ðam ðe *to the one who* 11
þam þe hi ær ahte *to the one who owned it before* 16
þan = þam 10
þanon forð *from then on* 19
þas þing *these things* 5
þas *these* 11
þe *to you* 18
þe *the* 20

þe *which, who* (relative pronoun) 4, 6, 7
þe *or* 14
þeah *though* 18
ge-þeah *flourished* 20
þearf *need* 19
þearflic *profitable* 18
þeawas *virtues* 8
þegenas *thegns* 7
ðegenlice *in a thegnly manner* 20
þegenriht thegnly *legal status* 20
þegnas *thegns* 7
þegnlice *in a thegnly manner* 20
þeh, þeah *although* 18
þencan *think; intend* 6, 13
þene = þæne *the* 19
þeode: þeod *nation* 14
þeoden *prince* 20
þeodscipe *nation, people* 7
þeow *servant* 13
þes *this* (masc.) 11
þing *thing or things* 5
þingum: for hwilcum þingum *for what reason* 15
þiss, þis *this* (neuter) 11
þohte *thought, intended* 6, 13
þone *the* (masc. acc.) 7, 10
þonne: swiftre þonne *swifter than* 3
þonne *then* 12, 16
þonne *when* (conj.) 5
þonne... þonne *when... then* (see þa... þa) 6
þreo hund *three hundred* 12
þrinnes *Trinity* 22
þritig *thirty* 12
þrydda *third* 17
þrymm *glory* 17
þryþ *power* (used with personal names) 1
þu *you* (sing.) 18
þuhte *seemed* 6
þurh *through* 6

þus, þus *thus* 8
þusend *thousand* 12
ge-þydan *associate* 22
þyllic *such a* 15
þyncan *seem* 6

ufon *up above* 12
uhtna gehwam *every morning* 22
unbefohten *without a fight* 21
unbesacan *uncontested* 11
unbesacen *uncontested* 19
unbesmiten *untarnished* 13
unbliþe *unhappy* 16
unc *the two of us* (dual) 22
uncer, uncre *our* (dual) 18, 22
under *under* 3
underfangen *received* (past part.) 17
underhnigan *sink under* 3
unforboden *unforbidden* 11
unforhte *fearless* 21
unlagu *injustice, wrong* 17
unnan *grant* 11
unnendre heortan *with a willing heart* 11
unriht injustice: unriht alecgan *put down injustice* 7
unswicende *faithful, undeceitful* 7
up *up* 20
uparist *rises* 5
upcyme *ascendancy* 22
upp: upp afligeð *flies up* 16
ura our: ura leofa hlaford *our dear lord* 7
ure cyning *our king* 6
ure Drihten *our Lord* 1
ure gastlica broðor *our spiritual brother* 7
urne *our* (masc. acc.): ðeah we urne broðor ofslean *if we kill our brother* 13
urum our: in urum life *in our life* (dat.) 1, 20, 21

ut *out* 4
(ge)utlagode man *they outlawed* 4
uton *let us* 13

wæg, weg *wave* 3
wælle *stream* 10
wæpna *weapons* (genitive) 21
wære *was* (subj.) 7, 12
wæron, wæran *were* from wesan 4
wæs *was* 1
wæstm-as *fruits* (plural) 5
wæt *wet* 5
wæter *water* 21
wæterleas *waterless* 13
wanað *wanes* 5
wat *know* 4
ge-wat *departed, went* 18, 21
we *we* 3
(ge)weald *dominion* 20
wealdan *wield, control* 21
weall *wall* 22
weard, ward *guardian* 1
wearm *warm* 5
wearð *became* 4
(ge)wearð *occurred* 14
wearð ... ofslægen *he was slain* 4
weaxað *grows, waxeth* 5
wedd *pledge* 8
weder *weather, storm* 22
weg *way* 10
weg, wæg: on wege *on the wave* 12
wegfarend *wayfaring* 13
wege þu *wave* (imperative) 15
wel: hine wel lærde *instructed him well* 1
welig *wealthy* 8
wenan *expect* 15
(ge)wende *returned, went* 4
wendon *they went* 19
weofod *altar* 7
weold *ruled* from wealdan 11

Weolintun *Wellington* **20**

weop *wept* **20**

weorod 17 = werod *troop*

weorð *worth, worthy* **20**

weorðan *become* **12**

weorðlic *worthy*: **mid weorðlican weorode** *with a worthy retinue* **17**

weorðscipe *honour* **17**

wende *supposed* **22**

wepan *to weep* **20**

wer *man* **16, 22**

wer *wergild, compensation* **19**

wera *of men* **15**

weras *men* **12**

weredon *they defended* **21**

werige *keep* **17**

werlic *masculine* **15**

werod *troop, force* **12, 21**

wesan *to be* **3**

west *west* **10, 16**

west riht *westwards* **10**

west weard *westwards* **18**

wexseð and wanað *waxes and wanes* **5**

wic *trading centre; dairy farm* **12**

wicg *horse* **12**

wicinga *of the Vikings* **21**

wicneras *bailiffs* **18**

widdor *more widely* **22**

wif *woman, wife* **6, 8, 10, 18**

wif *women* **22**

wiflic *feminine* **15**

wig *battle* **1, 21**

wig, wih *sacred place, image* **10**

wiga: wigan *warriors* **21**

wigheard *battle-hard* **21**

wihaga *battle-wall (of shields)* **21**

wiht *creature* **3, 12**

Wiht *Isle of Wight* **4**

Wihtland *Isle of Wight* **17**

wildeor, wilddeor *wild beast* **13**

willa will: eower willa *your wish* **15**

willan *to want, to wish* **15, 21**

wilnode: ic symle wilnode *I always wanted* **15**

wine *friend* **1, 20**

winter *winter* **5**

winterlæhte *it became winter* **19**

wis *wise* **19**

wisdom *wisdom* **2**

wiste knew: þeh he hit ær wiste *though he had known it before* **18**

witan *counsellors* **19**

witan *know* **4**

wið: freondræden wið *friendship with* **6**

wið: god wið yfele *good against evil* **4**

wið: wið Deorhyrste *near Deerhurst* **4**

wið: wið ða fynd *against the foe* **21**

wið: wið ðrittigum penegum *in exchange for thirty pennies* **13**

witnys, witnes *knowledge, witness* **7**

ge-witnes: to gewitnesse *as witness* **19**

witodlice *indeed, so* **6**

wlonc *proud* **10, 22**

wolde *would* **19**

womb, wamb *stomach* **12**

wong, wang *plain, uncultivated field* **3**

word *word* **7**

wordcwidas *words, sayings* **22**

worold *world* **7**

woruld *world* **1, 4**

wrætlice *wondrously* **12**

wrat *wrote* **16**

(ge)wrecan *avenge* **13**

wrecend *avenger* **13**

(ge)wregde *accused* **6**

Wridewellan *Wordwell* **11**

(ge)writ *letter, writ, document* **7**

(ge)writen *written (past part.)* **16**
wrixlan *exchange* **22**
wucena *of weeks* **12**
wudu *wood* **2**
wuldor *glory* **3**
wuldre *with glory* **22**
wulf *wolf* **1**
æt Wulfamere *at Woolmer* **19**
wulfstan *Wulfstan* **21**
wundor *wonder, miracle* **3**
wundriende *marvelling* **16**
wundrum *with wonders* **12**
(ge)wunian *remain* **4**
wurdon *they became* **8**
wurð *price* **14**
wurðlice *honourably* **17**
wurþmynt *honour* **17**
wurþra *richer* **8**
wurðscipe *honour* **13**
wyllað *we want* **5**
wylle *I want:* **ic wylle beon** *I wish to be* **7**
wylle: þu...wylle *you want* **15**

wynn *joy* **7, 20**
wynsam *delightful* **17**
(ge)wyrcan *construct, make* **2, 5, 6**
(ge)wyrcean *construct, make* **6**
wyrcð *makes* **5**
wyrtgemang *spice mixture* **13**
wyrð *becomes* **5**
wyrðscype *honour* **1, 17**

ycan *increase* **22**
yfel *evil* **2**
ylc: se ylca *the same person* **16**
yld: on his ylde *in his old age* **6**
ymbe about: ymbe þa feower timan *about the four seasons* **5**
ymbutan *round about* **6**
yrfe: on ece yrfe *as a permanent inheritance* **11**
yrmð *misery, crime* **14**
ys *is* **13**
ytemest *last* **5**
yð *wave* **22**

Appendices

Appendix I

The seven classes of Old English strong verbs

In dictionaries of Old English, strong verbs are identified by the class number to which they belong:

infinitive	class	present	past	past plural	past participle
drīfan	I	drīfð	drāf	drifon	(ge)drifen
cēosan	II	cȳst	cēas	curon	(ge)coren
singan	III	singð	sang	sungon	(ge)sungen
cuman	IV	cymð	cōm	cōmon	(ge)cumen
gifan	V	gifð	geaf	gēafon	(ge)gifen
swerian	VI	swereð	swōr	swōron	(ge)sworen
cnāwan	VII	cnǣwð	cnēow	cnēowon	(ge)cnāwen

It may be helpful to compare the modern English equivalents:

Class I	drive, drove, driven
Class II	choose, chose, chosen
Class III	sing, sang, sung
Class IV	come, came, come
Class V	give, gave, given
Class VI	swear, swore, sworn
Class VII	know, knew, known

Appendix II

Map of southern Britain, with names in Old English:

Credits